# ELISEO RODRIGUEZ

# Monolatry

*Jewish and Christian*

RYAN SKY

First published by Ryan Sky Media 2025

Copyright © 2025 by Eliseo Rodriguez

All rights reserved. No part of this publication may be reproduced, stored or transmitted in any form or by any means, electronic, mechanical, photocopying, recording, scanning, or otherwise without written permission from the publisher. It is illegal to copy this book, post it to a website, or distribute it by any other means without permission.

Eliseo Rodriguez asserts the moral right to be identified as the author of this work.

Eliseo Rodriguez has no responsibility for the persistence or accuracy of URLs for external or third-party Internet Websites referred to in this publication and does not guarantee that any content on such Websites is, or will remain, accurate or appropriate.

Scripture quotations marked (LSB) are taken from the Legacy Standard Bible®, Copyright © 2021 by The Lockman Foundation. Used by permission. All rights reserved. Managed in partnership with Three Sixteen Publishing Inc. LSBible.org and 316publishing.com.

Scripture quotations marked (ESV) are from the ESV® Bible (The Holy Bible, English Standard Version®), copyright © 2001 by Crossway, a publishing ministry of Good News Publishers. Used by permission. All rights reserved.

Unless otherwise indicated, all Scripture quotations are taken from the New American Standard Bible® (NASB), Copyright © 1995 by The Lockman Foundation. Used by permission. All rights reserved. www.lockman.org

Rediscovering What Was Always There

This book was written by the author as an original work of theological synthesis. While generative AI tools were used to assist in editing, restructuring, and refining language throughout the drafting process, all core ideas, theological positions, and arguments originated with the author.

The use of AI was limited to enhancing clarity, accessibility, and tone, and was carefully guided to preserve the author's voice and intent. No content was copied or adapted from external theological publications or other authors without clear citation. All Scripture quotations are used in accordance with public domain or appropriately licensed translations.

The final manuscript reflects the author's own convictions, insights, and theological creativity, supported by biblical exegesis and historical research.

Theology is not about invention—it is about discovery. It is the sacred work of recognizing what God has already revealed and realigning ourselves with truth that may have been buried, distorted, or overlooked.

This book is not an attempt to create something new, but to recover something ancient. I believe that the framework presented here—what I describe as monolatry—was always embedded in the biblical witness. It is a vision in which YHWH alone is uncaused, supreme, and worthy of worship, while other divine beings exist in a real but subordinate relationship to Him. This model is not foreign to Scripture—it rises from it.

Likewise, the concept I refer to as dynamic eternity is not a theological innovation. Others have spoken of God's relational nature in various ways, and the Bible itself portrays a God who acts, wills, speaks, sends, and responds. I do not claim these ideas as my own. As Ecclesiastes says, there is nothing new under the sun. If these insights hold any truth, they belong to God alone.

What I have done here is to observe, to question, and to follow the biblical pattern wherever it leads—even when that path departs from popular doctrine. My aim is not to be original, but to be faithful—to let the Scriptures speak plainly, and to frame their witness in ways that honor both their depth and their clarity.

I pray this work will help others see what was always there—and that it will stir in you a deeper awe for the God who alone is worthy of worship.

— Eliseo Rodriguez

First edition

ISBN: 979-8-218-75270-5

This book was professionally typeset on Reedsy.
Find out more at reedsy.com

# Contents

| | |
|---|---|
| *Preface* | v |
| *Abbreviations* | vii |
| *Dedication* | ix |
| Introduction | 1 |

## I  Part One

| | |
|---|---|
| 1  Defining Monolatry – Israel's Theological Framework | 5 |
| 2  Divine Plurality and Yahweh's Supremacy | 21 |
| 3  The Hidden Framework of the Hebrew Bible | 31 |

## II  Part Two

| | |
|---|---|
| 4  From Exile to the Second Temple — How Monolatry Endured | 45 |
| 5  Philo's Logos and the Bridge Between Jewish Thought and... | 66 |
| 6  The Targums, Memra, and Shekhinah | 78 |
| 7  Qumran (Dead Sea Scrolls) and Other Second Temple Evidence | 86 |
| 8  Wisdom and Logos: Mediators of the Divine Mind | 93 |

## III  Part Three

| | |
|---|---|
| 9  The New Testament in Light of Monolatry | 111 |
| 10  Qumran's Exalted Figures and Yeshua as King-Priest | 141 |
| 11  Key NT Passages Showing Subordination Within Monolatry | 154 |
| 12  God Granted Yeshua Revelation, Throne, and Authority | 168 |

| | | |
|---|---|---|
| 13 | Messianic Jews After Yeshua – Maintaining Jewish Traditions... | 181 |
| 14 | The "Two Powers" Controversy and the Jewish-Christian Divide | 204 |
| 15 | The Apostolic Fathers and Early Christian Diversity | 209 |
| 16 | From Jewish Monolatry to Christian Monolatry | 228 |
| 17 | The Apex of Christian Monolatry: The Theology of Eusebius of... | 246 |
| 18 | "How the Bible Reveals an Eternal God Who Acts, Begets, and... | 252 |
| 19 | The Road to Nicaea (325 A.D.) Revisited with Balancing... | 272 |
| 20 | The Athanasian Shift: Rewriting Christian Doctrine | 296 |
| 21 | Doctrine by Decree: How Imperial Power Forged a New... | 307 |
| 22 | Why We've Never Heard This Story | 311 |
| 23 | The Unbroken Thread | 321 |

| | |
|---|---|
| *A Word to the Reader* | 324 |
| *Appendix: The Foundational Creeds* | 326 |
| *Bibliography* | 328 |
| *Further Reading: A Guide for Your Continued Journey* | 333 |
| *Glossary of Key Terms* | 336 |

# Preface

This book began with tension—tension between what I had been taught, and what I was starting to read for myself.

I became a Christian within a Trinitarian framework. Like many, I was deeply sincere in that faith. But over time, certain verses began to stand out in ways I couldn't ignore. Revelation 3:12—where Jesus speaks of "my God" four times in a single verse—was one of them. John 17:3, where Jesus refers to the Father as "the only true God," was another. And yet, these had to be balanced with verses like John 1:1, "the Word was God."

I wasn't trying to undermine anything. I was trying to **reconcile** what I believed with what I read. But the more I tried to harmonize these passages within traditional Trinitarian theology, the more I realized the framework itself couldn't quite contain them.

I didn't go to church leaders. I went to the Bible. And then to church history. What I found there reshaped my theology—and this book is the culmination of that journey.

But the story has a personal side too. I once tried to explain these ideas—very gently—to a close friend of my wife and I. I only mentioned a few verses. But the reaction was immediate and painful. The relationship was damaged beyond repair. We were never given the chance to talk it through.

In response, I did something that, looking back, was probably more hopeful than wise: I wrote a book just for her. A year's worth of thought and care poured into pages she never read. It wasn't well written, and it wasn't meant for the public. It was an attempt to communicate what I hadn't been allowed to say—to show that these questions weren't rebellion, but reverence. I ended up publishing it anyway, so that effort wouldn't feel wasted.

But this book is different. This is the **mature version**—the full thought, laid out carefully, built not just from grief but from years of study. It's meant for anyone who has asked, quietly or out loud, *What if the Bible doesn't say what I think it says?*

You don't have to be a scholar to read this, though scholars will find it carefully documented. Whether you're a believer, a skeptic, or just someone drawn to the ancient textures of Scripture, I invite you to read slowly, think deeply, and give these ideas fair hearing.

Not every reader will agree. That's okay. This book isn't written to win arguments—it's written to recover something I believe the biblical authors themselves assumed: a theology built not on suppression of divine plurality, but on the **exclusive majesty of YHWH** within a richly layered spiritual realm.

Thank you for giving this book a chance. It means more than you know.

—Eliseo Rodriguez

# Abbreviations

**General**
- **A.D.** — *Anno Domini*, "in the year of the Lord"
- **BCE** — Before Common Era
- **cf.** — *confer*, meaning "compare"
- **e.g.** — *exempli gratia*, "for example"

**Biblical Texts and Versions**

- **DSS** — Dead Sea Scrolls
- **ESV** — English Standard Version
- **LSB** — Legacy Standard Bible
- **LXX** — The Septuagint (the ancient Greek translation of the Hebrew Bible)
- **MT** — Masoretic Text (the standard medieval Hebrew text of the Bible)
- **NASB95** — New American Standard Bible (1995 Update)
- **NT** — New Testament
- **OT** — Old Testament

**Ancient Manuscripts**

- **𝔓66 (P66)** — Papyrus 66 (Bodmer II), a near-complete codex of the Gospel of John from the late 2nd/early 3rd century.

- **𝔓75 (P75)** — Papyrus 75 (Bodmer XIV-XV), a codex from the early 3rd century containing large portions of Luke and John.
- **Codex Sinaiticus (א)** — A major uncial codex from the 4th century containing the entire New Testament.
- **Codex Vaticanus (B)** — A major uncial codex from the 4th century containing the majority of the New Testament.

**Qumran/Dead Sea Scrolls**

- **1Q, 4Q, 11Q, etc.** — Numbered caves of Qumran where manuscripts were found (e.g., **4Q246** refers to manuscript #246 found in Cave 4 at Qumran).
- **1QS** — The Community Rule (Serekh HaYahad)
- **1QM** — The War Scroll
- **11Q13 (11QMelch)** — The Melchizedek Scroll from Cave 11

# Dedication

To my lovely wife Trina—

your love, patience, and strength have carried me through every chapter of this journey.

You are my companion, my encourager, my pearl of great price. Your existence in my life is the greatest blessing I have ever had.

This book would not exist without you. Thank you. To God be the glory.

# Introduction

For centuries, believers and scholars alike have assumed that the Bible teaches **strict monotheism**—the idea that only one God exists, and all other so-called "gods" are either imaginary or false. This belief has shaped religious doctrine, worship practices, and entire cultures.

But what if that assumption isn't what the Bible actually says?

What if Scripture tells a more layered and surprising story—one in which **other divine beings** exist, not as threats or illusions, but as **real spiritual entities** under the authority of a singular Supreme God? What if, instead of strict monotheism, the Bible presents **monolatry**: the belief that while many gods exist, only one—**YHWH**—deserves worship?

This may sound like a subtle distinction. But it changes everything—from how we read the Bible, to how we understand the spiritual world, to how we think about God's relationship with creation and the role of the Messiah.

Throughout this book, you'll encounter familiar verses that suddenly feel unfamiliar—texts that speak of heavenly councils, divine hierarchies, and other elohim under God's rule. These are not obscure footnotes. They are part of the Bible's foundational worldview.

We won't unpack all of this here—that's what Chapter 1 is for. But here's the central shift this book proposes: The Bible doesn't say, *"No other gods exist."* Instead, it consistently proclaims, *"No other god is worthy of your worship."*

This is the core of **biblical monolatry**. And understanding it may not just change how you interpret the Bible—it could reshape how you see God's authority, the nature of divine beings, and your own place in the spiritual order.

This book will also explore a related but often overlooked idea: that **God's eternity is dynamic**—not static or unmoved, as later theology often claimed, but responsive, relational, and ordered. In contrast to a God frozen outside time, the Bible presents a God who engages, reacts, and enacts His will through layered divine agency.

We will unpack these themes gradually, chapter by chapter. Some sections will go deep into ancient texts, historical context, and theology. But whether you're a scholar or a curious reader, this journey is for you.

It may challenge your assumptions, but it will also deepen your insight into Scripture—and invite you to see the majesty of YHWH not as a lone being in the void, but as the Most High within a vibrant and ordered divine realm.

Let's begin.

I

Part One

# 1

# Defining Monolatry – Israel's Theological Framework

For more than millennia, Jewish and Christian traditions have taught that the Bible affirms strict monotheism—the belief that only one God exists, and all others are false, imaginary, or demonic. But is that truly what the Bible says?

This book begins with a necessary claim: the Hebrew Bible does not teach strict monotheism. Instead, it reveals a framework best described as monolatry—the belief that while many divine beings (elohim) exist, only one—YHWH—is worthy of worship.

*It is crucial for the reader to understand that* **much of modern scholarship has analyzed these ancient texts from within a default framework of strict, philosophical monotheism.** *When this later, rigid definition is used as the starting point, any biblical or Second Temple text that acknowledges a plurality of divine beings is inevitably viewed as a "remnant of polytheism" or a "binitarian compromise." But what if that starting assumption is wrong? This book argues that* **if we instead begin with monolatry**—*the exclusive worship of one supreme God among other real, but subordinate, divine beings—as the authentic biblical framework,* **the evidence looks entirely different.** *The tensions and contradictions that scholars have tried to explain away were never contradictions* *to the ancient writers. They are only problems when viewed through the wrong theological lens. By restoring the original monolatrous context, we will see that these texts are not a record of a failed evolution toward monotheism, but the consistent expression of a coherent and stable theological worldview.*

Before diving into biblical texts, we need to define the key terms that shape theological assumptions.

## Clarifying the Terms

### *Monotheism*

Monotheism is typically defined as the belief that only one God exists, to the exclusion of all others. In this view, all other so-called "gods" are either false, imaginary, or demonic. This idea has profoundly shaped Jewish and Christian theology alike. But is it truly what the Bible teaches?

Several biblical passages challenge the assumption that divine plurality is excluded:

- "Then the Lord said to Moses, "See, I make you as God to Pharaoh, and

# DEFINING MONOLATRY – ISRAEL'S THEOLOGICAL FRAMEWORK

your brother Aaron shall be your prophet." (Exodus 7:1, NASB95)[1][2]
- "God takes His stand in the congregation of God; He judges in the midst of gods." (Psalm 82:1, LSB)[3]
- "When the Most High gave to the nations their inheritance, when he divided mankind, he fixed the borders of the peoples according to the number of the sons of God." (Deuteronomy 32:8, ESV)[4]

These passages don't align well with strict monotheism. Instead, they suggest that the biblical worldview includes multiple divine beings—elohim—who exist under the authority of one uncreated God, Yahweh. This framework more accurately reflects monolatry, not monotheism: the

---

[1] For when God has a scarcity of good men, He makes those who are not so good the rulers and governors of the better sort; but when He has an abundance of them, then He tries and examines the best, and selects the most approved, to whom He entrusts the general command and government of the others. And he is appointed to be a god, not in appearance, but in reality, being looked upon as the god of the foolish part of the soul, which is figured by Pharaoh. For it is said, "I have made you a god to Pharaoh."
Source: Philo, *On the Life of Moses*, Book I, Section 158.

[2] Listen then, O ye initiates, to these sacred mysteries. "When he saith, I am the God who was seen by you in the place of God" (Gen 31:13). He here means the most ancient God. But the name of God is also applied to others… for He calls the man of perfect virtue also God… as when He says to Moses, "I have made thee a god to Pharaoh" (Exodus 7:1). And he gave this title also to the mind, not waiting for it to be made perfect; so that no one should ever dare to trust in himself as being already perfect.
Source: Philo, *That the Worse Is Wont to Attack the Better*, Sections 161-162.

[3] "Jesus answered them, "Has it not been written in your Law, 'I said, you are gods'? "If he called them gods, to whom the word of God came (and the Scripture cannot be broken), do you say of Him, whom the Father sanctified and sent into the world, 'You are blaspheming,' because I said, 'I am the Son of God'?" (John 10:34–36, LSB)

[4] The reading "sons of God" is preserved in the oldest manuscript evidence, including the Dead Sea Scrolls (4QDeutq) and the Septuagint (the ancient Greek translation of the Hebrew Bible). This contrasts with the later Masoretic Text's "sons of Israel." The scholarly consensus is that "sons of God" is the original reading, which was likely altered by later scribes who were uncomfortable with its theological implications of divine plurality.
See: Michael S. Heiser, *The Unseen Realm: Recovering the Supernatural Worldview of the Bible* (Bellingham, WA: Lexham Press, 2015), 113-116. See also Emanuel Tov, *Textual Criticism of the Hebrew Bible*, 3rd ed. (Minneapolis: Fortress Press, 2012), 269.

exclusive worship of one God among many.[5]

## Polytheism

Polytheism affirms the existence of many gods, often worshiped equally or in rivalry. Ancient cultures like Egypt, Canaan, and Greece operated this way—each with its own pantheon of deities representing nature, power, fertility, war, and fate.

Yet the Bible, while acknowledging the reality of other divine beings, consistently forbids their worship:

- "'For I will go through the land of Egypt on that night, and will strike down all the firstborn in the land of Egypt, both man and beast; and against all the gods of Egypt I will execute judgments—I am the Lord." (Exodus 12:12, NASB95)
- "For great is the Lord and greatly to be praised; He is to be feared above all gods. For all the gods of the peoples are idols, But the Lord made the heavens." (Psalm 96:4–5, NASB95)

These verses reflect not a denial of other gods' existence, but a polemic against their power and authority. Yahweh is not one among equals—He is the Creator, supreme over all.

---

[5] The idea of monolatry as a historical phase in Israel's religion was first systematized by 19th-century scholar Julius Wellhausen. More recently, scholars like Mark S. Smith have explored Israel's "polytheistic background" and the Ugaritic texts that show a conceptual world where a high god presided over a pantheon of lesser divine beings. While many scholars view monolatry as a transitional phase toward what they see as a later, "purer" monotheism, this book argues that the monolatrous framework itself is the consistent and foundational theology of the biblical text.

See: Mark S. Smith, *The Origins of Biblical Monotheism: Israel's Polytheistic Background and the Ugaritic Texts* (Oxford: Oxford University Press, 2001), 1-76.

## Henotheism

Henotheism acknowledges the existence of many gods, but worships only one—often based on time, tribe, or personal choice. This model allows allegiance to shift depending on context or convenience.

But the Bible rejects such flexible devotion. It demands exclusive, unchanging loyalty to Yahweh:

- "You shall have no other gods before Me." (Exodus 20:3, NASB95)
- "You shall not follow other gods, any of the gods of the peoples who surround you," (Deuteronomy 6:14, NASB95)

These commands don't suggest Yahweh is simply the preferred deity of Israel—they present Him as the only one worthy of allegiance. He is not merely the national god of one tribe among many; He is the uncreated Creator and Sovereign over all.

## Monolatry: The Biblical Model

Monolatry recognizes divine plurality but restricts worship to the one God who is uncreated, sovereign, and utterly supreme.

The Bible does not deny the presence of other elohim; rather, it commands total loyalty to Yahweh alone.

Unlike polytheism, monolatry doesn't allow worship of many. Unlike henotheism, it forbids switching devotion between deities. Monolatry recognizes divine plurality but restricts worship to the one God who is uncreated, sovereign, and utterly supreme.

- YHWH's Transcendence: Why He Alone Is Worshiped

The Bible teaches that Yahweh is uncreated, the eternal source of all things. Other elohim may be divine, but they exist only by His will.

This transcendence doesn't mean Yahweh is distant or disconnected. Instead, the biblical model presents a structured reality: Yahweh governs through divine agents, not because He is aloof, but because His authority flows relationally. Like rays from a flame, divine agency participates in Yahweh's purpose without being equal to Him.

Monolatry affirms that:

- Yahweh is alone in being uncreated
- Other divine beings exist by His design
- Worship belongs to Him alone

## A Crucial Distinction: Christian Monolatry vs. Latter-day Saint Theology

It is essential at the outset to draw a clear and firm distinction between the framework of Christian Monolatry presented in this book and the theology of the Church of Jesus Christ of Latter-day Saints (LDS). While Latter-day Saints also reject the classical Trinity and affirm a plurality of divine beings, their foundational claims are fundamentally different from the biblically-grounded monolatry of the early Church.

The Christian Monolatry described in this work is built on principles derived from the Hebrew Bible and early Christian witness. The LDS framework, by contrast, is based on extra-biblical revelations unique to its tradition, leading to several key differences:

1. **The Nature of God the Father:** Christian Monolatry affirms that God the Father is, and has always been, the unbegotten, transcendent, and supreme Spirit who is the single source of all things. In contrast, a core tenet of LDS theology is that God the Father was once a mortal man who progressed to godhood and possesses a physical body of flesh and bones.
2. **The Origin of the Son:** Christian Monolatry teaches that the Son is the only begotten of the Father, uniquely deriving His being from the

Father's own nature before time. LDS doctrine teaches that Jesus was the first of many spirit children begotten by a Heavenly Father and a Heavenly Mother in a pre-mortal existence. In this view, all humans are Jesus's spirit-siblings.

3. **The Goal of Salvation:** The biblical framework presents salvation as being brought into a relationship with God through His Son. LDS theology includes the doctrine of eternal progression, where faithful humans can themselves progress to become gods and goddesses, a concept summarized in the well-known saying: "As man now is, God once was: As God now is, man may be". This is entirely foreign to the monolatrous model, which maintains a permanent and absolute distinction between the one uncreated God and all created or begotten beings.

While both frameworks challenge traditional Trinitarianism, they are not the same. Christian Monolatry is a recovery of the original, biblically-attested worldview of the apostles and the early Church. It is a theology of one supreme God, one unique divine Son, and one created order. It should not be confused with any other theological system.

## A Further Distinction: Christian Monolatry vs. Jehovah's Witness Theology

Just as it is important to distinguish Christian Monolatry from Latter-day Saint theology, it is equally crucial to differentiate it from the teachings of the Jehovah's Witnesses. While Jehovah's Witnesses also reject the doctrine of the Trinity and affirm the supremacy of God the Father (whom they refer to exclusively as Jehovah), their Christology is fundamentally different from the monolatrous framework of the early Church.

The Christian Monolatry described in this book is built on the premise that the Son is eternally begotten *from the Father's own essence*, thereby sharing His divine nature as a true, descendant Son. Jehovah's Witness theology, however, is a form of Arianism, which teaches that the Son is not begotten from God's nature but was His very first *creation*.

Here are the three most critical distinctions:

1. **The Nature of the Son:** Christian Monolatry affirms that the Son is divine by nature because He is the only one begotten directly from the Father ("like begets like"). In stark contrast, Jehovah's Witnesses teach that Jesus is a **created being**.[6] They believe he was the first and highest of all God's creations and that in his pre-human existence, he was **Michael the archangel**.[7] This makes him **a creature**, not a divine Son by nature.[8]

2. **The Meaning of "God" in John 1:1:** The New World Translation, the Bible used by Jehovah's Witnesses, translates John 1:1 as "the Word was with God, and the Word was **a god**". This translation supports their view that Jesus is a lesser, created "mighty god" but not God Almighty. Christian Monolatry, as articulated by theologians like Eusebius, affirms that the Son is rightly called "God" because He is the unique offspring of the Father and shares His divine nature, not because He is a lesser, **created** deity.

3. **The Holy Spirit:** In Christian Monolatry, the Holy Spirit is under-

---

[6] "Thus, the Bible shows that Jesus is a created being, a part of the creation produced by God. He was not the Creator but was created by God to be His agent in subsequent creative works."

   **Source:** *The Watchtower*, "Jesus Christ—The Key to the Knowledge of God," February 15, 1992, p. 5.

[7] "So the evidence indicates that the Son of God was known as Michael before he came to earth and is known also by that name since his return to heaven where he resides as the glorified spirit Son of God."

   **Source:** Watch Tower Bible and Tract Society, *Reasoning from the Scriptures* (Brooklyn, NY: Watchtower Bible and Tract Society of New York, Inc., 1989), p. 218.

[8] "Jesus is Jehovah's most precious Son—and for good reason. He is called 'the firstborn of all creation,' for he was God's first creation. (Colossians 1:15) There is something else that makes this Son special. He is the 'Only-Begotten Son.' (John 3:16) This means that Jesus is the only one directly created by God."

**Source:** Watch Tower Bible and Tract Society, *What Does the Bible Really Teach?* (Brooklyn, NY: Watchtower Bible and Tract Society of New York, Inc., 2014), p. 41.

stood as a distinct, personal agent, subordinate to both the Father and the Son. Jehovah's Witnesses deny the personhood of the Holy Spirit altogether, teaching that it is not a person but is God's impersonal "active force," like electricity.

While both Christian Monolatry and the theology of the Jehovah's Witnesses are subordinationist, they are not the same. Christian Monolatry is a theology of **one God and one divine, begotten Son**. The theology of the Jehovah's Witnesses is a theology of **one God and one created, angelic son**. This distinction is fundamental and cannot be overlooked.

**Modern Assumptions vs. Biblical Language**

Mainstream theology—especially post-biblical Jewish and Christian thought—has often assumed a strict monotheistic framework. But the biblical language suggests something else:

"God takes His stand in the congregation of God; He judges in the midst of gods." (Psalm 82:1, LSB)

Deuteronomy 32:8–9 (Dead Sea Scrolls reading) –
   "When the Most High gave the nations their inheritance,
   When He separated the sons of man,
   He set the boundaries of the peoples
   According to the number of the sons of God.
   For Yahweh's portion is His people;
   Jacob is the allotment of His inheritance."

"Micaiah said, "Therefore, hear the word of the Lord. I saw the Lord sitting on His throne, and all the host of heaven standing by Him on His right and on His left. "The Lord said, 'Who will entice Ahab to go up and fall at Ramoth-gilead?' And one said this while another said that. "Then a spirit came forward and stood before the Lord and said, 'I will entice him.' "The

Lord said to him, 'How?' And he said, 'I will go out and be a deceiving spirit in the mouth of all his prophets.' Then He said, 'You are to entice him and also prevail. Go and do so.'" (1 Kings 22:19–22, NASB95)

These are not metaphorical flourishes. They describe a divine council structure, not a God-alone theology. The Bible reveals a heavenly court in which Yahweh reigns supreme, but not alone. This court includes members who deceive or can deceive, inferring fallen or imperfect members.

# Biblical Patterns That Support Monolatry

Throughout Scripture, Yahweh is portrayed as supreme among real spiritual beings (elohim), not as the only spiritual being. This consistent pattern affirms monolatry—the exclusive worship of Yahweh among other elohim:

- "For You are the Lord Most High over all the earth; You are exalted far above all gods." (Psalm 97:9, NASB95)
- "For the Lord your God is the God of gods and the Lord of lords, the great, the mighty, and the awesome God who does not show partiality nor take a bribe." (Deuteronomy 10:17, NASB95)
- "I kept looking Until thrones were set up, And the Ancient of Days took His seat; His vesture was like white snow And the hair of His head like pure wool. His throne was ablaze with flames, Its wheels were a burning fire. "A river of fire was flowing And coming out from before Him; Thousands upon thousands were attending Him, And myriads upon myriads were standing before Him; The court sat, ..."I kept looking in the night visions, And behold, with the clouds of heaven One like a Son of Man was coming, And He came up to the Ancient of Days And was presented before Him. "And to Him was given dominion, Glory and a kingdom, That all the peoples, nations and men of every language

# DEFINING MONOLATRY – ISRAEL'S THEOLOGICAL FRAMEWORK

Might serve Him. His dominion is an everlasting dominion Which will not pass away; And His kingdom is one Which will not be destroyed." (Daniel 7:9–14, NASB95)

These passages depict a divine hierarchy in which Yahweh reigns supreme, and other beings—even exalted ones like the "Son of Man"—receive authority from Him.

## Monolatry in the New Testament

The New Testament doesn't abandon the biblical framework of divine hierarchy—it builds on it. Early believers in Yeshua affirmed Yahweh's supremacy while recognizing the exalted role of Christ. This isn't trinitarian co-equality imposed on the text; it reflects a monolatrous hierarchy consistent with the Hebrew Scriptures.

- "For even if there are so-called gods whether in heaven or on earth, as indeed there are many gods and many lords, yet for us there is but one God, the Father, from whom are all things and we exist for Him; and one Lord, Jesus Christ, by whom are all things, and we exist through Him." (1 Corinthians 8:5–6, NASB95)
- "For this reason also, God highly exalted Him, and bestowed on Him the name which is above every name, so that at the name of Jesus every knee will bow, of those who are in heaven and on earth and under the earth, and that every tongue will confess that Jesus Christ is Lord, to the glory of God the Father." (Philippians 2:9–11, NASB95)
- "Then I looked, and I heard the voice of many angels around the throne and the living creatures and the elders; and the number of them was myriads of myriads, and thousands of thousands, saying with a loud voice, "Worthy is the Lamb that was slain to receive power and riches and wisdom and might and honor and glory and blessing." And every

created thing which is in heaven and on the earth and under the earth and on the sea, and all things in them, I heard saying, "To Him who sits on the throne, and to the Lamb, be blessing and honor and glory and dominion forever and ever." And the four living creatures kept saying, "Amen." And the elders fell down and worshiped." (Revelation 5:11–14, NASB95)

These texts affirm that worship (proskyneō) mediated through Jesus, yet always directed to the glory of the Father. Divine authority flows from the top—the Father initiates, the Son mediates, the Spirit enacts. This structure maintains hierarchy, not metaphysical sameness.

# Why Monotheism Doesn't Fit the Bible

The term monotheism doesn't reflect the Bible's actual language or framework. The Scriptures repeatedly use the word elohim for beings other than Yahweh—without mocking them as imaginary or demonic. These beings are sometimes judged, commissioned, or acknowledged as real spiritual entities under God's rule.

- "God takes His stand in the congregation of God; He judges in the midst of gods." (Psalm 82:1, LSB)
- "When the Most High gave to the nations their inheritance, when he divided mankind, he fixed the borders of the peoples according to the number of the sons of God. But the Lord's portion is his people, Jacob his allotted heritage." (Deuteronomy 32:8–9, ESV)

Scholars sometimes attempt to redefine monotheism to accommodate this, but it's a patch—not a solution. The biblical model is not:
"Only one God exists."
It's:

# DEFINING MONOLATRY – ISRAEL'S THEOLOGICAL FRAMEWORK

"Only one God is uncreated and supreme."

That's monolatry—and it aligns more faithfully with the Bible's own vocabulary and worldview.

## Why This Matters

Understanding monolatry helps resolve long-standing tensions in biblical interpretation. It clarifies how the Bible can affirm both the existence of other elohim and the exclusive worship of Yahweh.

Monolatry makes sense of:

- The Bible's divine hierarchy
- Yahweh's unique transcendence
- The exalted role of Yeshua without collapsing into metaphysical contradiction

It also explains why later doctrinal systems—however well-intended—often rewrote or reinterpreted the biblical framework to fit philosophical models like monotheism or trinitarian co-equality.

## *How Theology Rewrote the Text*

Over time, both Jewish and Christian theology reshaped the way divine plurality was understood—often in response to external pressures:

- Rabbinic Judaism, especially after the rise of Christianity, worked to eliminate divine plurality in Scripture to protect God's oneness from

perceived theological threats.[9]
- Church councils in the early centuries of Christianity restructured divine agency into a metaphysical Trinity—equal in essence, but often flattening the clear hierarchy seen in earlier biblical texts.
- Modern Bible translations sometimes obscure divine plurality by following later Hebrew manuscripts rather than earlier ones. For example, Deuteronomy 32:8 is often rendered "sons of Israel" instead of "sons of God."

These changes—textual, theological, and political—have obscured the Bible's original monolatrous framework, replacing it with a strict monotheism shaped more by doctrinal defense than original context.

## Conclusion: Recovering the Biblical Framework

Monolatry is not a compromise—it's the key to recovering the Bible's internal logic. Rather than forcing Scripture into rigid philosophical molds, monolatry invites us to:

- Take the Bible's language seriously
- Read its divine structure faithfully
- Avoid the forced reinterpretations required by later theology

---

[9] The seminal work on the rabbinic suppression of divine plurality is Alan F. Segal's *Two Powers in Heaven*. Segal's research documents the rabbinic efforts to define a stricter monotheism against what they saw as the heretical threat from early Christian and Gnostic interpretations that seemed to posit a second, rival divine figure. This book argues that much of the "two powers" thinking the rabbis struggled against, particularly from Christians, was not a belief in two rival gods but was the framework of Christian Monolatry—a recognition of God's exalted, subordinate agent.

See: Alan F. Segal, *Two Powers in Heaven: Early Rabbinic Reports about Christianity and Gnosticism* (Leiden: Brill, 1977).

# DEFINING MONOLATRY – ISRAEL'S THEOLOGICAL FRAMEWORK

Strict monotheism cannot fully account for the divine council, the plurality of elohim, or the exalted role of Yeshua. But monolatry can—without dismissing biblical authority or violating the oneness of worship owed to Yahweh.

The Bible's message isn't that only one being exists.

It's that only one is uncreated, supreme, and worthy of worship.

That's monolatry. And it's the foundation of everything in this book.

# Reader's Guide:

## *Monolatry in Plain Terms*

**So... What Is Monolatry?**

If this chapter felt dense, here's the big idea boiled down:

- **Monotheism** = Only one God exists. All others are false or demonic.
- **Polytheism** = Many gods exist and can be worshiped.
- **Henotheism** = Many gods exist, and one is worshiped—but that choice can change.

The Bible doesn't fully match any of these.

Instead, the Bible teaches **monolatry**:

- Many spiritual beings exist—
- but only Yahweh is to be worshiped.

## *Key Points:*

- The Bible uses **elohim** for other beings—not just Yahweh (e.g., angels, divine agents, even Moses).
- God never says these other beings are imaginary—He says they're **not**

**to be worshiped**.
- Yahweh is **unique** because He's uncreated. Everything else exists because of Him.
- These other beings are **real**—but they are under His authority.

## Why This Matters

Understanding monolatry helps explain:

- Why the Bible talks about a **divine council**
- Why other "gods" are **judged or acknowledged**
- How **Yeshua** is exalted by God
- Why **idol worship** is condemned so strongly

## In Short:

The Bible's message isn't

- "Only one being exists."

It's:

- "Only one is supreme, uncreated, and worthy of worship."

That's **monolatry**—and it's the foundation for everything in this book.

# 2

# Divine Plurality and Yahweh's Supremacy

For centuries, interpreters have approached the Hebrew Bible through the lens of strict monotheism, assuming that Israel's theological framework was always singular and exclusive. However, the biblical text presents a different picture—one where divine plurality exists within a structured hierarchy, with Yahweh reigning supreme.

The Bible does not claim that other divine beings are mere illusions. Instead, it presents a reality in which YHWH commands a council of spiritual beings, assigns roles to celestial agents, and interacts with the world through visible representatives. Though YHWH is eternal and unbound by time, He engages with His creation by means of emissaries—divine agents who enter temporal reality on His behalf. The challenge is not whether the Bible acknowledges other divine entities, but how it consistently portrays Yahweh as above them all.

## What This Chapter Covers

This chapter explores how the Hebrew Bible supports a divine hierarchy centered on YHWH, not strict philosophical monotheism. Specifically, we will examine:

- The meaning and usage of key Hebrew terms: Elohim, El, Elyon, and Adonai
- The divine council motif, in which YHWH governs a supernatural assembly
- Biblical texts that affirm a layered spiritual realm, rather than a solitary deity

Understanding Israel's theology requires a closer look at how divine titles are used. These Hebrew words are often translated into English as "God" or "Lord," but they carry specific theological weight:

Elohim – A grammatically plural term used for YHWH, but also applied to other spiritual beings, such as angels (Psalm 8:5), the disembodied dead (1 Samuel 28:13), and even human judges (Exodus 22:9).

El – A generic word for "god" in Semitic languages. Sometimes used as a poetic or shortened form of YHWH, but also appears in broader ancient Near Eastern contexts.

Elyon - Meaning "Most High," this title emphasizes God's supreme status among the elohim (see Deuteronomy 32:8–9).

Adonai – A reverent substitution for the divine name YHWH, translated "Lord" in most English Bibles. It signifies rulership and authority rather than exclusive divine identity.

## *Elohim – A Word That Defies Simplicity*

The term Elohim appears over 2,500 times in the Hebrew Bible. Though plural in form, it frequently governs singular verbs, creating interpretive tension.

> *"In the beginning God created the heavens and the earth." (Genesis 1:1, NASB95)*

# DIVINE PLURALITY AND YAHWEH'S SUPREMACY

Why is a singular God given a plural name?

**Possible Explanations:**

- **Plural of Majesty:** A common suggestion, but it fails to explain how Elohim applies to others besides YHWH.
- **Divine Council Theory:** YHWH is the singular supreme Elohim, presiding over lesser elohim.
- **Category of Beings:** Elohim refers to any inhabitant of the spiritual realm—angels, spirits of the dead, or even human judges.

In short, "Elohim" does not mean only one divine being exists—it reflects a category, while YHWH stands as its uncaused and supreme member.

## Genesis 1:26 – "Let Us Make Man"

> "Then God said, "Let Us make man in Our image, according to Our likeness; and let them rule over the fish of the sea and over the birds of the sky and over the cattle and over all the earth, and over every creeping thing that creeps on the earth."" (Genesis 1:26, NASB95)

This verse has sparked endless speculation. Who is "Us"?

**Traditional View: The Royal "We"**

- Often used by monarchs.
- **Problem:** No evidence of this usage in ancient Hebrew. Especially fails in Genesis 3:22: "The man has become like one of Us." That phrase demands at least two real entities.

**More Plausible: The Divine Council**

- Supported by other scenes (Job 1; 1 Kings 22).

- **But:** Would all divine beings share YHWH's image?

**Strongest Option: Divine Intermediary**

YHWH may be addressing a specific agent through whom He creates:

This divine agent, later described as the Angel "in whom is My Name," speaks and acts with full divine authority. In Exodus 3:12, this same agent says to Moses, "You shall worship God at this mountain"—even though Moses is already speaking with Him. This layered interaction reinforces that a subordinate intermediary may bear the name and status of Elohim, not as YHWH Himself, but as His visible representative. Through such agents, YHWH remains transcendent and timeless, yet fully active within creation—affirming the structure of dynamic eternity.

> "By the word of Yahweh the heavens were made, And by the breath of His mouth all their host." (Psalm 33:6, LSB).

YHWH sends an angel "My name is in him" (Exodus 23:20–22).

This being shares YHWH's image and is involved in creation. That image is then passed to humanity.

## *The Divine Council in Scripture*

The Hebrew Bible depicts a structured spiritual realm—a divine council with YHWH enthroned at its head:

- Psalm 82 – YHWH judges among the gods (elohim).
- 1 Kings 22:19–22 – YHWH consults with heavenly beings.
- Job 1:6 – The "sons of God" appear before YHWH.
- Daniel 7:13–14 – The "Son of Man" is exalted before the Ancient of Days.

These are not metaphors for human judges. They are real spiritual beings, subordinate to YHWH.

## Psalm 82: A Challenge to Strict Monotheism

Psalm 82 begins with a startling claim that stands in direct opposition to strict monotheism: "God takes His stand in the congregation of God; He judges in the midst of the gods." (Psalm 82:1, LSB).

This passage does not describe a solitary God but a divine courtroom. The first "God" (*Elohim*) is YHWH, who presides over a council of other divine beings, also called "gods" (*elohim*). He holds them accountable for their unjust rule, declaring:

> "I said, 'You are gods, and all of you are sons of the Most High. Nevertheless you will die like men and fall like any one of the princes.'" (Psalm 82:6–7, NASB95)[10]

The identities are unambiguous:

- They are **real gods**, not human metaphors. They are condemned to die "like men," a fate that only makes sense if they are not human to begin with.
- They are **subordinate**, titled "sons of the Most High," a term for divine beings in God's council.
- They are **judged** for their failure, confirming their delegated authority

---

[10] The scholarly consensus on Psalm 82 has shifted significantly in recent decades. While older interpretations often suggested the "gods" were merely human judges, most modern Old Testament scholars now affirm that the psalm depicts a literal scene in the heavenly council where Yahweh judges subordinate divine beings for their corrupt governance of the nations. The language used, particularly "sons of the Most High," and the sentence that they will "die like men," strongly indicates that the subjects of judgment are non-human.

See: Michael S. Heiser, "Monotheism and the Divine Council," in *The Unseen Realm*, 39-44. For a more technical academic discussion, see also the entry for "Divine Council" in the *Dictionary of Deities and Demons in the Bible*, edited by Karel van der Toorn, Bob Becking, and Pieter W. van der Horst.

is subject to YHWH's supreme judgment.

Strict monotheism, which denies the existence of other gods, cannot account for this scene. Monolatry, which acknowledges them but subordinates them to a supreme YHWH, explains it perfectly.

### John 10:34–36: Yeshua Affirms the Divine Council

Centuries later, Yeshua Himself invoked this passage to defend His own divine identity against accusations of blasphemy.

> *"Jesus answered them, 'Has it not been written in your Law, "I said, you are gods"? If He called them gods, to whom the word of God came (and the Scripture cannot be broken), do you say of Him, whom the Father sanctified and sent into the world, "You are blaspheming," because I said, "I am the Son of God"?'" (John 10:34–36, LSB)*[11]

Yeshua's argument is a masterclass in monolatrous reasoning:

1. **He confirms the premise of Psalm 82:** He affirms that Scripture calls other beings "gods."
2. **He establishes biblical authority:** He states this scriptural witness "cannot be broken," cementing the reality of these other gods as an unchangeable fact of the biblical worldview.
3. **He argues from lesser to greater:** If subordinate beings who merely *received* God's word can be called "gods," how can it be blasphemy for the one whom the Father uniquely "sanctified and sent" to claim the

---

[11] Jesus's defense in John 10 is a direct appeal to the monolatrous logic of Psalm 82. He affirms the scriptural precedent that beings other than the Father can be called "gods." New Testament scholar Larry W. Hurtado notes that Second Temple Judaism had various ways of conceptualizing "divine agency," which allowed for a chief agent (like the Son) to be uniquely exalted without violating the commitment to one God. Jesus's argument fits perfectly within this framework: if lesser divine beings can bear the title *elohim*, how much more so can the one whom the Father uniquely sanctified and sent?

See: Larry W. Hurtado, *One God, One Lord: Early Christian Devotion and Ancient Jewish Monotheism*, 3rd ed. (London: T&T Clark, 2015), 34-40.

title "Son of God"?

His defense does not argue for equality with the Father but for a biblically consistent, exalted status within a divine hierarchy. This framework perfectly aligns with Yeshua's other statements where He refers to the Father as the "only true God" (John 17:3) and "my God" (John 20:17). For Yeshua, the reality of the divine council was not a theological problem but a foundational truth that explained His own unique role as the Father's supreme agent.

## Deuteronomy 32:8–9 – YHWH Assigns the Nations

**Textual Variants:**

- Masoretic Text (MT): "sons of Israel"
- Dead Sea Scrolls / Septuagint (LXX): "sons of God"

The older reading makes more sense:

- Israel did not exist when nations were divided (Gen 11).
- "Sons of God" fits the divine council motif.

YHWH assigns oversight to lesser gods—but keeps Israel for Himself.

## Why These Texts Were Suppressed

Rabbinic Judaism rejected divine plurality to avoid overlap with early Christianity. Christianity, influenced by Greek metaphysics, redefined divine hierarchy into Trinitarian co-equality. Modern Bible translations sometimes obscure divine plurality by following later Hebrew manuscripts rather than earlier ones. For example, Deuteronomy 32:8 is often rendered "sons of Israel" instead of "sons of God."

But when we return to the text itself, we see a consistent picture: Divine hierarchy—not denial of plurality.

## *The Bible's Polemic Against Idolatry*

The Bible mocks idols—but not because other gods aren't real. It's because they are inferior and powerless compared to YHWH.

**Examples:**

- Isaiah 44:9–20 – A man burns half a log for warmth, then worships the other half.
- 1 Kings 18:27 – Elijah mocks Baal: "Maybe he's on a trip—or in the bathroom!"
- Deut 32:17 – Israel sacrifices to "demons, not God."
- 1 Cor 10:20 – Paul echoes: pagan sacrifices = sacrifices to demons.

These critiques affirm monolatry:

- The gods exist.
- They are spiritually dangerous.
- But YHWH alone is to be worshiped.

## *The First Commandment: Not Denial—But Devotion*

*"You shall have no other gods before Me." (Exodus 20:3, NASB95)*

This isn't a statement of exclusivity in existence, but in worship.

> *"For great is the Lord and greatly to be praised; He is to be feared above all gods." (Psalm 96:4, NASB95)*
> *"Who is like You among the gods, O Yahweh? Who is like You, majestic in holiness, Fearsome in praises, working wonders?" (Exodus 15:11, LSB)*

The Bible assumes divine plurality—but commands exclusive allegiance.

## Monolatry in the New Testament

Paul continues the same framework:

> *"For even if there are so-called gods whether in heaven or on earth,* **as indeed there are many gods and many lords**, *yet for us there is but one God, the Father, from whom are all things and we exist for Him; and one Lord, Jesus Christ, by whom are all things, and we exist through Him." (1 Corinthians 8:5–6, NASB95)*

- 1 Corinthians 10:20 – Idols are tied to real spiritual beings (demons).[12]

This is not monotheism in a philosophical sense. It is covenantal monolatry:

---

[12] The biblical authors frequently associate the worship of idols with the worship of real, but malevolent, spiritual entities. Paul's statement that pagan sacrifices are offered "to demons and not to God" is a direct continuation of the theology found in Deuteronomy 32:17. This perspective does not deny the existence of other spiritual powers; rather, it identifies them as corrupt and forbids their worship, thereby reinforcing the exclusive claim of Yahweh.
See: Michael S. Heiser, "The Gods as Demons," in *The Unseen Realm*, 111-113.

- Many gods exist.
- Only YHWH is supreme.

## *Summary: Key Takeaways from Chapter 2*

- The Bible uses plural divine terms like Elohim, El, and Elyon.
- YHWH is part of a divine council but rules alone.
- Psalm 82 and Deuteronomy 32 affirm real divine beings under YHWH.
- The First Commandment demands loyalty, not theological math.
- Idol worship is condemned—not because idols represent fiction, but because they represent lesser, unworthy gods.
- Paul affirms this model in the New Testament.

# 3

# The Hidden Framework of the Hebrew Bible

Reader's Guide: Chapter 3 at a Glance
What Most People Assume
Strict monotheism: "There is only one God. All other so-called gods are fake or imaginary."

But the Bible itself suggests something more nuanced—more layered—and far more ancient.

**What This Chapter Reveals**

- **Genesis 19:24 & Amos 4:11** – These verses show two YHWH figures acting together—one on earth, one in heaven. → This is not contradiction. It reflects YHWH working through His divine agent—often identified as the Angel of YHWH.

This chapter doesn't claim the Bible promotes polytheism. It simply explores whether the term strict monotheism fully captures the Bible's own language about God and other divine beings.

For generations, a profound truth has been hiding in plain sight—a forgotten reality buried beneath layers of later theology. This truth was once acknowledged openly, embedded in Israel's earliest worldview. But over time, it was reinterpreted, suppressed, and nearly erased. Most modern readers approach the Bible with a specific assumption: that Israel's religion was always strictly monotheistic—that YHWH ruled alone, and that all other so-called gods were fictitious or demonic. But what if that assumption is wrong? What if the Hebrew Bible presents not the denial of other divine beings, the biblical text presents a different picture—one where divine plurality exists within what scholars now identify as Jewish monolatry: a worldview in which many real divine beings exist, but only one—YHWH—is uncreated, supreme, and worthy of worship.

## What This Chapter Will Show

This chapter challenges the notion of strict monotheism and presents overwhelming biblical evidence for a worldview known as monolatry:

- Monolatry acknowledges many divine beings, but reserves worship for one—YHWH.
- These beings are real, powerful, and active—but they are not equal to YHWH.
- This view affirms YHWH's unrivaled supremacy, while allowing for a divine structure beneath Him.

We'll examine two key ideas:

1. **Genesis 19:24 & Amos 4:11** – Two YHWHs acting together—an early witness to divine agency.
2. **Implications for Israel's faith** – Why Israel's theology reflects exclusive worship, not exclusive existence.

## Daniel 10 – Spiritual Rulers Over Nations

Daniel 10 confirms the divine council framework described in Deuteronomy 32. Here, a heavenly being describes spiritual resistance in terms of national-level rulers:

> *"But the prince of the kingdom of Persia was withstanding me for twenty-one days; then behold, Michael, one of the chief princes, came to help me, for I had been left there with the kings of Persia." (Daniel 10:13, NASB95)*

Key Observations

These "princes" are not human kings—they are spiritual entities assigned to nations. The "Prince of Persia" is a hostile divine being, resisting YHWH's purposes. Michael, described as "one of the chief princes," is the spiritual protector of Israel. This scene perfectly aligns with Deuteronomy 32:8–9:

YHWH assigns authority over the nations to other divine beings, but keeps Israel for Himself.

## Genesis 19:24 – Two YHWHs?

# MONOLATRY

> *"Then Yahweh rained on Sodom and Gomorrah brimstone and fire from Yahweh out of heaven."* (Genesis 19:24, LSB)[13]

Why does the verse mention Yahweh twice? One figure (Yahweh) is on earth, executing judgment. The second Yahweh is in heaven, sending down fire. This distinction is not stylistic or poetic—it is theological.

**Key Observations**

- The verse presents two distinct actors, both referred to as Yahweh.
- One is present on earth, having visited Abraham and spoken with Lot.
- The other remains in heaven, the unseen Most High.

This echoes other divine agency patterns in Scripture, where a visible representative bears the Name and acts on behalf of the transcendent Yahweh.

This reading harmonizes with Genesis 18–19:

- Yahweh appears to Abraham as one of three "men."
- Two of them go on to Sodom (angels).
- One, speaking directly as Yahweh, lingers and judges the city.
- The fire comes "from Yahweh out of heaven"—showing both presence and transcendence.

Intermediary, Not Identity Confusion

The figure on earth is not a second deity, nor is this Trinitarian complexity.

---

[13] The syntax of Genesis 19:24, which mentions Yahweh on earth raining fire "from Yahweh out of heaven," has been a subject of extensive theological discussion. Pre-critical commentators often saw this as an early glimpse of the Trinity. However, many modern scholars now recognize it as a prime example of the biblical authors' "binitarian" or monolatrous worldview, where a visible, embodied Yahweh (often identified as the Angel of the Lord) acts on behalf of the invisible, transcendent Yahweh in heaven. This preserves a distinction between God's agent and God as the ultimate source.

See: Michael S. Heiser, *"Two Powers in Heaven,"* in *The Unseen Realm*, 143-156. Heiser refers to this as the *"Second Yahweh"* tradition.

It is the biblical pattern of divine representation:

- The Angel of Yahweh often speaks as Yahweh, yet is distinct from Him.
- This visible agent bears divine titles and even receives honor—but always representationally for the Most High.

The use of the same name (Yahweh) shows delegated authority, not ontological equality. This is not contradiction, nor polytheism. It is monolatry: YHWH reigns alone, even when acting through His visible agent.

## *The Angel of YHWH – Divine Agent, Not a Mere Messenger*

The Angel of YHWH is not just a dependent being:

- He speaks as God,
- Bears God's name,
- Channels honor/reverence,
- Yet is distinct from the unseen Most High.

This fits with the Genesis 19:24 pattern—YHWH works through His divine agent, not because He is limited, but because His nature includes relational agency. This agent is not a rival god or a created angel in the conventional sense. Rather, he functions as YHWH's embodied presence—appearing distinct, yet bearing YHWH's name, and authority.

## Amos 4:11 – Third-Person Self-Reference

> "I overthrew you, as God overthrew Sodom and Gomorrah, And you were like a firebrand snatched from a blaze; Yet you have not returned to Me," declares Yahweh. (Amos 4:11, LSB)

This passage is easily overlooked, yet it presents the same divine duality seen in Genesis 19:24—and references the very same event: the judgment upon Sodom and Gomorrah.

**Key Observations**

- YHWH is speaking in the first person, declaring judgment: "I overthrew you…"
- But then refers to "God" in the third person: "as God overthrew Sodom…"
- Then returns again to the first person: "Yet you have not returned to Me."

This shift is not poetic flourish—it reflects two divine agents, both referred to as God, just as Genesis 19:24 had "YHWH raining fire from YHWH out of heaven." Amos, centuries later, recalls this exact event, reinforcing a dual-agency model deeply embedded in Israel's theological memory.

Why This Matters

This isn't a literary quirk. It's part of a consistent biblical pattern:

- YHWH speaks through a visible agent who also bears His Name.
- That agent can be spoken of as "God" in third person, even while YHWH speaks.
- This affirms divine agency—not contradiction. YHWH remains transcendent while operating relationally through His authorized intermediary.

## The Name and the Agent – Divine Authority Through Representation

In ancient Israelite theology, bearing the Name of YHWH was not a mere title—it was a delegation of divine presence and power. This principle is embodied most clearly in the Angel of YHWH, who is sent by God, speaks as God, and commands obedience because the divine Name is 'in him' (Exodus 23:21).[14]

A helpful parallel can be found in the role of a prophet, who often delivered messages in the first person as God's authorized mouthpiece. However, the Angel of YHWH operates on a profoundly higher level. He does not merely speak *for* God; he personifies the very presence and authority *of* God, acting as His visible agent in the world.

### Exodus 3 – The Burning Bush and the Angel

*"And the Angel of Yahweh appeared to him in a blazing fire from the midst of a bush... When Yahweh saw that he turned aside to look, God called to him from the midst of the bush..." (Exodus 3:2, 4, LSB)*

This theophany begins with the Angel of YHWH, yet the speaker is alternately called Yahweh and God. Later, the speaker identifies Himself: "I am the God of your father, the God of Abraham, the God of Isaac, and the God of Jacob." (Exodus 3:6, LSB) This is not a contradiction — it's the veil being drawn back. YHWH's presence is manifested through a divine intermediary who carries His Name, authority, and speech.

---

[14] The statement that God's "Name" is "in" the Angel is theologically significant. In ancient Near Eastern thought, the name was not merely a label but a representation of one's essence, authority, and presence. For the Angel to have Yahweh's name in him was a delegation of Yahweh's own authority, which is why this specific Angel could command obedience and forgive sin—prerogatives normally reserved for God alone.

See: Larry W. Hurtado, "The 'Angel of the Lord,'" in *One God, One Lord: Early Christian Devotion and Ancient Jewish Monotheism*, 3rd ed. (London: T&T Clark, 2015), 37-40.

MONOLATRY

## Exodus 23 – The Angel in Whom Is My Name

*"Behold, I am going to send an angel before you to keep you and to bring you into the place which I have prepared. Be on guard before him and obey his voice; do not be rebellious toward him, for he will not pardon your transgression, for My name is in him." (Exodus 23:20–21, LSB)*

This angel is:

- Sent by YHWH,
- To lead Israel,
- With power to pardon or judge sin,
- Because YHWH's Name is in him.

No created being carries that kind of authority unless fully authorized as a representative embodiment of YHWH. The "Name" here indicates full investiture — a theological concept echoed in the Targums through the Memra of YHWH.
    The Meaning of "Angel" (Messenger) Implies Representation
    The Hebrew word mal'akh (רְאָלַמ), translated "angel" or "messenger," is a functional title, not an ontological one. It signals a representative role — a being sent to speak or act on behalf of another. In the case of the Angel of YHWH, the messenger:

- Bears YHWH's Name,
- Speaks with His authority,
- Commands the same respect,
- Yet remains subordinate to YHWH Himself.

This title reinforces the principle of divine agency: the Angel is of YHWH, not YHWH unmediated. He is visible, relational, and sent. The authority he carries does not originate in himself — it is delegated.

## Why This Matters

- YHWH remains uncaused and transcendent.
- Yet His will is executed in history through His agent.
- This agent may be called "YHWH" or "Elohim" because he bears the Name, not because he is ontologically equal.

This model supports monolatry, not Trinitarian consubstantialism. Worship is always directed to the one true God, but His agent may appear, speak, and even be addressed as God — because YHWH wills it so. This same pattern is affirmed in the New Testament: "No one has seen God at any time; the only begotten God who is in the bosom of the Father, He has explained Him." (John 1:18, LSB)[15] Here, too, we see the relational distinction: one invisible, unbegotten God (the Father), and one visible, begotten God (the Son), who mediates the presence of the unseen. This is not polytheism or consubstantialism—it is monolatrous agency, perfectly aligned with the Angel of YHWH model. John 1:18, LSB. This verse preserves the same monolatrous structure found in the Hebrew Bible: one unbegotten, invisible God (the Father), and one begotten, visible God (the Son) who reveals Him. The text does not describe co-equality or consubstantiality, but relational hierarchy and agency. That the "only begotten God" is the one who makes the unseen God known is precisely what we see with the Angel of YHWH — one who bears the Name, speaks as God, and yet is subordinate to the One who sent Him.

---

[15] The textual variant "only begotten God" (*monogenēs theos*) is widely accepted by modern textual critics as the original reading of John 1:18, as it is found in the earliest and best manuscripts. Scholars like Bart D. Ehrman, while not personally affirming the theology, argue that this phrasing reflects an early, pre-Nicene "binitarian" Christology where the Son is a distinct, second divine being who is subordinate to the Father, the "one true God." This framework is remarkably consistent with the Old Testament's depiction of a visible, divine agent revealing the invisible, supreme God.

See: Bart D. Ehrman, *How Jesus Became God: The Exaltation of a Jewish Preacher from Galilee* (New York: HarperOne, 2014), 224-228.

## *Representing the Invisible Through Dynamic Eternity*

This entire structure reflects the reality of dynamic eternity: YHWH, the uncaused God, remains outside of time, yet acts within time through His begotten Son. The Son is not a created messenger but the pre-temporily generated son/agent who enters creation by the Father's will. He is not independent, yet not controlled like a puppet—He acts freely in perfect obedience, mirroring the Father's will as His visible presence.

One might picture it this way: just as a person interacts in a digital world through an avatar, the begotten Son embodies YHWH's agency within creation. But unlike a game piece, this divine agent is alive, conscious, and in loving submission to the One who begot Him. He enters the created order not just to represent, but to redeem. When Yeshua became human, it was as if the divine avatar stepped inside the broken system to offer a way out a way to upgrade to eternal life before the program is erased. This is not mythology; it is the mystery of a Father and Son in pretemporality, expressed in agency, love, and purpose. This is the heart of monolatry: the one unbegotten God remains supreme, but He is known, seen, and worshiped through the One He sent.

## *Summary: What This Chapter Has Shown*

- Daniel 10 confirms that divine beings govern nations—but Israel belongs to YHWH.
- Genesis 19 and Amos 4 show two YHWHs acting in concert—one seen, one unseen.
- Yeshua quoted these truths to defend His divine status within a monolatrous structure.

This isn't new theology—it's ancient theology, recovered. Strict monotheism cannot explain these passages. Monolatry can.

**Core Building Blocks**

- **Monolatry** = One Supreme God (YHWH), many real subordinate divine beings
- Not polytheism (no equality among gods)
- Not strict monotheism (doesn't deny others exist)
- Not Trinitarianism (doesn't flatten hierarchy into co-equality)

**Common Objections—Answered**

- "The Shema proves strict monotheism."
- → No. "YHWH is one" affirms uniqueness, not aloneness. It's about supremacy, not numerical exclusivity.
- "Other gods are just idols."
- → The Bible mocks idols (wood, stone) but affirms real spirits behind them (Deut 32:17, 1 Cor 10:20).

**Why This Changes Everything**

- The Bible's theology is not embarrassed by divine plurality—it just insists YHWH alone is worthy of worship.
- Yeshua quotes Psalm 82 to defend His divine identity.
- Ancient Israel saw a divine hierarchy, not a closed universe with just one being.
- The earliest Christians inherited this monolatrous worldview.

✧ Bottom Line

The Hebrew Bible reveals a cosmic courtroom, a divine council, and a God who reigns supremely—but not solitarily.

II

Part Two

# 4

# From Exile to the Second Temple — How Monolatry Endured

**T**he Devil and the Enduring Divine Council

One of the strongest affirmations that the divine council remained an operative concept in post-exilic Jewish thought is the continued presence of rebellious divine beings, especially the Satan. In Job 1:6, we encounter a scene of heavenly deliberation:

"Now it was the day that the sons of God came to stand before Yahweh, and Satan also came among them." (Job 1:6, LSB)

This passage unmistakably portrays a formal divine council where YHWH presides, and where Satan—the accuser or adversary—is not only acknowledged but actively engaged. The "sons of God" (בְּנֵי הָאֱלֹהִים) are presented as divine beings under YHWH's rule, confirming a cosmic hierarchy that had not been abandoned, even in the post-exilic period.

Importantly, this adversarial being continues to operate throughout the biblical story. Nowhere is Satan said to have ceased to exist after this council. In fact, his presence intensifies across the Second Temple period and into the New Testament. Paul calls him "the god of this world" in 2 Corinthians 4:4:

"in whose case the god of this age has blinded the minds of the unbelieving so that they might not see the light of the gospel of the glory of Christ, who is the image of God." (2 Corinthians 4:4, LSB)[16]

This is a crucial point: a subordinate, rebellious divine being is still called "god" (theos) in the New Testament era. Even as an adversary, the title persists. This confirms that the biblical category of "god" (elohim/theos) was not limited exclusively to YHWH, even in later Jewish and Christian contexts.

Similarly, Daniel 10 describes cosmic conflict involving angelic figures like Michael and hostile entities like the "prince of Persia." These "princes" are more than metaphors—they are spiritual powers assigned to nations, functioning as part of an enduring cosmic bureaucracy:

Michael is "one of the chief princes," a guardian over Israel (Dan 10:13, 21).

The "prince of Persia" resists YHWH's purpose.

While not every appearance of a divine being signals a full council session, these accounts clearly demonstrate that the divine hierarchy still functions, populated by loyal and hostile agents. Even without a formal meeting scene, the network of spiritual governance envisioned in passages like Psalm 82 or 1 Kings 22 remains intact.

Thus, the devil—who was once present in the divine council—continues in his role until the eschaton. His authority is temporary and derivative, but his existence proves that the divine council was never fully disbanded, only reframed.

---

[16] The scene in Job 1:6 is a clear depiction of the divine council, with "the Satan" (a title meaning "the accuser") presenting himself among the other "sons of God." This shows that adversarial beings were still considered part of the heavenly assembly. Paul's reference to "the god of this age" in 2 Corinthians 4:4 continues this tradition, acknowledging a real, albeit subordinate and rebellious, spiritual authority over the unbelieving world.

*See: Michael S. Heiser, "The Divine Council," in The Unseen Realm (Bellingham, WA: Lexham Press, 2015), 39-44. For Paul's use of this concept, see Heiser, "The god of this world," in The Unseen Realm, 297-299.*

## Renamed, Not Removed: The Persistence of Subordinate "Gods"

The persistence of divine plurality beyond the Hebrew Bible is not limited to narratives of Satan or angelic warfare. It is reflected in Jewish theology, paraphrase, and philosophy, demonstrating that the idea of subordinate "gods" under YHWH was never fully abandoned—only transformed.

Consider Philo of Alexandria, the first-century Jewish philosopher whose writings heavily influenced both Hellenistic Judaism and early Christian theology. Philo speaks of the Logos—God's rational principle and mediator—as a "second god":

> *Why is it that he speaks as if of some other god, saying that he made man after the image of God, and not that he made him after his own image? [Genesis 9:6]. Very appropriately and without any falsehood was this oracular sentence uttered by God, for no mortal thing could have been formed on the similitude of the supreme Father of the universe, but only after the pattern of the second deity, who is the Word of the supreme Being; since it is fitting that the rational soul of man should bear before it the type of the divine Word; since in his first Word God is superior to the most rational possible nature. But he who is superior to the Word holds his rank in a better and most singular pre-eminence,* (Philo, *Questions and Answers on Genesis, II.62*)[17]

---

[17] Philo's description of the Logos as a "second god" (*deuteros theos*) is one of the most significant developments in Second Temple theology. As a Hellenistic Jewish philosopher, Philo sought to harmonize the Hebrew Scriptures with Greek philosophy. His Logos doctrine, which presents a divine but subordinate intermediary, is a sophisticated expression of the monolatrous framework and had a profound influence on early Christian thinkers who were grappling with how to articulate the divine identity of Jesus.

See: Larry W. Hurtado, "Philo's 'Second God' and the 'Divine Man,'" in *One God, One Lord: Early Christian Devotion and Ancient Jewish Monotheism*, 3rd ed. (London: T&T Clark, 2015), 41-50. See also David Winston, *Logos and Mystical Theology in Philo of Alexandria* (Cincinnati: Hebrew Union College Press, 1985).

Though Philo is careful to qualify the Logos as subordinate to the supreme God, he is equally clear in using the term "god" (θεός). This illustrates that Jewish thinkers still used divine language for YHWH's agents without collapsing into polytheism. The term "god" retained a legitimate, though derivative, usage within a monolatrous framework.

Likewise, the Targums—Aramaic paraphrases of the Hebrew Bible—regularly use the Memra ("Word") of YHWH as a mediating figure. In places where the Hebrew Bible says "YHWH," the Targum inserts "the Word of YHWH" acting, speaking, or appearing. For example:

> *Exodus 19:17 (Targum Onkelos):* "Moses brought the people out to meet the Word of YHWH."

The Memra is not merely a poetic flourish; it is a theological innovation that preserves YHWH's transcendence while affirming divine action through a distinct, personalized agent.

These examples make clear that Jewish tradition maintained a functional divine hierarchy. Even if the language shifted from "gods" to "angels," "princes," "Logos," or "Memra," the reality behind the terms persisted.

Therefore, monolatry was never replaced by a strict exclusion of all other divine beings—is well supported. These beings were:

"Renamed, not removed."

They continued to act, mediate, oppose, and serve within YHWH's sovereign rule. The category of "god," while never applied unqualifiedly to any other being but YHWH, remained active, even when describing adversarial powers like the Devil.

The period from the Babylonian Exile (586 BCE) to the rise of Rome (63 BCE) stands as one of the most transformative in Jewish history. Political upheaval, foreign domination, and cultural exchange profoundly shaped Jewish identity and theology. And yet, rather than breaking from the theological foundations of the Hebrew Bible, this era refined and reinforced them.

Rather than eliminating divine plurality, post-exilic Jewish theology restructured and redefined the roles of divine beings. The worship of YHWH became more sharply exclusive, but the acknowledgment of a populated heavenly realm—complete with divine agents and angelic rulers—remained intact.

In short: monolatry was not abandoned; it matured.

This section will examine three pivotal periods that shaped the theology of Second Temple Judaism:

- **The Babylonian Exile (586–539 BCE)** – A crisis of faith prompts a renewed emphasis on YHWH's sovereignty over all nations.
- **The Persian Period (539–332 BCE)** – Contact with Zoroastrianism influences the development of angelology and cosmic dualism.
- **The Hellenistic Period (332–63 BCE)** – Exposure to Greek philosophy brings fresh language to ancient convictions, without displacing core monolatrous beliefs.

Each of these eras contributed to a Jewish theological vision in which YHWH alone is sovereign, yet He governs through a structured hierarchy of divine beings.

## *The Babylonian Exile: Crisis and Refinement*

The destruction of the First Temple in 586 BCE and the exile to Babylon marked a theological turning point for Israel. This was more than a national tragedy—it was a crisis of covenant identity. If YHWH was truly sovereign, why had He allowed His people to fall? Had the gods of Babylon, like Marduk, triumphed?

In response, Jewish theology didn't collapse—it recalibrated.

Prophets like Ezekiel and Second Isaiah (Isaiah 40-55) pushed beyond temple-centric worship and emphasized YHWH's cosmic reign. Ezekiel's vision of the mobile throne (Ezekiel 1) confirmed that YHWH's rule extended beyond Jerusalem—even into the heart of Babylon. This was no local deity bound to a single temple, but the King of all realms, traveling on wheels and wings.

And in Isaiah 45:5-7, we hear the unambiguous claim: ""I am Yahweh, and there is no other; Besides Me there is no God. I will gird you, though you have not known Me, That they may know from the rising to the setting of the sun That there is no one besides Me. I am Yahweh, and there is no other, The One forming light and creating darkness, Producing peace and creating calamity; I am Yahweh who does all these." (Isaiah 45:5–7, LSB) This text is often cited in support of strict monotheism, but its original intent was polemical, not metaphysical. Isaiah's declaration confronts the claims of Babylonian deities, asserting YHWH's supremacy over them because the true God has caused all, even the evil demons trying to divert worship to themselves—not denying their existence altogether. This is obvious in the last verse: "I am Yahweh who does all these", His being the source of all is why there is no other, no other cause, no other god who caused it all.

Importantly, divine plurality remained embedded in the worldview. For example, Daniel 10 introduces angelic "princes" over nations—figures like the "Prince of Persia" and "Michael, your prince." These are spiritual authorities operating under YHWH's dominion, echoing the divine council framework seen in Deuteronomy 32:8-9, where the nations were apportioned to the sons of God, while YHWH reserved Israel for Himself.

Rather than erasing earlier beliefs, the exile catalyzed a shift from national worship to cosmic sovereignty. The divine council framework endured, but now foreign gods were cast as powerless under YHWH's supreme dominion.

## *The Persian Period: Angelic Structure and Renewed Identity*

With the fall of Babylon and the rise of Persia in 539 BCE, the Jewish exiles were allowed to return and rebuild the Temple. This new era raised fresh theological questions: How should Israel remain distinct under a tolerant empire? Were Persian rulers operating under divine sanction? What roles did angelic beings play in cosmic governance?

This period did not produce a rejection of divine plurality but rather a deepened sense of order. Under Persian influence—particularly Zoroastrian dualism—Jewish thought refined its understanding of spiritual forces. Zoroastrianism presented a cosmic battle between light and darkness, and while Judaism never adopted its dualistic theology, similar language began to appear in Jewish apocalyptic literature.

The development of angelology accelerated. Figures like Michael, Gabriel, and Raphael emerged not as independent deities but as high-ranking servants within YHWH's court. Zechariah 3, for instance, presents a celestial courtroom where the Angel of YHWH mediates and Satan accuses, all under YHWH's oversight. Daniel 7's vision reinforces the same structure—YHWH enthroned as the Ancient of Days, with thrones set for His heavenly attendants.

This was not a dilution of monotheism. It was a consolidation of monolatry: YHWH alone was worshiped, but His governance involved a highly structured divine hierarchy.

## The Hellenistic Period: Philosophy Meets Divine Mediation

The conquest of the Near East by Alexander the Great in 332 BCE introduced Greek language, culture, and philosophy into Jewish life. This created both pressure and opportunity: Jewish thinkers had to articulate their theology using new intellectual categories without compromising their core commitments.

Rather than abandoning divine plurality, the Jewish response to Hellenism was to reframe it philosophically. Angelic intermediaries, the divine council, and exalted figures were not discarded—they were explained in ways that resonated with Platonic and Stoic thought.

The Septuagint, the Greek translation of the Hebrew Scriptures, subtly emphasized divine transcendence. Diaspora Jews—especially in Alexandria—grappled with Greek ideas through figures like Philo of Alexandria, who described the Logos as God's rational agent, mediating between the ineffable divine and the created world. This Logos, while not equal to YHWH, was depicted as a subordinate, preeminent force through whom YHWH governed.

This intellectual framework helped preserve the core of monolatry: YHWH remained the uncreated, supreme source, while the Logos (like Wisdom or the Angel of YHWH in earlier texts) acted as His agent.

Second Temple texts reflect this ongoing synthesis:

- Tobit 12:15 speaks of Raphael as one of seven angels who stand in the divine presence.
- 1 Enoch 46 introduces the "Son of Man" as a glorified but subordinate figure.
- The Dead Sea Scrolls develop cosmic dualism and angelic warfare—without ever suggesting a rival to YHWH's ultimate authority.

The Hellenistic period didn't produce theological rupture. It produced linguistic and conceptual refinement. Jewish thinkers learned to defend the same hierarchical cosmos—rooted in monolatry—using Greek philosophical tools.

## Post-Exilic Literature and the Persistence of the Divine Council

Contrary to the assumption that divine plurality disappeared after the exile, post-exilic Jewish literature preserves and even develops the divine council motif. While YHWH's supremacy is consistently affirmed, these texts depict a complex heavenly realm populated by angels, archangels, and exalted figures who function under His rule.

Two key prophetic passages illustrate this:

- **Daniel 7** presents a vivid courtroom scene: "Thrones were set in place… the Ancient of Days took His seat… thousands upon thousands served Him." This echoes earlier divine council imagery (like Psalm 82) and introduces a new exalted figure—"one like a Son of Man"—who is given authority but remains subordinate to the Ancient of Days.
- **Zechariah 3** portrays a heavenly tribunal where the Angel of YHWH mediates between Joshua the High Priest and Satan. The Angel represents divine authority while remaining distinct from YHWH, reaffirming the intermediary structure seen throughout earlier texts.

These post-exilic visions did not suppress the idea of a divine hierarchy—they transformed it into apocalyptic imagery, suited for a people living under foreign rule and seeking cosmic justice.

This theological trajectory continues in intertestamental literature:

- Tobit 12:15 identifies Raphael as one of seven angels who "stand before the glory of the Lord," implying a heavenly structure of privileged beings.
- 1 Enoch 46 builds on Daniel, introducing the "Son of Man" as a messianic judge enthroned beside the Ancient of Days—an exalted but subordinate figure.
- The Qumran texts (e.g., 1QM, the War Scroll) depict angelic armies engaged in cosmic conflict under YHWH's direction. Figures like Michael, the Prince of Light, are not independent powers but agents of divine justice.

These writings reinforce the same pattern: YHWH is unique, but not alone. His reign includes a heavenly administration, a divine court in which others participate, but none rival.

This enduring structure of divine mediation and hierarchy demonstrates that monolatry was not replaced—it matured. The divine council became the stage for visions of judgment, redemption, and the hope of restoration, setting the theological foundation for later messianic expectations.

## *The Gods Who Remain: Renamed, Not Removed*

Though the explicit term "gods" (elohim) fades in much of later Jewish literature, the beings it once described do not vanish. They are renamed, not removed. What were once called "sons of God" or "elohim" in texts like Deuteronomy 32 and Psalm 82 become mal'akhim—messengers or angels—in the Second Temple period. This shift is linguistic, not ontological. "Angel" (mal'akh/angelos) denotes a function—a messenger—not an essence. These beings are still subordinate divine agents, whether obedient or rebellious, operating under YHWH's rule. Their subordination is emphasized by the title "messenger," but their divine status is never entirely erased—especially since YHWH Himself referred to them as "gods."

This point is confirmed by Yeshua, who cites Psalm 82:6—"I said, you are gods"—and adds, "Scripture cannot be broken" (John 10:34-35). His statement affirms the enduring authority of that declaration. The beings called "gods" were not demoted by men, nor should the term be theologically overwritten. Instead, their divine identity is reframed under stricter monolatrous clarity.

This elevated status continues subtly in both the Targums and Philo's writings. In the Targums, the Memra (Word) often replaces the name of God Himself, functioning not as a lesser being but as God's personal and powerful agent. Rather than weaken divine mediation, this language elevates it—a more reverent way to refer to divine action without compromising YHWH's transcendence. Similarly, Philo refers to the Logos as "the second God" or "image of God," indicating that the term 'god' was still in use for subordinate divine agents, though within a strict philosophical hierarchy. In both cases, the category of "god" was preserved—but refined, reverently redirected, and structurally contained within Jewish monolatry.

## Jewish Angelology and the Hierarchy of Divine Beings

As Jewish thought developed in the Second Temple period, one of the most significant theological refinements was the elaboration of angelology—the study of divine messengers and their roles. The word angel (Hebrew mal'akh, Greek angelos) means "messenger." It describes a role or function, not an essence or rank. In Scripture, an "angel" can be a low-ranking spirit—or an exalted being who bears God's name and authority. What defines them is their mission, not their metaphysical category. Far from diminishing YHWH's supremacy, this growing angelic hierarchy clarified the distinction between the Most High and His divine agents.

One of the most important continuities from the Hebrew Bible into Second Temple thought is that the divine council didn't vanish—it adapted. The beings once called "gods" (elohim) in passages like Psalm 82 or Deuteronomy 32 were never portrayed as equals to YHWH. Their new designation as "messengers" or "angels" reflects their function, not their nature. In fact, the term angel (mal'akh in Hebrew, angelos in Greek) carries no ontological weight—it simply means "one sent." Whether high-ranking like Michael or rebellious like the "prince of Persia," these beings remain subordinate participants in the divine administration. Even the devil, referred to as the "god of this world" (2 Cor 4:4), is framed within this hierarchy—not as a rival deity, but as a rebellious subordinate. This preserves a crucial theme: the divine realm includes both loyal and fallen members of the council. The ongoing cosmic conflict is not between YHWH and a true rival, but between obedient and disobedient agents within His sovereign domain.

While angels are present throughout the Hebrew Bible, post-exilic texts present a more structured divine order:

- Psalm 103:20-21 speaks of angels who "do His bidding" and are "ministers who do His will," confirming their subordinate status as servants of YHWH.

- Daniel 10 introduces "princes" over nations—spiritual rulers like the "prince of Persia" and "Michael, one of the chief princes." These figures suggest that divine authority is mediated through ranked angelic beings, consistent with the divine council model seen in Deuteronomy 32 and Daniel 7.
- Zechariah 1 describes angels patrolling the earth and reporting back to the Angel of YHWH, portraying an organized network of divine messengers functioning within YHWH's command.

This more detailed hierarchy is further refined in intertestamental literature:

- Tobit 12:15 names Raphael as one of seven angels who enter before YHWH's glory. This matches 1 Enoch 20, which lists seven archangels—Michael, Gabriel, Raphael, Uriel, Raguel, Sariel, and Remiel—each assigned a distinct cosmic role.

These developments show that divine plurality was not abandoned; rather, it was formalized into an ordered celestial administration with YHWH as supreme ruler. Each angel operates on His behalf, never as an independent or competing power.

A particularly important figure within this hierarchy is the Angel of YHWH. This being often speaks as YHWH, yet is distinguished from Him:

- In Exodus 3, the Angel appears in the burning bush, yet speaks with divine authority, identifying as "the God of Abraham, Isaac, and Jacob."
- In Judges 2, the Angel of YHWH claims to have brought Israel out of Egypt—again speaking with divine prerogative.

This figure becomes the basis for later mediating concepts, such as the Memra (Word) in the Targums and the Logos in Philo's writings, both of which describe divine intermediaries who act for YHWH but are not equal to Him.

Jewish angelology, then, reinforces monolatry. It affirms that while many spiritual beings populate the divine realm, only YHWH is uncreated, sovereign, and worthy of worship. The angels, archangels, and divine messengers reflect His will, never supplant it.

## *The Influence of Persian and Hellenistic Thought on Jewish Angelology*

The development of Jewish angelology during the Second Temple period did not occur in isolation. As Jewish communities interacted with surrounding cultures—particularly during the Persian and Hellenistic eras—they absorbed certain ideas that shaped but did not redefine their theological framework. These influences helped clarify the role of divine intermediaries within the boundaries of monolatry.

Persian Influence: Cosmic Struggle and Angelic Order

Under Persian rule (539-332 BCE), Jewish thought came into contact with Zoroastrianism, a religion characterized by stark cosmic dualism. In Zoroastrian belief, the universe is divided between the good deity Ahura Mazda and the evil spirit Angra Mainyu, with spiritual beings aligned on both sides of a cosmic war.

While Jewish theology never adopted this dualism outright, it did reflect similar themes:

- Daniel 10 describes angelic princes engaged in conflict—Michael assisting the angelic messenger opposed by the "prince of Persia." This spiritual warfare echoes the Zoroastrian model, though Daniel remains firmly monolatrous: all beings, good or evil, exist under YHWH's authority.
- 1 Enoch and the War Scroll (1QM) expand on this theme, depicting

battles between the forces of light and darkness, led by angels such as Michael and opposed by Belial (Satan). Again, these figures are never portrayed as equals to YHWH, but as players within His divine strategy.

Thus, Persian thought contributed to the structure and narrative framework of Jewish apocalyptic literature, but did not alter its theological core. YHWH remains unchallenged in supremacy, even as He governs through angelic intermediaries engaged in cosmic conflict.

Hellenistic Influence: Philosophical Mediation and Divine Reason

Following Alexander the Great's conquests (332 BCE), Greek philosophy exerted significant influence on Jewish intellectual life, especially in Diaspora communities like Alexandria. This period saw the integration of Platonic and Stoic ideas into Jewish theology, leading to more abstract formulations of divine mediation.

- **Platonism** emphasized a transcendent, unchanging divine source and a world of intermediary forms or beings. This lent itself well to Jewish concepts of divine Wisdom (Chokhmah) and later, Logos (Word) as cosmic agents who executed YHWH's will.
- **Stoicism** introduced the Logos as the rational principle ordering the universe. Jewish thinkers adapted this to articulate YHWH's relationship with creation—without implying a second deity.

Most notably, Philo of Alexandria described the Logos as God's "firstborn," His chief messenger, and the agent through whom the world was made. Yet Philo did not equate the Logos with YHWH Himself; instead, he emphasized that the Logos, while divine, was subordinate and derivative— a continuation of the Angel of YHWH tradition, not a replacement for YHWH.

These Greek concepts gave Jewish theology philosophical vocabulary to express already-existing beliefs about divine mediation. The structure remained monolatrous: YHWH is the sole, uncreated source, and all intermediaries—be they angels, Logos, or Wisdom—act on His behalf.

Synthesis: Cultural Adaptation, Theological Consistency

While Persian and Greek influences introduced new categories and imagery, they did not introduce polytheism into Jewish theology. Instead, they helped sharpen distinctions:

- Between YHWH as the uncaused cause, and all other spiritual entities as derived agents.
- Between worship of the Most High and acknowledgment of divine intermediaries who serve Him.

The result was a more sophisticated angelology, fully compatible with the monolatrous framework of the Hebrew Bible. Jewish thought maintained a clear divine hierarchy, now explained in more precise terms to engage with the philosophical and religious ideas of the time.[18]

---

[18] The Second Temple period was a time of significant cultural and theological synthesis. Scholars widely acknowledge that contact with Persian Zoroastrianism influenced the development of Jewish angelology and its more structured cosmic dualism (the conflict between light and darkness). Similarly, the encounter with Hellenistic philosophy provided Jewish thinkers like Philo with a new vocabulary (such as *Logos*) to articulate their long-held beliefs about divine mediation to a Greek-speaking world. These influences did not replace the native monolatrous framework but provided new ways to express it.
See: Martin Hengel, *Judaism and Hellenism: Studies in Their Encounter in Palestine During the Early Hellenistic Period* (Philadelphia: Fortress Press, 1974). For Persian influence, see Edwin Yamauchi, *Persia and the Bible* (Grand Rapids, MI: Baker Books, 1990).

## The Targums and Divine Mediation in Jewish Thought

As Jewish communities adapted to life in the Diaspora, especially in Aramaic-speaking regions, they developed Targums—Aramaic paraphrases and interpretations of the Hebrew Scriptures. These were not mere translations; they were theological commentaries that preserved the biblical message while clarifying key ideas for new cultural contexts.

One of the most striking theological features of the Targums is their use of intermediary language to speak of YHWH's interaction with the world—particularly through terms like Memra (Word of YHWH), Shekinah (Divine Presence), and Yeqara (Divine Glory).

The Memra: The Word as Divine Agent

The Memra (Aramaic for "Word") emerges in the Targums as a theologically significant expression of YHWH's active presence, particularly in moments of creation, revelation, and covenant.

Examples include:

**Genesis 1:3 (Targum Neofiti):** "And the Memra of the Lord said: 'Let there be light'; and there was light according to the decree of his Memra."
**Psalm 33:6 (Targum Jonathan):** "By the Memra of the Lord were the heavens were made, and by the speech of his mouth all their hosts."

This parallels both Philo's Logos as the instrument of creation and the Wisdom tradition (e.g., Proverbs 8) that described divine agency in cosmic order.

Revelation and Covenant

The Memra is the communicative and relational aspect of YHWH—His Word that speaks, guides, and makes covenant:

- **Psalm 91:2** (Targum Jonathan): "In His Memra I will trust."
- **Genesis 28:20-21** (Pseudo-Jonathan): "If the Memra of YHWH will be my Helper… then the Lord shall be my God."

Here, the Memra bridges the gap between God's unapproachable transcendence and His nearness in relationship—just as the Angel of YHWH did in Exodus 23.

Judgment

Like the Angelic agents in apocalyptic literature, the Memra also executes divine judgment:

- **Deuteronomy 9:3** (Onkelos): "The Memra of the Lord is a consuming fire."

This mirrors the function of the Angel of YHWH in Numbers and Judges, and aligns with apocalyptic visions of divine intervention (e.g., 1 Enoch, War Scroll).

Protection

The Memra is also a shield, helper, and source of comfort:

- **Exodus 33:22** (Onkelos): "I will cover you with my Memra."
- **Isaiah 41:10** (Jonathan): "Fear not, for my Memra is your support."
- **Psalm 91:2** (Jonathan): "In His Memra I will trust."

This protective function recalls Michael's role in Daniel and the Qumran scrolls—as a guardian of Israel under YHWH's authority.

This development represents a striking theological elevation. Whereas earlier intermediaries like angels or divine beings functioned as messengers or warriors, the Memra introduces a more refined paradigm: a timeless agent who enacts God's will within time, preserving God's transcendence while achieving relational immediacy. Like Philo's Logos, the Memra stands at the threshold between eternity and temporality—an embodiment of dynamic eternity. In this model, God remains untouched by time, yet fully present through His agent, who bears His name and authority. In this way, the Memra becomes the most elevated form of mediation in Jewish monolatry: an agent through whom all things are made, judged, protected, and revealed—yet never mistaken for the Supreme Himself.

Comparing Memra, Logos, and the Angel of YHWH

The Memra occupies the same theological space we've previously examined in the Angel of YHWH and Philo's Logos: a divine intermediary who speaks for God, acts on His behalf, and carries out His will.

| Feature | Memra (Targums) | Logos (Philo) | Angel of YHWH (Tanakh) |
|---|---|---|---|
| Role | Mediator of divine speech and action | Cosmic rational principle | Divine messenger and agent |
| Identified as Divine? | Yes, as divine Helper (Gen 28:20-21) | Yes, called a "second God" (Q&A 2.62) | Yes, speaks as YHWH (Exod 23:-22) |
| Messianic Expectation? | Indirectly, in divine agency | No explcic messianic role | Indirectly, as divine ruler (Zech 3:1-5) |

Taken together, these figures reflect a unified Jewish theology of divine plurality within monolatry, where one supreme God rules through appointed agents. The Memra, like the Logos and Angel of YHWH, makes God knowable without compromising His singularity.

The Shekhinah: God's Indwelling Presence

While the Memra conveys divine action and Word, the Shekhinah (from רכש, "to dwell") represents God's manifest presence—especially within the Temple or among the people.

The Targums frequently use Shekhinah in place of direct references to YHWH's presence:

- In Exodus 25:8, where God says, "I will dwell among them," the Targum Onkelos reads: "I will cause my Shekhinah to dwell among them."
- In Deuteronomy 4:7: "What nation is so great as to have their God near?" the Targum Neofiti answers: "For the **Shekhinah of the Lord our God is nigh**"

The Shekhinah functions like the Yeqara (Glory) or the divine kavod in Ezekiel and Isaiah's visions—transcendent yet local, awesome yet relational.

Together, Memra and Shekhinah encapsulate divine communication and presence. They offer a nuanced way for post-exilic and Second Temple Jews to speak of God's activity without compromising His transcendence.

In Summary:

- **Memra** – God's Word in action: speech, creation, covenant, judgment
- **Shekhinah** – God's Presence dwelling among His people

Together, they express how YHWH remains utterly transcendent while acting intimately through chosen agents

## Conclusion: A Framework of Mediation within Monolatry

The Targums, though post-biblical in form, reflect an older, consistent theology: YHWH governs the world through structured divine agency. Whether through Memra, Shekhinah, the Angel of YHWH, or Philo's Logos, we observe the same pattern:

1. God remains the uncaused Cause, utterly unique and supreme.
2. His Word, Presence, and agents carry out His will, speaking, protecting, judging, and creating.

3. Worship remains directed to YHWH alone, while His intermediaries are honored but not adored.

This continuity affirms that early Christian claims about a divine mediator were not theological novelties, but deeply rooted in Jewish thought. The Memra especially offers a direct parallel to the Johannine Logos, setting the stage for understanding Yeshua as the Word made flesh.

## *Looking Ahead*

With the theological foundation of the Memra now established, we are prepared to explore how this idea converged with emerging messianic expectations, and how it shaped early Jewish-Christian interpretation of Yeshua's identity.

In the next chapter, we will examine how the concept of the Word, understood through the lens of the Targums, Philo, and the Hebrew Scriptures, comes to full expression in the New Testament's presentation of Messiah as both divine and subordinate—a mediator perfectly situated within the Jewish tradition of monolatry.

# 5

# Philo's Logos and the Bridge Between Jewish Thought and Early Christology

Philo of Alexandria (c. 20 BCE–50 CE), a Hellenistic Jewish philosopher, played a pivotal role in articulating how Jewish theology could speak meaningfully to a Greek-speaking world. His concept of the Logos—a rational, divine intermediary—became one of the most significant bridges between Second Temple Jewish monolatry and early Christian Christology.

As we've seen, Jewish thought during the Second Temple period had already developed a rich theological framework: YHWH reigned supreme, while subordinate divine agents such as angels, the Memra, Wisdom, and the Angel of YHWH acted under His authority. Philo's Logos continued this tradition, offering a philosophically refined way to speak of divine mediation without compromising YHWH's supremacy.

This chapter explores Philo's intellectual context, the multifaceted nature of the Logos in his writings, its continuity with Jewish intermediaries, and its influence on New Testament theology and the Church Fathers.

## Philo's Intellectual World

Living in Alexandria—a hub of Jewish and Hellenistic learning—Philo was educated in both the Hebrew Scriptures and Greek philosophy. His goal was to show that the Torah was not only compatible with philosophical reason but superior to it. To that end, he interpreted the Hebrew Bible allegorically, using Platonic and Stoic categories to express Jewish truths.

Some of his most influential works include:

- **Legum Allegoriae** (Allegorical Interpretation): Applying Platonic ideas to Genesis.
- **De Opificio Mundi** (On the Creation): Harmonizing Genesis 1 with Greek cosmology.
- **Quis Rerum Divinarum Heres** (Who Is the Heir of Divine Things?): Exploring themes of mediation and inheritance.

Philo's thought is thoroughly Jewish in content, yet expressed in the language of Greek metaphysics—making him a critical link between Jewish monolatry and Greco-Roman philosophical theology.

## *The Logos in Philo's Theology*

In Philo's writings, the **Logos** (Greek for "Word" or "Reason") is the central mediator between God and creation. It is at once divine and subordinate—a reflection of the same structured hierarchy we've traced throughout Second Temple Judaism.

### 1. The Logos as Divine Mediator

Philo calls the Logos the "eldest Son of God," portraying him as a bridge between the transcendent God and the material world:

> *"For the Father of the universe has caused him to spring up as the eldest son, whom... he calls the firstborn."*
> — Confusion of Tongues *146*

He describes the Logos as continually interceding for humanity:

> *"And this same Word is continually a suppliant to the immortal God on behalf of the mortal race, which is exposed to affliction and misery; and is also the ambassador, sent by the Ruler of all, to the subject race.*
> *"*— Who Is the Heir of Divine Things? *205*

In this single sentence, Philo masterfully captures the dual function of the Logos, providing a conceptual framework that powerfully resonates with the New Testament's description of Jesus. Philo's **"suppliant,"** who continually pleads for humanity, finds its direct counterpart in the New Testament, where Jesus is our **"Advocate with the Father" (1 John 2:1)**. This role is defined even more explicitly when Paul calls Jesus the **"one mediator between God and men" (1 Timothy 2:5)**. At the same time, Philo's **"ambassador,"** who represents God's authority downward to the world, perfectly aligns with Jesus's mission as the one sent from the Father to reveal Him.

The structural parallel is undeniable: both Philo's philosophy and the early Church's theology envisioned a supreme God who interacts with humanity through a single, unique, and subordinate divine intermediary. This shared framework demonstrates how the monolatrous view was maintained in both traditions. The model is not one of co-equal trinity but of divine hierarchy, where the mediator—whether called Logos, Advocate, or Son—functions as the Father's exclusive agent.

This recalls the function of the **Angel of YHWH** and the **Memra**, both of whom serve as divine agents acting on YHWH's behalf, yet never rivaling His authority.

## 2. The Logos as the "Second God"

Philo goes so far as to call the Logos a "second god" (*deuteros theos*)—but crucially, always subordinate to the Supreme:

> *"Why is it that he speaks **as if of some other god**, saying that he made man after the image of God, and **not** that he made him **after his own image**? (#Ge 9:6). Very appropriately and without any falsehood was this oracular sentence uttered by God, for **no mortal thing could have been formed on the similitude of the supreme Father** of the*

*universe, **but only after the pattern of the second deity, who is the Word** of the supreme Being"*
— Questions and Answers on Genesis *II.62*[19]

This terminology mirrors what we've seen in Jewish apocalyptic literature: exalted figures such as the **Son of Man** in 1 Enoch, or **Melchizedek** in the Dead Sea Scrolls, who act with divine authority but never eclipse YHWH's supremacy.

Importantly, when Philo uses the phrase "second god," he does not imply polytheism or equality with the Supreme. Rather, he follows a pattern visible throughout Jewish scripture: divine beings may be called "god" or even bear the divine name, yet always operate under YHWH's supreme will. This is consistent with Psalm 82, where YHWH Himself uses the term "gods" for subordinate beings, affirming the legitimacy of the title without surrendering His unrivaled authority.

## 3. The Logos as Creative Word

Philo identifies the Logos as the divine Word through which creation came into being:

---

[19] Philo's description of the Logos as a "second god" (*deuteros theos*) is a pivotal moment in the development of Second Temple theology. As a Hellenistic Jewish philosopher, Philo sought to harmonize the Hebrew Scriptures with Greek philosophy. His Logos doctrine, which presents a divine but subordinate intermediary, is a sophisticated expression of the monolatrous framework and had a profound influence on early Christian thinkers who were grappling with how to articulate the divine identity of Yeshua.

See: Larry W. Hurtado, "Philo's 'Second God' and the 'Divine Man,'" in *One God, One Lord: Early Christian Devotion and Ancient Jewish Monotheism*, 3rd ed. (London: T&T Clark, 2015), 41-50. See also David Winston, *Logos and Mystical Theology in Philo of Alexandria* (Cincinnati: Hebrew Union College Press, 1985).

*Philo describes the Logos as the 'image of God,' through which the world was framed* (On the Creation *24-25*).

This echoes the biblical tradition where God speaks creation into existence (Genesis 1) and aligns with the Wisdom of Solomon:

> *"You made all things by Your Logos."*
> — Wisdom of Solomon *9:1–2*

Again, we see continuity with the **Memra** in the Targums, which acts as YHWH's spoken agent in both creation and covenant.

### 4. The Logos as Angelic Commander

Philo merges the Logos with angelic tradition by presenting him as the commander of the divine host:

> *"To the one who is first, the eldest Logos, He has entrusted the care of the sacred army."*
> — On Dreams *1.239*

This aligns the Logos with the **Angel of YHWH**, the divine warrior and covenant messenger seen throughout the Hebrew Bible.

### 5. The Logos as Divine Reason (Nous)

Philo also identifies the Logos with divine rationality—*Nous*—which sustains the cosmos, describing it as the divine reason that "binds and holds together all things" (*On the Migration of Abraham* 6). This Philonic concept shows remarkable harmony with the New Testament's description of Jesus's cosmic role. The Apostle Paul, for instance, writes that in Jesus "all things hold together" (Colossians 1:17) and makes an even more direct parallel in his letter to the Corinthians. There, he explains that while all things are *from* God the Father, it is through "one Lord, Jesus Christ, **by whom are all things**" (1 Corinthians 8:6). In both frameworks, the transcendent God engages with and sustains creation through a single, divine agent. This harmony between Philo's Logos and Paul's Christology powerfully demonstrates a shared worldview rooted in monolatry, where a supreme God operates through His exclusive, world-ordering agent.

The term *god* (θεός / elohim) in these contexts should not be misunderstood as implying equality with YHWH. In both Hebrew and Greek usage, it could designate exalted beings or agents who bear divine authority without being self-existent or worthy of worship. Just as the Targums often apply the name YHWH to the Memra, so too does Philo assign the title "god" to the Logos—not to create a second independent deity, but to describe a fully empowered intermediary acting by divine commission.

## *Logos, Memra, and the Providential Bridge*

The parallels between Philo's Logos and the **Memra** of the Targums are striking. Both function as YHWH's active agent, both are referred to as the instrument of creation, and both stand in between the transcendent God and the created order.

While Philo spoke to a Hellenistic Jewish audience, the broader providential result was that Gentiles, steeped in philosophical notions of the Logos, were prepared to understand John's claim:

> *"And the Logos became flesh and dwelt among us."*
> — John 1:14

This theological bridge enabled Jewish and Gentile audiences alike to grasp the radical claim of **Yeshua as the Logos**: a personal manifestation of the same divine mediator spoken of by both Hebrew and Hellenistic traditions.

## *Philo and the New Testament Logos*

John's Gospel opens with a formulation deeply reminiscent of Philo:

> *"In the beginning was the Logos, and the Logos was with God, and the Logos was God."*
> — John 1:1

What would have been radical is not the idea of a divine Logos, but that this Logos became flesh. John's Gospel does not invent new metaphysics—it redeploys familiar Jewish categories: Word, Image, Wisdom, and Glory. These concepts, already functioning as mediators in Jewish theology, are gathered and applied to Yeshua in a profoundly personal and historical form.

This echoes Philo's language of the Logos being both divine and distinct, the firstborn of God, and the agent of creation. Colossians 1:15–17, describing Messiah as "the image of the invisible God" and "firstborn over all creation," further reflects this conceptual lineage.

The **Church Fathers** also carry Philo's influence:

- **Justin Martyr** identifies Jesus as the Logos and the pre-existent Angel of YHWH.
- **Irenaeus** emphasizes the Logos as eternally begotten yet subordinate to the Father.
- **Clement of Alexandria** describes the Logos as the rational mediator between God and the world—divine reason incarnate.[20]

Philo, though not a Christian, helped shape the categories through which early believers articulated the divine identity of Yeshua within the framework of Jewish monolatry.

---

[20] The early Christian apologists frequently identified the personified Wisdom of Proverbs 8 with the pre-existent Christ. Figures like Justin Martyr and Tertullian explicitly used this passage to argue for the Son's pre-existence and his role as the agent of creation, seeing a direct continuity between the *Chokhmah* (Wisdom) of the Hebrew Bible and the *Logos* of John's Gospel.

See: Jaroslav Pelikan, *The Christian Tradition: A History of the Development of Doctrine, Vol. 1: The Emergence of the Catholic Tradition (100-600)* (Chicago: University of Chicago Press, 1971), 188-191.

## Conclusion: Philo's Lasting Impact

Philo's Logos doctrine demonstrates that divine mediation was not a foreign or Christian innovation—it was deeply rooted in Jewish theology, developed further through Greek philosophical expression, and adapted by early Christians to describe the unique role of the Messiah.

Importantly, Philo never departed from **monolatry**:

- The Logos is always subordinate to YHWH.
- Worship is reserved exclusively for the Supreme God.
- The Logos functions as agent, not as rival.

Early Christian theology, particularly in the Johannine tradition, built upon this model—radically personalizing the Logos as Yeshua, but without abandoning the monolatrous structure inherited from Jewish thought.

Philo's contribution lies not in creating something new, but in clarifying what was already present in Israel's scriptures: that YHWH governs through Word, Wisdom, and Agent. His Logos concept gave these truths a philosophical voice, setting the stage for their fuller embodiment in the emerging Christian story—all within the enduring framework of Jewish monolatry.

Even Eusebius of Caesarea, writing in the fourth century, recognized Philo's theological instincts as aligned with Christian truth. In *Ecclesiastical History*, he describes Philo as a wise man whose writings "harmonized with the doctrines of the Church," especially in his understanding of divine mediation and the Logos. This endorsement reflects how early Christian thinkers saw continuity, not contradiction, between Philo's Jewish monolatry and their own developing Christology.

Eusebius of Caesarea affirmed Philo's value to Christian theological heritage. In *Praeparatio Evangelica* 7.21, Eusebius calls Philo a Hebrew interpreter of Scripture who rightly explained the divine image and Logos. He praises Philo's insight that man was made not in the image of the Supreme God, but "in the likeness of the second God, who is the Word [Logos] of the other." This, Eusebius notes, was spoken with "great beauty and wisdom." Philo's formulation—of a subordinate Logos who bears the image and reason of God—harmonized so closely with Christian Logos theology that Eusebius could cite him as an authoritative precursor, not a rival.[21]

This reception confirms that Philo's Jewish monolatry—structured hierarchy under one supreme God—formed a natural theological bridge to early Christian monolatry. For both, the Logos is not an equal rival to God Most High, but a divinely appointed intermediary, a rational and personal extension of YHWH's will.

---

[21] Eusebius of Caesarea, one of the most important historians and theologians of the early fourth century, held Philo's work in high regard. In his *Ecclesiastical History*, he praises Philo and notes the harmony between his Logos theology and Christian doctrine. This endorsement by a key pre-Nicene figure demonstrates that the early church saw the monolatrous, hierarchical framework of Philo not as a theological problem, but as a legitimate and valuable precursor to its own Christology.
See: Eusebius, *Ecclesiastical History*, Book II, Chapters 16-18.

## Moving Forward

The next chapter will explore the **Targumic Memra**, the Aramaic counterpart to Philo's Logos. There, we'll see how Jewish translations and paraphrases of the Hebrew Bible consistently presented the **Word of YHWH** as His divine agent, reinforcing the same theological logic that prepared the ground for early Christology.

# 6

# The Targums, Memra, and Shekhinah

As Jewish communities moved further from Hebrew as a spoken language, the need arose to make Scripture accessible through paraphrased translations. The result was the Targums—Aramaic renderings of the Hebrew Bible that went beyond mere translation. They offered interpretive glosses, theological expansions, and, crucially, preserved Second Temple Jewish concepts of divine mediation.

Among their most distinctive contributions is the introduction of two powerful theological terms: Memra ('Word')[22] and Shekhinah ('Divine Presence')—each offering a way to maintain YHWH's transcendence while dynamically expressing His nearness through mediated relationship. These terms reflect the same monolatrous structure we have seen throughout earlier chapters: YHWH remains supreme, but His interactions with the

---

[22] The use of *Memra* ("Word") in the Aramaic Targums is a key feature of post-biblical Jewish theology. Scholars note that the *Memra* is not merely a substitute for the divine name but functions as a distinct agent through which God creates, reveals, and makes covenants. This allowed the Targumists to preserve God's transcendence while affirming His active involvement in the world through a divine intermediary.

See: Daniel Boyarin, "The Gospel of the Memra: Jewish Binitarianism and the Prologue to John," *Harvard Theological Review* 94, no. 3 (2001): 243–284. See also Bruce Chilton, *The Isaiah Targum: Introduction, Translation, Apparatus, and Notes* (Collegeville, MN: Liturgical Press, 1987).

world are mediated through exalted yet subordinate agents.

As with the Logos in Philo's theology and the Angel of YHWH in biblical texts, the Memra and Shekhinah operate within a theological system that affirms divine plurality without compromising the uniqueness or supremacy of YHWH. This chapter will explore how the Targums express that structure, laying further groundwork for later Jewish and Christian theological developments.

## The Role of the Targums in Jewish Thought

The Targums were not simply word-for-word translations. They were liturgical tools used in synagogue settings to interpret the Scriptures for an Aramaic-speaking audience. In doing so, they served as a theological bridge, shaping how Jewish communities understood divine agency, revelation, and presence.

In their interpretive work, the Targums consistently:
- Avoided anthropomorphic descriptions of God.
- Inserted interpretive commentary to clarify theological meaning.
- Introduced terminology like Memra and Shekhinah to describe how God acted in the world.

Much like Philo's Logos, the Memra provided a way to speak of God's activity in creation, covenant, and judgment, while maintaining a strong sense of God's transcendence.

The Memra: YHWH's Word as Divine Mediator

The Memra appears in place of the direct name of YHWH in many key biblical texts. Where the Hebrew Scriptures simply state, "God said," or "YHWH appeared," the Targums often insert "the Memra of YHWH"—a theological term that encapsulates divine agency.

Rather than being a mere euphemism, the Memra operates like the Logos or Angel of YHWH: a distinct but subordinate expression of God's presence and will. As with previous intermediaries, the Memra:
- Speaks, creates, and judges.
- Acts in covenantal relationships.
- Carries divine authority while remaining distinct from YHWH's essence.

Let's look more closely at how the Targums deploy the Memra in four key theological categories.

Memra in Action: Four Theological Functions

1. Creation

The Memra is introduced as the creative agent, echoing both Genesis and Psalm language:
- Genesis 1:3 (Targum Neofiti): "And the Memra of the Lord said, 'Let there be light.'"
- Psalm 33:6 (Targum Jonathan): "By the Memra of the Lord were the heavens made."

This parallels both Philo's Logos as the instrument of creation and the Wisdom tradition (e.g., Proverbs 8) that described divine agency in cosmic order.

2. Revelation and Covenant

## THE TARGUMS, MEMRA, AND SHEKHINAH

The Memra is the communicative and relational aspect of YHWH—His Word that speaks, guides, and makes covenant:

• Psalm 91:2 (Targum Jonathan): "In His Memra I will trust."

• Genesis 28:20–21 (Pseudo-Jonathan): "If the Memra of YHWH will be my Helper… then the Lord shall be my God."

Here, the Memra bridges the gap between God's unapproachable transcendence and His nearness in relationship—just as the Angel of YHWH did in Exodus 23.

3. Judgment

Like the Angelic agents in apocalyptic literature, the Memra also executes divine judgment:
• Deuteronomy 9:3 (Onkelos): "The Memra of the Lord is a consuming fire."

This mirrors the function of the Angel of YHWH in Numbers and Judges, and aligns with apocalyptic visions of divine intervention (e.g., 1 Enoch, War Scroll).

4. Protection

The Memra is also a shield, helper, and source of comfort:
• Exodus 33:22 (Onkelos): "I will cover you with my Memra."
• Isaiah 41:10 (Jonathan): "Fear not, for my Memra is with you."

This protective function recalls Michael's role in Daniel and the Qumran scrolls—as a guardian of Israel under YHWH's authority.

This development represents a striking theological elevation. Whereas earlier intermediaries like angels or divine beings functioned as messengers or warriors, the Memra introduces a more refined paradigm: a timeless agent who enacts God's will within time, preserving God's transcendence while achieving relational immediacy. Like Philo's Logos, the Memra stands at the threshold between eternity and temporality—an embodiment of dynamic eternity. In this model, God remains untouched by time, yet fully present through His agent, who bears His name and authority. In this way, the Memra becomes the most elevated form of mediation in Jewish monolatry: an agent through whom all things are made, judged, protected, and revealed—yet never mistaken for the Supreme Himself.

Comparing Memra, Logos, and the Angel of YHWH

The Memra occupies the same theological space we've previously examined in the Angel of YHWH and Philo's Logos: a divine intermediary who speaks for God, acts on His behalf, and carries out His will.

| Feature | Memra (Targums) | Logos (Philo) | Angel of YHWH (Tanakh) |
|---|---|---|---|
| Role | Mediator of divine speech and action | Cosmic rational principle | Divine messenger and agent |
| Identified as Divine? | Yes, as divine Helper (Genesis 28:20-21) | Yes, called a "second God" (Questions & Answers 2.62) | Yes, speaks as YHWH (Exodus 23:20-22D) |
| Messianic Expectation? | Indirectly, in divine agency | No explicit messianic mesianic role | Indirectly, as divine (Zechariah 3:1-5) |

*Taken together, these figures reflect a unified Jewish theology of divine plurality within monolatry, where one supreme God rules through appointed agents. The Memra, like the Logos and Angel of YHWH, makes God knowable without compromising His singularity.*

The Shekhinah: God's Indwelling Presence

While the Memra conveys divine action and Word, the Shekhinah (from רכש, "to dwell") represents God's manifest presence—especially within the Temple or among the people.

The Targums frequently use Shekhinah in place of direct references to YHWH's presence:

In Exodus 25:8, where God says, "I will dwell among them," the Targum reads: "I will cause my Shekhinah to dwell among them."

In Deuteronomy 4:7: "What nation is so great as to have their God near?" the Targum Neofiti answers: "Whose Shekhinah is with them."

The Shekhinah functions like the Yeqara (Glory) or the divine kavod in Ezekiel and Isaiah's visions—transcendent yet local, awesome yet relational.

Together, Memra and Shekhinah encapsulate divine communication and presence. They offer a nuanced way for post-exilic and Second Temple Jews to speak of God's activity without compromising His transcendence.

In Summary:
- Memra – God's Word in action: speech, creation, covenant, judgment
- Shekhinah – God's Presence dwelling among His people
- Together, they express how YHWH remains utterly transcendent while acting intimately through chosen agents

Conclusion: A Framework of Mediation within Monolatry

The Targums, though post-biblical in form, reflect an older, consistent theology: YHWH governs the world through structured divine agency. Whether through Memra, Shekhinah, the Angel of YHWH, or Philo's Logos, we observe the same pattern:

God remains the uncaused Cause, utterly unique and supreme.

His Word, Presence, and agents carry out His will, speaking, protecting, judging, and creating.

Worship remains directed to YHWH alone, while His intermediaries are honored but not adored.

This continuity affirms that early Christian claims about a divine mediator were not theological novelties, but deeply rooted in Jewish thought. The Memra especially offers a direct parallel to the Johannine Logos, setting the stage for understanding Yeshua as the Word made flesh.

Looking Ahead

With the theological foundation of the Memra now established, we are prepared to explore how this idea converged with emerging messianic expectations, and how it shaped early Jewish-Christian interpretation of Yeshua's identity.

# 7

# Qumran (Dead Sea Scrolls) and Other Second Temple Evidence

The Second Temple period was a defining era for Jewish theology, shaping the theological landscape that early Christianity would later emerge from. During this time, various Jewish sects debated divine agency, messianic figures, and the function of divine intermediaries within a monolatrous framework. Though these groups differed in specifics, they shared a fundamental commitment to the worship of one supreme God—YHWH—who worked through subordinate divine agents.

The Qumran community, often identified with the Essenes, provides invaluable insights into Second Temple Jewish thought. Their Dead Sea Scrolls (DSS) reveal a theology structured around divine mediation, angelic hierarchies, and eschatological expectations—all of which align with the broader Jewish tradition while anticipating concepts later developed in early Christianity. This chapter explores the theological significance of Qumran's writings by addressing the following questions:

- How did Qumran conceptualize divine agency?
- What role did divine intermediaries play in their theology?
- How do their texts compare with Philo's Logos and the Targums' Memra?

# QUMRAN (DEAD SEA SCROLLS) AND OTHER SECOND TEMPLE EVIDENCE

- Did Qumran preserve monolatry while engaging with divine plurality?

By analyzing these themes, we bridge the gap between Second Temple Judaism and the theological developments of early Christianity, demonstrating that Christological concepts arose within, rather than apart from, Jewish theological traditions.

## Overview of Chapter Structure

## Qumran Community and Their Theology

- The historical and theological background of Qumran and the Dead Sea Scrolls.
- Their beliefs on divine mediation, messianic expectations, and angelic figures.
- Key texts such as 1QM (War Scroll), 1QHa (Thanksgiving Hymns), and 11QMelchizedek.

## Common Threads with Philo and the Targums

- Comparison of Qumran's divine mediation framework with Philo's Logos and the Targums' Memra.
- How these traditions reflect a shared commitment to monolatry while engaging with divine agency.

## Transition into the New Testament

- How first-century Jewish thought laid the foundation for Christology.
- The Qumranic expectation of a divine-human messianic figure and its parallels with early Christian theology.

## Qumran Community and Their Theology
### Divine Hierarchy

## MONOLATRY

The Songs of the Sabbath Sacrifice (4Q400–407) depict a celestial priesthood performing liturgy in heaven. These angels are arranged in structured ranks, acting under YHWH's supreme authority:

> *"Praise the God of the exalted [angels]... O [divine] spirits of knowledge, truth, and righteousness in his glorious kingdom, [praise] the exaltation of His name." (4Q403 1 i 30–31)*

The Community Rule (1QS) refers to the Prince of Light and the Angel of Darkness:[23]

> *"He has appointed the Prince of Light to assist us in all our ways, and the Angel of Darkness to act against us." (1QS 3:20–21)*

These figures, while powerful, remain subordinate agents within YHWH's command structure.

### Angels and Mediators

Qumran texts frequently describe angels and exalted humans as God's agents:

- **4Q246**: "He will be called the Son of God, and they will call him the Son of the Most High. His kingdom will be an everlasting kingdom."

---

[23] The dualism of the Qumran community, particularly the figures of the Prince of Light and the Angel of Darkness (also called Belial), reflects a developed angelology with a clear cosmic hierarchy. While influenced by Persian thought, this framework remains monolatrous, as both figures are created beings who operate under the ultimate sovereignty of the one God.

*See:* James C. VanderKam, "The Angelic World," in *An Introduction to Early Judaism*, 2nd ed. (Grand Rapids, MI: Eerdmans, 2022), 154-157.

(4Q246 2:1–4)[24]
- **4Q521 (Messianic Apocalypse)**: "He will heal the wounded, revive the dead, and bring good news to the poor."
- **1QS 9:11**: "Until the coming of the Prophet and the Messiahs of Aaron and Israel."

These messianic expectations include both priestly and kingly figures who serve under divine commission.

**Scriptural Interpretation**

The pesharim interpret Scripture in light of the community's theology:

- **4Q175 (Testimonia)**: Brings together Deuteronomy 18:18, Psalm 2, and Isaiah 11 to describe a prophetic and royal Messiah.
- **4Q285 ( Formerly *The Pierced Messiah* now conquering Messiah)**: Once thought to describe a "pierced Messiah," the corrected reading of fragment 4Q285 now points to a powerful "killing Messiah" who triumphs over his enemies. This revised understanding does not weaken the links to the New Testament but strengthens them in a different direction. It aligns this Qumranic expectation with the apocalyptic vision of Jesus in Revelation 19—not as the lamb who was slain, but as the conquering "Word of God" on a white horse who

---

[24] The Aramaic text known as 4Q246, or the "Son of God" text, is one of the most significant pre-Christian manuscripts for understanding the background of the New Testament's Christological titles. Scholars note the striking parallels to the language used for Jesus in the Gospel of Luke (cf. Luke 1:32, 35). While the identity of the figure is debated (whether a historical king or a future messianic figure), the text clearly shows that the titles "Son of God" and "Son of the Most High" were used within a Jewish context for a supreme, eschatological agent of God before the time of Jesus.

See: Florentino García Martínez, *Qumran and Apocalyptic: Studies on the Aramaic Texts from Qumran* (Leiden: Brill, 1992), 162–179.

returns to execute divine judgment.[25]

- **4Q396 (Some Works of the Law):** Emphasizes covenant obedience and divine oversight.

These interpretations support the view of a suffering, victorious redeemer under YHWH's authority.

### Ritual and Eschatology

Purity laws reflect readiness for divine presence:

> "They shall be separated from the midst of the habitation of unjust men and shall go into the wilderness to prepare the way." (1QS 5:13–14)

The War Scroll (1QM) anticipates cosmic judgment:

> "The heavens and the earth shall obey the Prince of Light... he shall judge the wicked and destroy the Sons of Darkness." (1QM 13:10–11)

This eschatological vision connects with Christian texts like Revelation 19:11–16, which depicts Yeshua as divine warrior.

## Common Threads with Philo and the Targums
### Shared Theological Framework

Despite linguistic and cultural differences, Qumran, the Targums, and Philo all express a monolatrous theology in which subordinate agents serve under YHWH:

---

[25] The initial, highly publicized reading of this fragment as a "pierced" or "slain" Messiah has been almost universally rejected by subsequent scholarship. The scholarly consensus now affirms that the key Hebrew verb is best translated as "he will kill," referring to the messianic "Prince of the Congregation" who triumphs over his enemies. This interpretation aligns the text with other Qumranic expectations of a conquering, not a suffering, messianic figure.

*For a summary of the scholarly debate and consensus, see: Géza Vermes, The Complete Dead Sea Scrolls in English, Revised ed. (Penguin Classics, 2004), introduction to the text.*

- **Memra in Targums**: "And the Memra of the Lord created man in His image." (Targum Neofiti on Gen. 1:27)
- **Logos in Philo**: "The Logos is the eldest son, the high priest of creation." (De Confusione Linguarum 146)
- **Melchizedek in Qumran**: "Melchizedek will proclaim liberty... and execute judgment in the divine council." (11Q13 2:9–13)[26]

All three frameworks preserve the uniqueness of YHWH while using intermediary language.

## Transition into the New Testament

Early Christian thought did not invent divine mediation but inherited it:

- **4Q246's "Son of God"** → Luke 1:32 "He will be called Son of the Most High."
- **4Q521's miracles** → Matt. 11:5 "The blind receive sight... and the good news is proclaimed to the poor."
- **4Q285's conquering Messiah** → Revelation 19:11-16 "He judges and makes war... King of kings."[27]
- **Targumic Memra** → John 1:1 "In the beginning was the Word."
- **11Q13's Melchizedek** → Hebrews 7:17 "You are a priest forever after

---

[26] The Melchizedek scroll (11Q13 or 11QMelch) from Qumran depicts a heavenly figure named Melchizedek who carries out divine judgment and proclaims final atonement. This figure is an exalted divine agent, acting on God's behalf in the heavenly council. This text demonstrates that Second Temple Judaism contained traditions of powerful, heavenly mediators who fulfilled roles typically reserved for God, a key theological precedent for the New Testament's presentation of Jesus as the ultimate high priest and judge.

See: Andrei A. Orlov, "The Melchizedek Tradition," in *The Enoch-Metatron Tradition* (Tübingen: Mohr Siebeck, 2005), 95-101.

[27] The initial, highly publicized reading of this fragment (4Q285) as a "pierced" or "slain" Messiah has been almost universally rejected by subsequent scholarship. The scholarly consensus now affirms that the key Hebrew verb is best translated as "he will kill" or "they will kill," referring to the messianic "Prince of the Congregation" who triumphs over his enemies. This corrected reading provides a powerful parallel not to the crucifixion, but to the conquering, warrior Messiah depicted in Revelation 19.

the order of Melchizedek."
- **1QM's divine warrior** → Revelation 19:11–16 "He judges and makes war... King of kings."

## Conclusion

The Dead Sea Scrolls affirm that Jewish theology was rich with mediatory concepts that upheld monolatry. Divine agents like the Prince of Light, Melchizedek, and the "Son of God" in Qumran texts prepared the ground for early Christian Christology.

---

*For a summary of the scholarly debate and consensus, see: Géza Vermes, The Complete Dead Sea Scrolls in English, Revised ed. (Penguin Classics, 2004), in the introduction to the text. Vermes refers to it as 'The Messianic Leader (the Prince of the Congregation)'.*

# 8

# Wisdom and Logos: Mediators of the Divine Mind

While angels and divine agents represented YHWH's presence in specific moments of history or revelation, Jewish theology during the Second Temple period developed a more conceptual mediator—one that could account for the consistent, sustaining wisdom and order of the universe. This idea took form in two key figures: Wisdom (הַחָכְמָה, Chokhmah) in Hebrew tradition and the Logos (Λόγος) in Hellenistic Jewish philosophy.

Both concepts function as **personified expressions** of YHWH's will—divine, yet distinct from YHWH Himself. These figures were not separate deities but explanatory tools, helping Jewish thinkers understand how an utterly transcendent God could remain immanent in the world.

## Wisdom in the Hebrew Bible and Beyond

The Hebrew Bible presents Wisdom as **preexistent, creative**, and **near to God**—but always **subordinate**:

**Proverbs 8:22–31 (LBS)**: Wisdom speaks, saying, "Yahweh possessed me at the beginning of His way, Before His deeds of old.... I was beside Him, *as a master workman*"[28]

- → She is present at creation, but not co-eternal or self-existent.

One of the most debated verses in this tradition is Proverbs 8:22, where Wisdom declares, "Yahweh possessed me at the beginning of His way." At first glance, this seems to place Wisdom within created time. However, the phrase "at the beginning" (רֵאשִׁית, *reshit*) means far more than a simple chronological start; it signifies **primordial primacy**. Wisdom is "acquired" or "possessed" by God not as the first act *in* time, but as the foundational act that precedes all created things, **including time itself**. As God's very first work, Wisdom's begetting must, by definition, operate outside of and before the unfolding of time-bound creation. She is the first, eternal expression of God's divine will.

This opens the door to what some scholars call a **dynamic eternity**: the idea

---

[28] The personification of Wisdom in Proverbs 8 is a key text for understanding the development of divine mediation in Jewish thought. Scholars note that Wisdom is depicted as being "possessed" or "acquired" by Yahweh "at the beginning of His way," establishing her as the first and highest of God's works, but still subordinate to Him. She is "beside Him, as a master workman," an agent through whom creation is ordered, not the uncaused source of creation itself.
See: Richard J. Clifford, "The Personification of Wisdom," in *The Anchor Yale Bible Dictionary*, ed. David Noel Freedman (New York: Doubleday, 1992), 6:960-962.

that something can be "brought forth" from God and yet not be contingent in the way created things are. It is eternal not by self-existence, but by being the first and inseparable act of God's will. Later Jewish thinkers—and eventually early Christians—would find in this verse a model for how divine mediation can be ancient, exalted, and foundational, without rivaling God's ultimacy.[29]

This portrait of Wisdom at creation may also illuminate the otherwise enigmatic statement in **Genesis 1:26**: *"Let us make man in our image, after our likeness."* While traditionally interpreted in a range of ways—angelic address, divine plurality, or rhetorical plurality—the presence of preexistent Wisdom offers another possible layer. If Wisdom is God's agent in creation, as Proverbs suggests, then this "us" may reflect the **dialogue between YHWH and His mediating agent**. The phrase *"in our image"* gains new depth: it points not to a visible form of God—who is invisible—but to **His**

---

[29] This verse became the central Old Testament battleground of the Arian controversy. As historian R.P.C. Hanson notes, it was a point of universal agreement among all parties—Arians, Nicenes, and subordinationists alike—that the figure of Wisdom in this passage referred to Christ. The Arians seized upon the Septuagint's translation, "The Lord **created** (*ektise*) me," as undeniable proof that the Son was a creature.

However, a theologian like Eusebius of Caesarea, who rejected the Arian view, offered a different interpretation. He argued that the word *ektise* did not have to mean "created out of nothing" as Arius claimed. In his work *On Ecclesiastical Theology*, Eusebius argued that in this context, it meant that the Father had **"established"** the Son as the head and principle of creation. For Eusebius, this did not imply the Son was a creature; rather, it affirmed his unique, pre-temporal begetting *from the Father* to be the agent through whom all other things were then made. This interpretation allowed Eusebius to preserve the Son's true divinity and pre-existence while maintaining his subordination to the Father as his source—a classic expression of the monolatrous framework.

See: R.P.C. Hanson, *The Search for the Christian Doctrine of God: The Arian Controversy 318-381* (Edinburgh: T&T Clark, 1988), 825-830. For Eusebius's specific exegesis, see Eusebius of Caesarea, *On Ecclesiastical Theology*, Book 3, Chapter 2.

**appointed image-bearing agent.**[30]

In this reading, the "image" of God is not a physical likeness but a **functional resemblance to the one through whom God creates and governs**—Wisdom. This interpretation parallels later Jewish and Christian traditions that speak of the Logos or Son as the visible Image of the invisible God (cf. Colossians 1:15), and it fits comfortably within Second Temple patterns of divine mediation. Humanity is made in the image of the one who embodies divine Wisdom—thus rooting human dignity not just in divine creation, but in **divine mediation.**

- **Sirach 24:3, 9** and **Wisdom of Solomon 7:25-26** echo this portrayal:
- → Wisdom is the "breath of God's power," the "reflection of eternal light"—a divine emanation, not an independent being.

These passages continue the **monolatrous logic** we've seen before: divine mediation is affirmed, but worship remains directed solely to YHWH.

---

[30] This interpretation is not a modern reconstruction but was a central theme in the theology of the early Church Fathers. They consistently identified the "Us" in Genesis 1:26 as a dialogue between God the Father and His pre-existent Son, the Word (Logos/Wisdom). **Justin Martyr** argued that God was conversing with "someone who was numerically distinct from Himself... a rational Being." **Irenaeus** identified the "Us" as the Father speaking to His "Hands"—the Son and the Holy Spirit—through whom He creates all things. **Origen** likewise stated that in Genesis 1:26, "God said: 'Let us make man to our image and likeness,' to insinuate... a plurality of persons... Father and Son and Holy Spirit." For these pre-Nicene theologians, this verse was a clear scriptural proof of a divine agent who was distinct from the Father yet active with Him in the act of creation.

See: *Justin Martyr, Dialogue with Trypho, 62; Irenaeus, Against Heresies, 4.20.1; Origen, quoted in patristic commentaries on Genesis 1:26.*

# WISDOM AND LOGOS: MEDIATORS OF THE DIVINE MIND

## *The Logos in Hellenistic Jewish Thought*

For Jews living in the Greek-speaking world—particularly in **Alexandria**—the figure of **Logos** became the philosophical counterpart to biblical Wisdom.

**Philo of Alexandria** (c. 20 BCE – 50 CE), a Jewish philosopher steeped in Platonic thought, describes the Logos as:

- The **rational principle** by which God created and ordered the universe.
- The **high priest** and **intercessor** who mediates between God and the world.
- A divine being who **bears the name of God**, but is never equated with the ultimate divine essence.

> Philo even applies the title "god" (θεός) to the Logos in a qualified sense, reflecting its divine function without compromising God's singular essence. Similarly, in the Aramaic Targums, the Memra frequently appears where the Hebrew text has YHWH—functioning as a reverent way to speak of God's action while preserving His transcendence.

> *nevertheless let him labour earnestly to be adorned according to his first-born word, the eldest of his angels, as the great archangel of many names; for he is called, the authority, and the name of God, and the Word, and man according to God's image, and he who sees Israel.* (On the Confusion of Tongues 146)

Philo's Logos builds on the tradition of **Wisdom** and the **Angel of YHWH**, reinterpreting them through a **philosophical lens** without abandoning their theological roots.[31]

## *Theological Continuity: No Break in Monolatry*

Despite their conceptual differences, both **Wisdom and Logos** fit comfortably within the broader framework of monolatry. They do not function as rival deities but as **expressions of YHWH's mind and will**:

- Like the **Angel of YHWH**, they bear divine authority but do not originate it.
- Like the **Memra** in the Targums, they mediate without competing for devotion.
- Like the exalted figures in **1 Enoch** or the **Qumran texts**, they are positioned within a **hierarchical divine order**.

The **absence of worship** directed toward Wisdom or the Logos in Jewish texts reinforces this point. While exalted, they are never recipients of prayer, sacrifice, or devotion. Worship remains fixed on YHWH alone.

---

[31] Philo of Alexandria's development of Logos theology is a critical bridge between Hebrew thought and Hellenistic philosophy. David Winston, a leading scholar on Philo, explains that Philo's Logos functions as God's creative and governing power, the "image of God," and the intermediary through whom the transcendent God interacts with the created world. This formulation is a philosophical refinement of the roles previously held by the personified Wisdom and the Angel of YHWH in the Hebrew Bible.

*See: David Winston, Logos and Mystical Theology in Philo of Alexandria (Cincinnati: Hebrew Union College Press, 1985), 15-28.*

# WISDOM AND LOGOS: MEDIATORS OF THE DIVINE MIND

*Preparing the Ground for Christological Thought*

By the time we reach the early first century, Jewish theological vocabulary is **rich with tools** for describing divine mediation: the **Angel of YHWH**, the **Memra**, **Wisdom**, and the **Logos** all provide frameworks for understanding **how YHWH can be both transcendent and active** in the world.

These frameworks would become especially significant in early Christian interpretations of Yeshua. As we will explore in the next chapter, many early believers **did not need to invent a new theology**—they simply applied existing Jewish concepts of divine mediation to a new, specific figure.

## Worship and Divine Mediation in the Second Temple Period

With so many intermediary figures and theological developments in play, it's worth asking: **How did these ideas affect actual worship?** Did Jewish liturgical life reflect the presence of divine mediators, or was worship kept strictly focused on YHWH?

The evidence from the Second Temple period shows that **Jewish worship remained monolatrous**, even while acknowledging a complex divine hierarchy. Intermediaries such as angels, Wisdom, the Memra, and the Logos were honored as expressions of God's governance—but **they were not objects of devotion**. Worship practices retained a clear focus: **exclusive reverence for YHWH**.

## Temple Worship: Centered on YHWH Alone

At the heart of Jewish religious life during this period was the **Jerusalem Temple**. Its rituals, sacrifices, and festivals all maintained the traditional biblical emphasis: worship directed solely to YHWH.

- **Daily offerings** (Exodus 29:38–42) and **festal observances** (Leviticus 23) were conducted in YHWH's name, with **no references to intermediary figures**.
- The **High Priest**—though functioning as a human mediator—entered the **Holy of Holies** only once a year (Leviticus 16), petitioning YHWH alone.
- Temple Psalms exalt YHWH's kingship (e.g., Psalm 99), reinforcing the **covenantal focus** of Israel's worship.

Even as theology grew more complex, worship remained theologically grounded in **singular devotion to YHWH**.

## Synagogue and Diaspora Worship: Mediators Acknowledged, Not Worshiped

Outside Jerusalem, especially in diaspora communities, synagogue worship and prayer developed alongside the Temple system. These settings **allowed greater theological flexibility**, and here we find more **explicit acknowledgment** of divine intermediaries:

- **Liturgical poetry and prayers** often invoked the presence of angels, particularly in cosmic worship scenes:

    *"Bless Him, all you hosts... Praise Him, you heavenly beings." (cf. Songs of the Sabbath Sacrifice, Qumran)*

- **The Qedushah prayer**, drawn from Isaiah 6:3, envisions **angels glorifying YHWH**—a motif later reflected in Christian worship (Revelation 4–5).

The Qedushah prayer perfectly illustrates this dynamic. In this central part of Jewish liturgy, the earthly congregation explicitly joins the angelic choirs in heaven, sanctifying God by reciting their very words from **Isaiah 6:3: 'Holy, holy, holy, is the LORD of hosts; the whole earth is full of His glory.'** This powerfully demonstrates: the angels are active *participants* in worship, but YHWH alone remains the sole *recipient* of that praise, a motif directly mirrored in the heavenly throne room scene of Revelation 4:8.

Importantly, even in these texts, **all worship is still offered to YHWH**. Angels and other mediators are present and active, but they never **receive** praise, sacrifice, or prayer themselves.

## The Role of the Memra in Liturgical Contexts

As discussed earlier, the **Memra**—the "Word" of YHWH—often replaces direct references to God in the Aramaic Targums. In worship, this allowed Jewish communities to express **God's presence and activity** without diminishing His transcendence:

- **Targum Neofiti (Genesis 28:20–21)**: "If the Memra of YHWH will be with me... then the Lord will be my God by his Word (Memra)."
- **Targum Onkelos (Exodus 3:12)**: "My Memra shall be with you."

Though prominent in synagogue readings and prayers, the Memra is **not invoked independently** of YHWH. It is a **theological bridge**, not a rival object of devotion.

## Summary: Structured Devotion, Singular Worship

The worship practices of Second Temple Judaism provide a lived expression of the theology developed throughout this chapter. In every case:

- **Intermediaries** are acknowledged and celebrated as participants in divine action.
- **YHWH alone** receives worship, prayer, and sacrifice.

- The **liturgical imagination** reflects divine hierarchy without deviating into polytheism.

This carefully balanced system aligns with the broader monolatrous framework we've traced: **plurality in the divine realm, unity in worship**.

## Theological Tensions: Monolatry vs. Emerging Monotheism

As Second Temple theology matured, it did not move in a single, unified direction. While monolatry—the belief in YHWH's sole worthiness of worship within a structured divine hierarchy—remained prevalent, **a competing impulse began to emerge**: one that sought to define God's uniqueness in increasingly exclusive and philosophical terms. This growing tension between **biblical monolatry** and **later monotheistic reinterpretation** shaped Jewish thought well into the Rabbinic period.

### *Monolatry's Enduring Presence*

The evidence for continued monolatry across post-exilic and Second Temple Jewish literature has been well established throughout this chapter. Key texts repeatedly reflect the same basic theological pattern:

- **YHWH remains the supreme, uncreated God** (Daniel 7; Isaiah 44).
- **Divine intermediaries** such as angels, the Angel of YHWH, Wisdom, the Logos, and the Memra operate under His authority.
- **Worship remains focused solely on YHWH**, even when these figures are exalted in role and proximity.

Rather than abandoning divine plurality, these texts **refine it**, articulating a cosmic hierarchy where all divine agents are dependent on and subordinate to YHWH.

## The Shift Toward Exclusivist Monotheism

Despite this, a **new theological tendency** emerges in some circles—a push to define YHWH's uniqueness in increasingly absolute terms. This shift was not uniform or immediate, but it began to take shape through:

- **Polemical language** in prophetic literature (e.g., Isaiah 45:5: "I am YHWH, and there is no other").
- **Editorial changes** in certain biblical texts, such as the alteration of Deuteronomy 32:8 from "sons of God" to "sons of Israel" in the Masoretic Text.
- **Rabbinic discomfort** with divine intermediaries, especially in reaction to early Christian claims about Yeshua.

This movement toward a **strict, exclusive monotheism** increasingly resisted the older framework of divine hierarchy.

## Was Divine Plurality Later Suppressed?

Theological revisionism seems to have occurred. While early Jewish texts freely depicted a populated heavenly realm under YHWH's rule, later writings began to **reinterpret or suppress** these ideas:

- **Targums** replace anthropomorphic or multiplicity-language with terms like *Memra* and *Shekinah*, abstracting divine action.
- **Rabbinic literature** polemicizes against "Two Powers in Heaven"—a charge likely rooted in opposition to Christian theology, but one that resulted in a wider rejection of intermediary figures altogether.
- **Biblical reinterpretation** reassigns passages once seen as references to divine beings (e.g., "let us make man" in Genesis 1:26) to angels or poetic language.

What had once been a **core feature** of Israelite theology became suspect, redefined, or abandoned in the face of new religious and cultural challenges.

## Competing Trajectories in Jewish Thought

Second Temple Judaism did not present a singular view of divine reality. Instead, it contained multiple strands:

- Some traditions (e.g., Daniel, 1 Enoch, Tobit, Philo) preserved and elaborated divine hierarchy within a **monolatrous framework**.
- Others (e.g., the Sadducees, later Rabbinic authorities) moved toward **strict monotheism**, downplaying intermediary figures and limiting divine agency to YHWH alone.
- Sectarian tensions, Greco-Roman philosophical influence, and growing distance from Christian theology all contributed to this divergence.

## Why This Tension Matters

Understanding the internal debates within Second Temple Judaism helps clarify why later theological conflicts arose between Jewish and Christian communities. It also reveals that **strict monotheism was not the original biblical or Second Temple model**, but rather **a later development**—one shaped by both polemical necessity and philosophical preference.

The next section will explore how **various Jewish sects—Pharisees, Sadducees, Essenes, and Hellenistic Jews—responded** to these theological tensions, offering a fuller picture of Second Temple theological diversity.

## Conclusion: Theological Continuity and the Legacy of Monolatry

Across the post-exilic and Second Temple periods, Jewish theology demonstrated remarkable continuity rather than rupture. Despite foreign rule, cultural upheaval, and intellectual cross-pollination, the underlying framework of monolatry held firm: YHWH was worshipped exclusively as the supreme, uncreated God, while divine intermediaries continued to function within a structured hierarchy.

Rather than diminishing the divine realm, Second Temple Jewish literature refined its understanding. Angelic beings such as Michael and Raphael, exalted figures like the "Son of Man," and theological concepts such as the Memra, Shekinah, and Logos all expressed YHWH's authority without challenging His singular supremacy. This continuity confirms that declarations of divine uniqueness in texts like Isaiah 44:24 were never intended as denials of divine plurality, but as polemical affirmations of YHWH's unrivaled status in the cosmic order.

Multiple strands of Jewish tradition—from prophetic visions to apocalyptic literature, from the Targums to the writings of Philo—reinforced this pattern. Even Jewish mysticism, with its elaborate heavenly hierarchies, maintained YHWH as the central, unapproachable source of divine governance.

At the same time, we have seen theological tensions emerge. Some strands of Judaism began moving toward a more restrictive, philosophical monotheism, particularly in reaction to the rise of Christianity. Others held firmly to the older model of divine mediation. These tensions did not produce a single theological outcome, but instead shaped the diverse landscape of Jewish thought going into the early Christian era.

## *Looking Ahead*

This foundation sets the stage for the next chapter, where we will examine how early Jewish-Christian thought built directly on the Second Temple understanding of monolatry. The idea of a divine mediator under YHWH—fully subordinate yet uniquely exalted—was not a foreign invention but a natural extension of existing Jewish categories.

The question before us now is not whether early Christianity introduced something new, but how it interpreted and extended the already well-established pattern of divine mediation. As we turn to the New Testament and early Christology, the continuity with Second Temple Jewish theology will come into sharper focus.

III

Part Three

*Chapter 9: The New Testament in Light of Monolatry*

# 9

# The New Testament in Light of Monolatry

The theological framework developed throughout this book has progressively built upon the concept of divine agency in Jewish thought. This foundation, rooted in the Hebrew Scriptures and further developed during the Second Temple period, finds its ultimate expression in the New Testament's presentation of Yeshua the Messiah. Every category of divine agency examined—the Memra (Word of YHWH), the Logos (Divine Reason), the Angel of YHWH, the Son of Man, the Messenger of YHWH, and the Exalted Lord—converges in Yeshua.[32]

---

[32] New Testament scholarship widely recognizes that the early Christians used categories from their Jewish heritage to understand and articulate the identity of Jesus. Larry W. Hurtado's work is seminal in demonstrating that early "high Christology" (the belief in a divine Christ) was not a late, Hellenistic invention but emerged very early within a Jewish context that allowed for a chief divine agent to be exalted alongside God without violating their monotheistic commitment.

See: Larry W. Hurtado, *One God, One Lord: Early Christian Devotion and Ancient Jewish Monotheism*, 3rd ed. (London: T&T Clark, 2015), 1-15.

Rather than introducing an entirely new theological concept, the New Testament operates within the same established patterns of divine agency found in earlier Jewish tradition. Yeshua is presented not as an innovation but as the full realization of the divinely appointed agent who executes the will of YHWH on earth and in heaven. The way He is identified with the Memra in John 1:1, the Logos as understood by Philo, the Angel of YHWH's authority in passages such as Exodus 23:20–21, the enthronement of the Son of Man in Daniel 7, and the Messianic function in Malachi 3:1 all demonstrate continuity rather than disruption.

The New Testament fully embraces the concept of monolatry—maintaining exclusive worship of the Most High God while acknowledging an exalted figure who operates with divine authority. However, the Jewish authorities after 70 CE rejected this framework, not because it lacked historical precedent, but because it was now inseparably tied to the Christian claim that Yeshua was the long-awaited divine agent of YHWH.

## *The Post-70 CE Jewish Suppression of Divine Plurality*

One of the most decisive moments in the Jewish-Christian theological split was the rabbinic rejection of the "Two Powers in Heaven" theology. As explored in earlier chapters, the period following the destruction of the Second Temple in 70 CE marked a theological turning point. Rabbinic leaders, facing the rise of Christianity, redefined the boundaries of monotheism by deliberately eliminating traditions that could be construed as supporting divine plurality.³³

This shift was not driven by a purely exegetical or theological necessity—it was a reaction to the growing Christian claim that Yeshua was the divine Son, exalted alongside YHWH. The New Testament's use of exalted intermediary figures to describe Yeshua forced the rabbis to respond. To counter the perception that Judaism supported any form of dual divine presence, they systematically erased traditions that allowed for an exalted intermediary who shared in YHWH's authority.

Before 70 CE, a variety of Jewish sects and writings reflected openness to divine agency through exalted figures. Apocalyptic literature such as 1 Enoch and 4 Ezra, wisdom traditions, and even early Targumic interpretations often described divine intermediaries who acted with divine prerogatives. The Son of Man figure in Daniel 7, the Angel of YHWH bearing His Name, the Memra in Aramaic translations, and Philo's Logos concept—all these pointed to an accepted theological category: a divine agent who was not identical to God but who operated with His power and authority.

However, after the Christian movement explicitly identified Yeshua with these figures, post-Temple Jewish leadership worked to disassociate Judaism from any theology that could support such an idea. The "Two Powers in Heaven" controversy emerged as a direct reaction: Christians affirmed

---

³³ Scholars like Daniel Boyarin and Alan Segal have argued that the rabbinic condemnation of the "Two Powers in Heaven" heresy was part of a process of "boundary making" between emerging Rabbinic Judaism and early Christianity. In this view, what had been acceptable theological speculation about a second divine figure within Second Temple Judaism was declared heretical precisely because Christians had identified that figure with Jesus of Nazareth.

See: Daniel Boyarin, "The Gospel of the Memra: Jewish Binitarianism and the Prologue to John," *Harvard Theological Review* 94, no. 3 (2001): 243–284. See also Alan F. Segal, *Two Powers in Heaven: Early Rabbinic Reports about Christianity and Gnosticism* (Leiden: Brill, 1977).

Yeshua as the exalted second figure alongside YHWH, while rabbinic Judaism rejected the entire category.

Thus, rather than disproving the claims of the New Testament, the rabbinic rejection of these traditions actually confirms that early Christian theology was drawing on legitimate, pre-existing Jewish concepts. The earliest followers of Yeshua were not importing pagan ideas or inventing divine plurality—they were affirming the role of a divine agent that had long existed in Jewish tradition. The rupture came not because Christians stepped outside of Judaism, but because Judaism narrowed its theological framework in response to the Christian identification of that agent with Yeshua.

Understanding this historical shift is essential. It highlights that the New Testament's portrayal of Yeshua as the exalted Lord was not a departure from Jewish theology, but a fulfillment of it—a fulfillment that post-70 CE rabbinic Judaism could no longer accommodate.

## *From Partial Understanding to Full Revelation of the Son*

A recurring theme throughout the biblical narrative is the progressive nature of revelation. While Israel always confessed that YHWH alone is God, the full identity of His divine agent was only partially understood under the Old Covenant. Figures such as the Angel of YHWH, Wisdom, the Memra, and the Logos served as veiled expressions of God's presence and power. Yet their true nature and identity remained obscured.

This concealment was not due to theological error but to divine purpose. According to the New Testament, God intentionally revealed His plans gradually, and only in Yeshua were the mysteries of divine agency fully disclosed.

Several New Testament passages make this veiling explicit:

- **2 Corinthians 3:14–16 (NASB 1995):** "But their minds were hardened; for until this very day at the reading of the old covenant the same veil remains unlifted, because it is removed in Christ. But to this day whenever Moses is read, a veil lies over their heart; but whenever a person turns to the Lord, the veil is taken away."
- **John 1:10–11 (NASB 1995):** "He was in the world, and the world was made through Him, and the world did not know Him. He came to His own, and those who were His own did not receive Him."
- **Luke 10:23–24 (NASB 1995):** "Blessed are the eyes that see the things you see, for I say to you, that many prophets and kings wished to see the things which you see, and did not see them, and to hear the things which you hear, and did not hear them."
- **Romans 11:25 (NASB 1995):** "For I do not want you, brethren, to be uninformed of this mystery… that a partial hardening has happened to Israel until the fullness of the Gentiles has come in."

These verses show that Israel, though blessed with divine revelation, could not yet perceive the full identity of God's agent. They recognized intermediaries like the Memra or Logos in concept, but the personal, eternal identity of that figure—as the Son of God—remained hidden.

The New Testament unveils this mystery. In **John 1:1–3 (NASB 1995):** "In the beginning was the Word, and the Word was with God, and the Word was God. He was in the beginning with God. All things came into being through Him, and apart from Him nothing came into being that has come into being."

And in **John 1:18 (NASB 1995):** "No one has seen God at any time; the only begotten God who is in the bosom of the Father, He has explained Him."

These declarations clarify that the Word (Logos)—long known to Jewish tradition—is in fact the divine Son who became incarnate in Yeshua. He is not merely a created messenger or abstraction but the very self-expression of YHWH, made flesh to dwell among humanity (**John 1:14**).

The rabbis, once confronted with this claim, were forced to make a decision. If they acknowledged Yeshua as the Logos or Memra made flesh, they would have to accept that God's intermediary was more than symbolic—He was personal and divine. Instead, rabbinic Judaism retracted its previous openness to such figures, reformulating theology in opposition to the Christian message.

Thus, the unveiling of the Son in the New Testament does not negate prior Jewish theology; it fulfills it. What was previously hidden behind the veil—God's ultimate agent—is now made known in Yeshua, the "only begotten God" who reveals the Father perfectly.

## *The Testimony of the Old Testament and the Prophets to Messiah*

A central claim of the New Testament is that Yeshua fulfills what was already written in the Hebrew Scriptures. The early followers of Yeshua did not believe they were inventing a new theology; rather, they believed that the Law, the Prophets, and the Writings all testified about Him. This belief was deeply rooted in Yeshua's own words and in apostolic teaching.

## Yeshua's Own Testimony: The Scriptures Speak of Him

Yeshua consistently affirmed that the Old Testament bore witness to His mission and identity. Yet He also acknowledged that many had failed to perceive its true message:

- **John 5:39–40 (NASB 1995):** "You search the Scriptures because you think that in them you have eternal life; it is these that testify about Me; and you are unwilling to come to Me so that you may have life."
- **Luke 24:25–27 (NASB 1995):** "And He said to them, 'O foolish men and slow of heart to believe in all that the prophets have spoken! Was it not necessary for the Christ to suffer these things and to enter into His glory?' Then beginning with Moses and with all the prophets, He explained to them the things concerning Himself in all the Scriptures."
- **Luke 24:44–45 (NASB 1995):** "Now He said to them, 'These are My words which I spoke to you while I was still with you, that all things which are written about Me in the Law of Moses and the Prophets and the Psalms must be fulfilled.' Then He opened their minds to understand the Scriptures."

In these statements, Yeshua makes it clear that the Old Testament pointed forward to Him. The failure to recognize this, according to Him, was due not to a lack of evidence but to spiritual blindness and hard-heartedness.

## The Prophetic Witness to the Suffering and Glory of the Messiah

The Hebrew Bible contains both portraits of a suffering servant and an exalted king. These themes are not contradictory but part of the same prophetic arc.

- **Isaiah 53:3–5 (NASB 1995):** "He was despised and forsaken of men, a man of sorrows and acquainted with grief... He was pierced through for our transgressions, He was crushed for our iniquities... and by His scourging we are healed."
- **Psalm 22:16–18 (NASB 1995):** "For dogs have surrounded me; a band of evildoers has encompassed me; they pierced my hands and my feet. I can count all my bones. They look, they stare at me; they divide my garments among them, and for my clothing they cast lots."
- **Daniel 7:13–14 (NASB 1995):** "And behold, with the clouds of heaven One like a Son of Man was coming... And to Him was given dominion, glory and a kingdom, that all the peoples, nations and men of every language might serve Him."
- **Psalm 110:1 (NASB 1995):** "The Lord says to my Lord: 'Sit at My right hand until I make Your enemies a footstool for Your feet.'" Yeshua directly applied this verse to Himself (see Matthew 22:44).

These passages combine to form a complex messianic expectation: the Messiah must suffer, be vindicated, and reign with divine authority. The New Testament presents Yeshua as the one who fulfills all of these roles—He is the Suffering Servant, the Son of Man given eternal dominion, and the enthroned Lord at YHWH's right hand.

**The Partial Understanding of the Old Testament Saints**

Although the Scriptures contained these prophetic truths, the people of the

Old Covenant did not fully comprehend them. The apostles described this as a "mystery" hidden for ages and only now revealed.

- **1 Peter 1:10–12 (NASB 1995):** "As to this salvation, the prophets who prophesied of the grace that would come to you made careful searches and inquiries… seeking to know what person or time the Spirit of Christ within them was indicating as He predicted the sufferings of Christ and the glories to follow."
- **Colossians 1:26–27 (NASB 1995):** "The mystery which has been hidden from the past ages and generations, but has now been manifested to His saints… Christ in you, the hope of glory."
- **2 Corinthians 3:14–16 (NASB 1995):** (as cited earlier) emphasizes the veil that covered Israel's understanding, removed only in Messiah.

The prophets, under inspiration, foresaw glimpses of the Messiah's suffering and exaltation. But they did not see the full picture until the revelation in Yeshua.

**Yeshua as the Revealer of the Father**

Yeshua does not merely fulfill prophecy—He reveals the very nature of God. He is the visible expression of the invisible God, the One who makes the Father known.

- **John 1:18 (NASB 1995):** "No one has seen God at any time; the only begotten God who is in the bosom of the Father, He has explained Him."

- **John 14:9 (NASB 1995):** "He who has seen Me has seen the Father."[34]

The Old Testament saints glimpsed the workings of divine agency—seeing angels, hearing the Word of the Lord, encountering the glory of YHWH. But only in the Son is the fullness of God's character, will, and personhood made known. This climactic revelation confirms that the New Testament is not a break from the Hebrew Scriptures but their fulfillment.

## II. Avoiding the "Trinitarian" Imposition

One of the greatest obstacles to understanding the New Testament's portrayal of Yeshua is the tendency to read it through the lens of later Trinitarian dogma. The doctrine of the Trinity—as formally articulated in the Nicene Creed (A.D. 325) and further developed at Constantinople (A.D. 381)—describes the Father, Son, and Holy Spirit as coequal and coeternal persons of one divine essence. However, this theological formulation did not exist during the time the New Testament was written.

The earliest Jewish followers of Yeshua did not conceive of the Trinity.

---

[34] The Johannine portrayal of Jesus as the one who "explains" or "makes known" the unseen Father (John 1:18) is a direct continuation of the divine agent christology found in Second Temple Judaism. The Son fulfills the role that figures like the Logos (in Philo) and the Memra (in the Targums) played: a divine intermediary who makes the transcendent God accessible and known to humanity.

See: Larry W. Hurtado, "The Divine Agent," in *One God, One Lord*, 34-40. Hurtado discusses how Jesus fits into the established Jewish category of a principal agent who can be spoken of in terms that are otherwise reserved for God.

Instead, they viewed Yeshua through the framework of **divine agency**, which had long been present in Jewish theology. He was the ultimate emissary of YHWH, vested with divine authority, honored and obeyed, but never worshiped as a separate, coequal deity. The New Testament maintains monolatry: the worship of one God—YHWH—while recognizing that YHWH acts through a chosen, exalted agent.

**Modern Readers' Presuppositions**

Modern Christian readers often assume that the divinity of Yeshua must be understood in Nicene terms. This assumption, however, can obscure how first-century Jewish believers actually viewed Him.

- They **affirmed Yeshua's exaltation** but within a **clear hierarchy**: YHWH remained supreme, and Yeshua was His anointed agent.
- Worship of Yeshua was **relational and derivative**: He was honored because the Father had given Him that place of honor (John 5:23).
- The **language of "Son of God" and "Lord"** did not imply coequality in nature with YHWH but instead denoted status and function within a divine order.

The danger in imposing later theological definitions onto the biblical text is that it risks distorting what the New Testament authors actually wrote and believed. Recovering their original, Jewish context allows for a clearer understanding of the early Christian message.

**Reading in Light of the Second Temple Context**

# MONOLATRY

To rightly interpret the New Testament's Christology, we must view it within the theological landscape of Second Temple Judaism. During this period, Jewish writings frequently explored the idea of **divine intermediaries**—figures such as Wisdom, the Angel of YHWH, the Logos (as in Philo), and the Memra (as in the Targums).

The New Testament presents Yeshua as fulfilling each of these intermediary roles, not as a novelty but as a natural extension of this Jewish tradition. He fits within a familiar pattern of **God working through an exalted agent**—one who bears God's name, speaks God's words, and enacts God's will.

For example:

- **John 1:18 (NASB 1995)** again captures this dynamic:
- "No one has seen God at any time; the only begotten God who is in the bosom of the Father, He has explained Him."
- This echoes both the Targumic Memra and Philo's Logos while preserving Yeshua's subordinate role as revealer.
- As previously explored, the concept of divine plurality in Jewish texts was later suppressed by rabbinic authorities, particularly after Christian theology made Yeshua its focal point.

In essence, **the Jewish rejection of divine plurality was a post-Christian development**, not the original state of biblical theology. The New Testament reflects a continuity with older Jewish thought, presenting Yeshua as **the culmination—not a contradiction—of divine agency.**

By shedding the assumptions of post-Nicene orthodoxy and restoring the Second Temple context, modern readers can better understand how the

New Testament intended to portray the Son: **not as an equal partner in a triune essence, but as YHWH's exalted and obedient emissary, who bears His Name and reveals His will.**

## III. Yeshua and the Father: The Climax of Divine Agency

The central argument of this book is that Yeshua's status in the New Testament is not a radical innovation, but the culmination of a long history of Jewish reflection on **divine intermediaries**. Across the Hebrew Bible and Second Temple writings, we've seen how YHWH works through agents—figures such as **the Angel of YHWH, the Memra, the Logos**, and **Wisdom**—who speak for Him, act in His name, and are at times indistinguishable from His presence.

The New Testament does not overturn this framework. Instead, it presents Yeshua as the final and fullest expression of it. He embodies every role these agents once played, now brought into focus in one person. Yet, crucially, **He remains subordinate to the Father**. The relationship is one of honor, obedience, and unity—but not equality in origin or authority.

### A. The Angel of YHWH → Yeshua as the One Sent by the Father

The Angel of YHWH was described in the Hebrew Scriptures as carrying God's name and authority. In **Exodus 23:20–21**, YHWH warns:

> "Behold, I am going to send an angel before you to guard you along

*the way... Be on your guard before him and obey his voice; do not be rebellious toward him, for he will not pardon your transgression, since My name is in him."*

This angel is not merely a created being. He bears the divine Name, speaks in the first person as YHWH, and acts with authority to forgive or withhold forgiveness.

Yeshua, too, claims to be the **sent One**, bearing the Father's authority and acting in obedience:

- **John 5:30 (NASB 1995):**
- "I can do nothing on My own initiative. As I hear, I judge; and My judgment is just, because I do not seek My own will, but the will of Him who sent Me."
- **John 12:49 (NASB 1995):**
- "For I did not speak on My own initiative, but the Father Himself who sent Me has given Me a commandment as to what to say and what to speak."

Yeshua's mission mirrors the Angel of YHWH—He speaks God's words, exercises God's power, and demands obedience. Yet He is always clear that His authority is **given**, not innate.

## B. The Logos in Philo → Yeshua as the Logos in John 1

Philo of Alexandria described the **Logos** as God's divine reason or intermediary between the transcendent Creator and the world. This Logos was seen as **God's firstborn, His image, and the means through which the cosmos was created**—but still subordinate.

The Apostle John uses this very concept:

- **John 1:1–3 (NASB 1995):**

"In the beginning was the Word, and the Word was with God, and the Word was God. He was in the beginning with God. All things came into being through Him, and apart from Him nothing came into being that has come into being."

Here, the Logos (Word) is with God and is God—but the language preserves a distinction. The Word is the agent "through" whom all things were made, not the uncaused Source. John's Logos, like Philo's, is **divine yet subordinate**.

**C. The Memra in the Targums → Yeshua as the "Word Made Flesh"**

In the Aramaic Targums, the **Memra (Word)** of YHWH is a divine agent who interacts with creation and Israel:

- **Genesis 1:27 (Targum Neofiti):**
- "And the Memra of the Lord created man in His image."
- **Exodus 19:17 (Targum Onkelos):**
- "Moses brought the people out of the camp to meet the Memra of the Lord."

The Memra is often used in place of direct references to God, preserving divine transcendence while allowing interaction with the world.

John builds directly on this idea:

- **John 1:14 (NASB 1995):**
- "And the Word became flesh, and dwelt among us, and we saw His glory, glory as of the only begotten from the Father, full of grace and truth."

This bold claim—that the role of the *Memra*, long known as the interface of divine presence, has now been embodied by a person—is the cornerstone of the New Testament's understanding of Yeshua. He is not a new, rival God, but rather the personal fulfillment of the **function** the Memra played. The divine agency once understood as the Father's active Word is now revealed to be a distinct person: the begotten Son, who has taken on flesh to mediate His Father's will.

## D. The Messenger of YHWH (Malachi 3:1) → Yeshua as the Consecrated One

In **Malachi 3:1**, YHWH says:

> *"Behold, I am going to send My messenger, and he will clear the way before Me. And the Lord, whom you seek, will suddenly come to His temple..."*

The New Testament applies this to both **John the Baptist** (the forerunner) and to **Yeshua**, who is the "Lord" entering the temple and enacting the covenant.

- **John 10:36 (NASB 1995):**
  - "Do you say of Him, whom the Father sanctified and sent into the world, 'You are blaspheming,' because I said, 'I am the Son of God'?"

*Yeshua is the messenger and the covenant-bearer, the one sanctified by God to reveal Him fully.*

## Yeshua as the Angel of YHWH—The Ultimate Divine Agent

The Angel of YHWH in the Hebrew Bible appears as God's supreme messenger—speaking with divine authority, performing acts of salvation and judgment, and at times even receiving honor. Yet he remains distinct from the Most High, functioning as God's visible representative. The New Testament presents Yeshua in exactly this role. He is not a second God, nor a competing divine force, but the one through whom YHWH has always mediated His presence, covenant, and deliverance. In doing so, it reveals the **new dimension** of truth: this divine messenger is none other than **God's only begotten Son**—the one expected by Israel to be its Savior and Deliverer.

The recognition that the Angel of YHWH was the pre-incarnate Son redefines earlier appearances of divine presence in the Old Testament.

From the burning bush to the Exodus, from guiding Israel to granting forgiveness (Zechariah 3:4), the Angel of YHWH was acting not simply as a servant, but as the very **Son of God**, dependent upon the will of the Father and commissioned to carry out His redemptive purpose. The New Testament declares that Yeshua is this very figure—not created like other messengers, but **begotten**, meaning He shares the divine nature of the Father while existing in perfect dependence upon Him.

This view upholds the full **ontological likeness** of the Son to the Father. As Paul affirms, Yeshua is in the "form of God" (Philippians 2:6), possessing the "fullness of deity" (Colossians 2:9), and the "exact representation" (Hebrews 1:3) of God's nature. Yet, this exalted identity is not independent—it is derived. He is the **"only begotten God"** (John 1:18, NASB95), which affirms both His divinity and His dependence on the Father for existence, purpose, and life. This is the heart of **Christian Monolatry**: one Supreme, unbegotten God—the Father—and one exalted, begotten Son, who mediates divine presence and authority.

This framework preserves the essence of **Christian Monolatry**: one ultimate God (the Father), who is worshiped through the Son, His visible and appointed image. The Son bears the divine name, executes divine acts, and receives reverence—but this honor is never independent of the Father. Instead, it is **representational**: to bow before the Son is to bow before the God who sent Him. The **honor** directed toward Yeshua is not a violation of monolatry, but its fulfillment—because the Son is not a second, autonomous deity. He is the **begotten God**, the exact representation of the Father, and the one through whom YHWH mediates His presence to the world. Thus, reverence offered to the Son always returns glory to the Father (Philippians 2:11), maintaining the exclusive worship of the One God while acknowledging His chosen agent.

| Angel of YHWH in the Old Testament | Yeshua in the New Testament |
|---|---|
| **Bears** YHWH's Name (Exodus 23:20-21) | I have manifiested Your Name John 17:6, NASB95 |
| **Speaks** as YHWH (Exodus 3:2-6) | I and the Father one (John 10:30, NASB95) |
| **Forgives sins** (Zechariah 3:3-4) | The Son of Man has authority on earth to forgive sins (Mark 2:10, NASB95) |
| **Receives honor//reverence** (Johuas 5:14) | Worshiped Him (Matthew 14:33, NASB95; John 9:38) |
| **Saves and leds Israel** (Exodus 14:19-20; Judges 2:1) | You shall call His name Jesus, for He will save His people (Matthew 1:21, NASB95) |
| **Judges on YHWH's behaff** (Genesis 18:25, Exodus 23:22) | The Father has given all judgement to the Sohn 5:22, NASB95) |

*This table illustrates the direct continuity between the Old Testament's chief divine messenger and the New Testament's exalted depiction of the Son. In both cases, we see not an autonomous deity, but a divine representative, fully authorized to act on behalf of the unseen God.*

## *Yeshua as the Angel of YHWH — The Ultimate Divine Agent*

To fully appreciate how the New Testament presents Yeshua, we must understand that the title "Angel of YHWH" in the Hebrew Bible was not meant to describe an ontological category, like a member of a separate species. Rather, it was a **functional role**—a title for the one who bore and enacted YHWH's authority in visible form. This figure often appears mysteriously: speaking in the first person as YHWH, receiving divine honor, forgiving sins, and even bearing the Name of God. Nowhere else in Scripture is such authority given to a standard created being.

The New Testament presents Yeshua as the **visible expression of this same authority**. He does what the Angel of YHWH did—but now incarnate, now as the Son, now as the long-awaited Messiah. What was once veiled in mystery is now revealed in full: the Angel of YHWH is not a mere theophany or created angel, but the one who was "in the beginning with God" and who is now made flesh (John 1:1–14 NASB95).

A central claim of **Christian Monolatry** is this: Yeshua is not an independent deity or a second god in competition with the Father. He is **the dependent God**, begotten from the Father, possessing the fullness of divine nature, yet existing always in submission to the will of the One who begot Him. He does not derive His identity autonomously, but relationally—as the exact image and Word of the Father. His divinity is not diminished by His subordination, nor is the Father's supremacy threatened by the Son's exaltation.

This framework maintains the strict **worship of one God**, while making space for the Son to be honored, **as the unique representative of that God**. In this light, honor offered to Yeshua is not a violation of monolatry—it is its ultimate expression. For as the Gospel of John records:

> *"...so that all will honor the Son just as they honor the Father. The one who does not honor the Son does not honor the Father who sent Him."* (John 5:23, NASB95)

In other words, the honor of the Son is **derivative, not independent**—it honors the sender by honoring the one sent.

## Yeshua Bears the Name of YHWH

In Exodus 23:20-21 (NASB95), YHWH speaks of sending His angel to guide Israel:

> *"Behold, I am going to send an angel before you to guard you along the way and to bring you into the place which I have prepared. Be attentive to him and obey his voice; do not be rebellious toward him, for he will not pardon your wrongdoing, since My name is in him."*

This angel is no ordinary messenger. He possesses the authority to forgive sins—something only God can do—and bears the very **Name** of YHWH, indicating His role as God's personal representative on earth.

The New Testament reveals that Yeshua **embodies this identity** in full clarity. In His high priestly prayer, He says:

> *"I have revealed Your name to the men whom You gave Me out of the*

*world..." (John 17:6, NASB95)*

And Paul writes:

*"For this reason also God highly exalted Him, and bestowed on Him the name which is above every name..." (Philippians 2:9, NASB95)*

This bestowal of the divine Name on Yeshua marks a climactic moment in the progression of divine agency: the one who was formerly veiled as the Angel of YHWH is now openly declared as the **Son** and **Messiah**, bearing the Name of YHWH not metaphorically, but fully—because **the Father has given it to Him**.

From the perspective of **Christian Monolatry**, this is precisely what qualifies Yeshua to receive obedience, and even honor/reverence. **He bears God's Name by divine appointment**. He is not a separate God, but the one through whom the one God is known and glorified. His authority is real, His status exalted, but always in submission to the will of the Father.

In this way, the New Testament shows that Yeshua's exaltation does not compete with YHWH's uniqueness—it expresses it. It fulfills the promise of the Angel who would carry God's Name and execute His covenant purposes, and it calls all creation to bow not to two gods, but to **one God revealed through His appointed Son**.

## Yeshua Speaks with Divine Authority, Yet Distinguishes Himself from the Father

Throughout the Hebrew Bible, the Angel of YHWH speaks not just on behalf of God but **as God**, using the first person in ways that signal divine prerogative. Yet even then, the narrative carefully preserves a distinction between the Angel and YHWH Himself—pointing to a representative figure who is divine in speech and action, but not independent in being.

For example:

> "The angel of the Lord appeared to him in a blazing fire from the midst of a bush... When the Lord saw that he turned aside to look, God called to him from the midst of the bush..."
> *(Exodus 3:2-4, NASB95)*

Here, the Angel and God are interchangeable in function but remain distinguishable in identity. This sets the precedent for how the **Son** is portrayed in the New Testament.

Yeshua reflects the same paradox. He speaks with the authority of YHWH, even invoking titles and statements that clearly echo the divine voice. For instance, in John 10:30 (NASB95), He says:

> "I and the Father are one."

Yet this is not a claim to ontological equality in the Nicene sense. Rather, it is an assertion of **perfect unity of purpose and will**. Just as the Angel bore the Name and executed the will of YHWH without being a freely undependent God, so too Yeshua fully embodies God's mission while **remaining subordinate to the One who sent Him.**

Yeshua frequently emphasizes this subordination:

> *"Truly, truly, I say to you, the Son can do nothing of Himself, unless it is something He sees the Father doing..."*
> (John 5:19, NASB95)

And again:

> *"I do nothing on My own, but I speak these things as the Father instructed Me."*
> (John 8:28, NASB95)

This pattern confirms a key tenet of **Christian Monolatry**: Yeshua shares in the authority, speech, and mission of YHWH **because the Father empowers Him to do so.** His divinity is real, but derived; His authority is full, but bestowed.

This avoids two critical errors:

- It does not reduce Yeshua to a mere human prophet or created angel.
- Nor does it elevate Him to a coequal deity in a way that violates the Shema.

Instead, it affirms that **Yeshua is the visible expression of the invisible God**, the one through whom the Father has chosen to reveal Himself—**His dependent Son**, glorified yet ever obedient.

In this framework, honor directed toward Yeshua is not idolatry, because it flows through the channel God Himself has appointed. It is an act of **honoring the Father by honoring His Son**—the One who bears His Name, speaks His word, and fulfills His covenant.

## Yeshua as the Supreme Messenger of YHWH

The Hebrew word for "angel," *mal'akh*, and the Greek term *angelos*, both mean "messenger." In Scripture, they describe both human envoys and heavenly agents, depending on context. But the **Angel of YHWH** stands apart from all others—He is not merely one of many servants, but **the unique personal representative** of YHWH Himself.

This background sharpens our understanding of how the New Testament depicts Yeshua: not as one among many messengers, but as the **supreme Messenger**, the one whom the Father sanctified, sent, and glorified.

Yeshua applies this identity to Himself:

> *"Do you say of Him, whom the Father sanctified and sent into the world, 'You are blaspheming,' because I said, 'I am the Son of God'?"* (John 10:36, NASB95)

Here, Yeshua does not claim equality with the Father. Rather, He emphasizes that He was **set apart** and **sent**—a divine emissary, consecrated for a mission. His role mirrors that of the Angel of YHWH in the Old Testament, but now made flesh and revealed as the **Son**.

This identification comes into focus in light of the prophecy of Malachi 3:1:

> *"Behold, I am sending My messenger, and he will clear a way before Me. And the Lord, whom you are seeking, will suddenly come to His temple; and the messenger of the covenant, in whom you delight, behold, He is coming," says the Lord of armies.*

This passage refers to two figures:

1. A forerunner (whom the NT identifies as John the Baptist).
2. The "messenger of the covenant," who **comes to the temple as "the Lord"**.

The early Christians saw this second figure as Yeshua—the divine emissary **bearing the authority of YHWH**, appearing suddenly in the temple, fulfilling His long-promised role as covenant restorer.

Thus, within the framework of **Christian Monolatry**, Yeshua functions as **the supreme Messenger of YHWH**:

- Not a created angel, but the one uniquely sanctified.
- Not a rival to God, but **the one who executes the will of the only true God** (John 17:3).

- Not merely sent, but **sent being the Son**, carrying the Father's Name and presence.

This distinction preserves the hierarchy of divine roles while honoring the full weight of Yeshua's identity. It affirms that God's ultimate self-disclosure—His voice, judgment, mercy, and redemption—comes through the person of Yeshua, **without breaching the monolatrous fidelity to YHWH alone.**

## *Yeshua as the Angel of YHWH and the Jewish-Christian Divide*

The identification of Yeshua as the Angel of YHWH stands as one of the most potent theological assertions in the New Testament—one that traces directly back to Jewish traditions of divine agency but ultimately became a fault line between early Christians and rabbinic Jews. This identification does not posit Yeshua as an independent deity or a created angelic being, but as the embodied presence of YHWH's own agency, the one who had always borne His Name and carried out His will.

In Christian Monolatry, this framework is preserved: Yeshua is divine because He is the agent through whom YHWH reveals Himself, yet He remains dependent on the Father for His life, authority, and mission. This balance—divine representation without independent supremacy—distinguishes the Christian claim from later Trinitarian formulations and also from rabbinic rejections.

## Pre-70 CE Judaism: Openness to Divine Agency

Before the destruction of the Second Temple, Jewish theology allowed for a range of intermediary figures with exalted authority. The Angel of YHWH was not merely an anonymous messenger, but one who spoke in the first person as God, forgave sins (Zechariah 3:4), and bore the divine Name (Exodus 23:20–21). The Memra in the Targums, the Logos in Philo's thought, and the exalted Son of Man in Daniel 7 each point to this theological openness—a monolatrous tradition that acknowledged divine agency without asserting multiple gods.

This theological diversity began narrowing significantly after the Temple's destruction.

## Post-70 CE Judaism: Defining Against Christian Claims

Once the early Christian community began proclaiming Yeshua as the embodiment of this divine agent—the very Angel of YHWH made flesh—rabbinic leaders were faced with a critical decision. To preserve Jewish identity in contrast to the growing Christian movement, they redefined acceptable monotheism to exclude any theological framework that could support a second, divine figure.

The result was a deliberate rejection of the "Two Powers in Heaven" theology. What had once been permissible speculation became a formal heresy. Talmudic sources condemn any interpretation that would place a second divine figure alongside YHWH, particularly one that could support the idea of Yeshua's exaltation.

## Christian Monolatry as a Preserved Heritage

Rather than departing from Jewish theology, the New Testament preserves the earlier framework. In calling Yeshua the "only begotten God" (John 1:18, NASB95), it affirms His genuine divinity while simultaneously emphasizing His dependent status: begotten, not unbegotten; revealed, not original; the agent, not the source. This is the cornerstone of Christian Monolatry.

Thus, the Jewish-Christian divide over Yeshua is not merely about who the Messiah is, but about how one defines the boundaries of devotion and the structure of divine agency. Christianity maintains that honoring the Son is honoring the Father, because the Son acts as the visible manifestation of the Father's will and Name (John 5:23; 17:6).

## Avoiding Ontological Missteps

To describe Yeshua as the Angel of YHWH is not to say He is a "created angel" in the sense of Michael or Gabriel. Rather, it is to say that He fulfills the *role* of YHWH's supreme messenger—the one through whom the Father reveals Himself, governs creation, and mediates redemption.

This avoids two theological extremes:

- **Anomoeanism**, which strips the Son of shared divine nature.
- **Nicene co-equality**, which erases the clear subordination and sentness the Son Himself acknowledges (John 5:30; 14:28).

Yeshua is not ontologically inferior in nature, but He is functionally subordinate. He is in the "form of God" (Philippians 2:6), the "exact representation" of the Father's essence (Hebrews 1:3), and yet "the Son can do nothing of Himself" (John 5:19, NASB95). This is the essence of Christian Monolatry: honoring the Son as the one appointed to bear the Father's authority, while never confusing the Son with the unbegotten Source.

## A Functional Framework Restored

By returning to this biblical understanding of "angel" as a functional title, we free the New Testament portrayal of Yeshua from post-biblical assumptions. He is not a rival deity, nor merely a man. He is the Angel—the Messenger—of YHWH in the fullest and final sense.

Christian Monolatry thus reclaims the framework that the earliest followers of Yeshua would have understood: one supreme God, and one divine messenger who speaks, judges, and saves in His Name.

# 10

# Qumran's Exalted Figures and Yeshua as King-Priest

Beyond the Angel of YHWH, the Logos, and the Memra, another vital stream of Second Temple Jewish thought comes from the Qumran community (Dead Sea Scrolls), which presents exalted individuals—sometimes blending the roles of king, priest, and heavenly judge—in ways that anticipate New Testament portrayals of Yeshua. These figures are never portrayed as coequal with YHWH, but they operate with extraordinary divine authority, reinforcing the pattern of functional subordination within Jewish monolatry.

## A. Messianic Priest-King Expectations

The Qumran scrolls reflect a dual-messiah expectation: one from the line of David (a royal figure) and one from the line of Aaron (a priestly figure). Some texts portray these as two distinct persons; others envision a single eschatological figure uniting both roles. Regardless, the idea emerges that

YHWH would raise up an agent endowed with cosmic significance—ruling Israel, restoring worship, and defeating evil.

This is not a violation of monolatry, but an expression of it: the priest-king figure acts as YHWH's human-divine emissary. This context enriches the early Christian claim that Yeshua fulfills both roles in one person: Son of David and eternal high priest.

## B. 11QMelchizedek – A Cosmic Melchizedek Figure

The scroll known as 11QMelchizedek offers a particularly striking example. It elevates Melchizedek—a mysterious priest-king from Genesis 14—into a heavenly deliverer and eschatological judge. He is portrayed as:

- **Judging heavenly beings**, implying dominion in the unseen realm.
- **Proclaiming liberty**, echoing the Jubilee of Leviticus 25.
- **Effecting atonement**, standing in a redemptive role once exclusive to God.

This Melchizedek is not God Himself, but his agent, bearing divine authority in the final judgment. The author of Hebrews draws from this concept but reveals its fulfillment in Yeshua, who is exalted not as an eternal being in isolation, but as the *appointed* high priest and king—God's chosen representative.³⁵

## C. 4Q246 – The "Son of God" Text

Another Qumran text, 4Q246 (often called the "Son of God" scroll), describes a figure identified with divine titles: "Son of God" and "Son of the Most High." These echo both Daniel 7 and Psalm 2. While interpretations differ, the scroll clearly envisions an individual who bears God's authority and ushers in an everlasting kingdom.

This kind of exalted human or angelic agent—divine in function but not coequal in being—lays the groundwork for understanding Yeshua's role within Christian Monolatry. He is not a rival to the Most High, but the one appointed to reflect and extend the Father's reign.³⁶

---

³⁵ The Melchizedek scroll (11Q13) from Qumran portrays a heavenly figure named Melchizedek who carries out divine judgment in the heavenly council and proclaims final atonement. This figure is an exalted divine agent, acting on God's behalf. This text is a key example of how Second Temple Judaism contained traditions of powerful, heavenly mediators who fulfilled roles typically reserved for God, providing a crucial theological precedent for the New Testament's presentation of Yeshua as the ultimate high priest and judge.

See: Florentino García Martínez, "Messianic Hopes in the Qumran Writings," in *The People of the Dead Sea Scrolls: Their Writings, Beliefs, and Practices* (Leiden: Brill, 1995), 159–189. See also Andrei A. Orlov, "The Melchizedek Tradition," in *The Enoch-Metatron Tradition* (Tübingen: Mohr Siebeck, 2005), 95–101.

³⁶ The Aramaic text known as 4Q246, or the "Son of God" text, is one of the most significant pre-Christian manuscripts for understanding the background of the New Testament's Christological titles. Scholars note the striking parallels to the language used for Jesus in the Gospel of Luke (cf. Luke 1:32, 35). While the identity of the figure is debated, the text clearly shows that the titles "Son of God" and "Son of the Most High" were used within a Jewish context for a supreme, eschatological agent of God before the time of Jesus.

## Yeshua as High Priest and Son of Man: Continuity with Qumran

The New Testament does more than adopt language from Qumran's eschatological expectations—it integrates and fulfills the very roles that the Qumran community anticipated. Yeshua is not just another priest or another king; He is the divinely appointed and exalted agent who unites priesthood and kingship in Himself, in full continuity with Jewish monolatrous tradition.

### A. Yeshua as the Melchizedekian High Priest (Hebrews 7)

The Epistle to the Hebrews explicitly identifies Yeshua with the mysterious priest-king Melchizedek, drawing on both Genesis 14 and Second Temple expectations:

> *"Being designated by God as High Priest according to the order of Melchizedek."*
> (Hebrews 5:10, NASB95)

Hebrews 7 explains that Yeshua's priesthood is:

---

*See: James C. VanderKam, "The 'Son of God' Text from Qumran," in An Introduction to Early Judaism, 2nd ed. (Grand Rapids, MI: Eerdmans, 2022), 160-162. See also Florentino García Martínez, Qumran and Apocalyptic: Studies on the Aramaic Texts from Qumran (Leiden: Brill, 1992), 162–179.*

- **Eternal**, not dependent on ancestry or Levitical lineage.
- **Divinely appointed**, not self-initiated.
- **Superior**, offering perfect mediation between God and humanity.

This does not make Yeshua a second deity, but the appointed priestly mediator through whom God offers atonement and intercession. His role parallels Qumran's exalted Melchizedek figure—but unlike speculative dualities, Yeshua's appointment is revealed and rooted in God's will, in full service to the Father's supremacy.

## B. Yeshua as the Danielic Son of Man (Mark 14:62)

When asked by the high priest to identify Himself, Yeshua replies with words that echo Daniel 7:

> "You shall see the Son of Man sitting at the right hand of Power, and coming with the clouds of heaven."
> (Mark 14:62, NASB95)

In Daniel's vision, the "Son of Man" approaches the Ancient of Days and receives glory, dominion, and a kingdom. The Qumran texts often depict a similar figure—heavenly, authoritative, and exalted. The New Testament applies this directly to Yeshua, who is:

- **Entrusted with divine dominion**, yet remains subordinate to the Father.
- **Glorified in heaven**, but not self-glorifying (cf. John 8:54).
- **The visible expression of God's authority**, yet never the Independent God.

Yeshua's identity as the Son of Man thus reflects the culmination of long-developing Jewish expectations. Yet, within Christian Monolatry, His exaltation never breaches the singular supremacy of the Father. The Son reigns because the Father enthrones Him. His glory redounds to the glory of the One who sent Him.

# Monolatry Preserved: Yeshua's Priest-King Role Without Rivaling the Father

Even as the New Testament draws on Qumran's exalted priest-king imagery and applies it to Yeshua, it remains unwavering in its monolatrous fidelity. The Father is always the supreme source of authority, and Yeshua's exaltation as priest and king is never presented as ontological rivalry, but as a divinely granted office within a clearly defined hierarchy.

## A. Yeshua Receives His Priesthood from God

Just as Melchizedek was chosen and appointed in Genesis 14 without reference to lineage or law, so Yeshua's priesthood is a divine gift, not a claim to independent power. Hebrews emphasizes:

> "So also Christ did not glorify Himself so as to become a high priest, but He who said to Him, "You are My Son, Today I have begotten You";" *(Hebrews 5:5, NASB95)*

Yeshua is not self-appointed. His priestly authority flows from the Father's initiative—preserving the framework where God alone is the origin of all divine function and office.

## B. Yeshua Submits His Kingdom to God (1 Corinthians 15:24–28)

Paul makes the monolatrous structure of divine rule clear:

> "Then comes the end, when He hands over the kingdom to the God and Father... For He must reign until He has put all His enemies under His feet... When all things are subjected to Him, then the Son Himself will also be subjected to the One who subjected all things to Him, so that God may be all in all."
> (1 Corinthians 15:24–28, NASB95)

The Father remains the ultimate purpose and terminus of divine governance. Yeshua's reign, though genuine and glorious, is derivative and subordinate. His submission at the end of the age does not diminish His glory—it confirms the monolatrous fidelity that defines Christian faith.

## C. The Father is "the Only True God" (John 17:3)

In His high priestly prayer, Yeshua identifies the Father with unequivocal clarity:

> "This is eternal life, that they may know You, the only true God, and Jesus Christ whom You have sent." *(John 17:3, NASB95)*

This distinction is essential. Yeshua acknowledges the Father as the ultimate God, while positioning Himself as the one sent—the Messiah, the intermediary through whom eternal life is mediated. He does not redefine God's oneness but reinforces it through His role as divine Son and representative.

# Convergence and Fulfillment: Yeshua as the Culmination of Qumran's Hopes

The New Testament does not merely borrow themes from Qumran—it fulfills them. The priestly and royal expectations that were articulated separately in the scrolls are unified in Yeshua, revealing a singular messianic figure who holds both offices in harmony, and does so without challenging the supremacy of the Father.

## A. A Single Figure Who Embodies Both Offices

Qumran literature often anticipated two messianic figures: one priestly and one royal. However, the Letter to the Hebrews shows that in Yeshua, the two roles are not divided but merged:

> "But He, having offered one sacrifice for sins for all time, sat down at the right hand of God..."
> (Hebrews 10:12, NASB95)

As priest, Yeshua offers the definitive atonement; as king, He is enthroned beside God. This convergence was not imagined in full by the Qumran sectarians, but the New Testament reveals it as the culmination of their longings.

## B. The "Son of God" Language from Qumran and the Gospels

The fragment 4Q246 from Qumran refers to a coming figure called "Son of God" and "Son of the Most High." While interpretations vary, the New Testament applies this very language to Yeshua:

> *"He will be great and will be called the Son of the Most High; and the Lord God will give Him the throne of His father David."*
> (Luke 1:32, NASB95)

Rather than a separate heavenly being or angelic redeemer, the Son is now revealed as the incarnate Messiah who embodies this title in both mission and identity.

## C. Not a Second God, but a Representative Fulfillment

In Christian Monolatry, Yeshua does not replace YHWH or act as a rival divine being. Instead, He completes the picture that Qumran began to sketch—a divine agent with priestly and royal authority, yet one whose power and glory flow entirely from the God of Israel.

> *"And because of it He must be made like His brothers in all things, so that He might become a merciful and faithful high priest... to make propitiation for the sins of the people."*

(Hebrews 2:17, NASB95)

Yeshua, both divine and human, both priest and king, fulfills Israel's ancient hopes not by rivaling God, but by perfectly reflecting His will.

# Conclusion: Yeshua as the High Priest-King in Early Christian Monolatry

The integration of Qumran's exalted messianic hopes with the identity of Yeshua completes the picture of Christian Monolatry. It affirms that Yeshua fulfills roles that had long been anticipated—King, Priest, Redeemer—without displacing the Father's unrivaled supremacy.

## *A. The High Priest-King as the Culmination of Divine Agency*

The New Testament authors, especially the writer of Hebrews, present Yeshua as the ideal culmination of various strands of Jewish expectation:

- Like **Melchizedek**, He is both king and priest.
- Like the **Son of Man** in Daniel 7, He is enthroned beside the Ancient of Days.
- Like the **Messenger of the Covenant**, He comes to the temple bearing

divine authority.
- Like the **Angel of YHWH,** He speaks and acts in the name of God Himself.

These overlapping identities converge in one person—the Son—who serves as the final and full expression of divine agency.

## B. Monolatry Preserved Through the Priest-King Motif

Importantly, none of these exalted roles require a departure from monolatry. The Father remains the one uncreated, independent God, the source of all authority and existence. Yeshua is exalted *because* the Father willed it and empowered Him to mediate His covenant.

> *"The Lord has sworn and will not change His mind, 'You are a priest forever according to the order of Melchizedek.'"*
> (Hebrews 7:21, NASB95)

This priesthood is eternal, not by nature, but by divine appointment. Yeshua's role is supreme and everlasting, yet rooted in dependence upon the Father.

## C. Reverance That Honors the Father Through the Son

Within this framework, Christian honor/reverence of Yeshua does not violate monolatry but rather affirms it. When believers honor the Son, they glorify the Father who sent Him, exalted Him, and placed His Name upon Him.

> "So that at the name of Jesus every knee will bow... and that every tongue will confess that Jesus Christ is Lord, to the glory of God the Father."
> (Philippians 2:10–11, NASB95)

And as Yeshua Himself stated:

> "So that all will honor the Son just as they honor the Father. The one who does not honor the Son does not honor the Father who sent Him."
> (John 5:23, NASB95)

In this way, the honor given to Yeshua is not a threat to the Father's glory but its extension. Christian Monolatry is thus preserved: honor/reverence directed to the Son is only valid insofar as it flows from the will of the Father and returns to Him in glory.

# 11

# Key NT Passages Showing Subordination Within Monolatry

Despite the exalted titles and divine functions attributed to Yeshua, the New Testament consistently affirms His subordinate relationship to the Father. This hierarchy is not a denial of His divinity, but a clarification of His role as the dependent Son—the one through whom the Father acts, speaks, and reveals Himself. This dynamic preserves Christian Monolatry by ensuring that worship and glory ultimately ascend to the Independent God, the Father.

## A. John 14:28 – "the Father is Greater than I"

In one of the clearest affirmations of subordination, Yeshua states:

> "You heard that I said to you, 'I am going away, and I am coming to you.' If you loved Me, you would have rejoiced because I am going to

## KEY NT PASSAGES SHOWING SUBORDINATION WITHIN MONOLATRY

*the Father, for the Father is greater than I."*
(John 14:28, NASB95)

This is not merely a comment about Yeshua's human nature, nor is it temporary. It reflects an enduring distinction of authority: the Father possesses greater status, existence, and sovereignty. The Son, though divine, remains *begotten* and dependent.[37]

## B. 1 Corinthians 15:28 – The Son Submits the Kingdom

Paul outlines the final eschatological vision in which all authority is returned to God the Father:

> *"When all things are subjected to Him, then the Son Himself will also be subjected to the One who subjected all things to Him, so that God may be all in all."*
> (1 Corinthians 15:28, NASB95)

---

[37] While later Trinitarian theologians interpreted this verse as referring only to Christ's human nature (his "economic" role), many pre-Nicene fathers, such as Origen and Eusebius, understood it as a statement about the eternal, hierarchical relationship between the Father and the Son. This reading, which affirms an ontological priority of the Father as the source of the Son, was the dominant view in the early Church.

See: R.P.C. Hanson, *The Search for the Christian Doctrine of God: The Arian Controversy 318-381* (Edinburgh: T&T Clark, 1988), 64-67. Hanson provides a thorough overview of how early theologians understood this passage.

This verse encapsulates the entire New Testament theology of **derived authority**. Yeshua rules because the Father gave Him the right to rule; He submits because the Father remains supreme. The Son's glory enhances—not diminishes—the singular glory of God.[38]

## C. John 1:18 – "The Only Begotten God"

The NASB95 and the LSB preserves one of the most striking affirmations of both Yeshua's divine status and His dependence:

> *"No one has seen God at any time; the only begotten God who is in the bosom of the Father, He has explained Him."*
> (John 1:18, NASB95)

This verse affirms two critical aspects:

1. **Yeshua is "God"** — not in a coequal sense, but as the **only begotten** one, the visible expression of the invisible Father.

---

[38] This passage, which describes the Son's final subjection to the Father, presents a significant challenge to later models of co-equal deity. New Testament scholars acknowledge that Paul is here describing a final and complete restoration of all things to God the Father as the ultimate source and goal. The Son's reign is depicted as a mediatorial one, which, having accomplished its purpose, is returned to the one who granted it.

See: Gordon D. Fee, *The First Epistle to the Corinthians*, New International Commentary on the New Testament (Grand Rapids, MI: Eerdmans, 1987), 756-759.

## KEY NT PASSAGES SHOWING SUBORDINATION WITHIN MONOLATRY

2. **He is in the bosom of the Father** — eternally close, yet distinct and subordinate. He reveals the Father, not Himself.

This unique wording preserves Christian Monolatry: it upholds the divinity of the Son without compromising the supremacy of the Father.

## D. Hebrews 1:8–9 – Messiah Is Called "God," Yet Anointed by "His God"

Hebrews offers a profound insight into this hierarchy:

> "But of the Son He says, "Your throne, O God, is forever and ever, And the righteous scepter is the scepter of His kingdom. "You have loved righteousness and hated lawlessness; Therefore God, Your God, has anointed You With the oil of gladness above Your companions." (*Hebrews 1:8–9, NASB95*)

Yeshua is addressed as "God," affirming His status. But He is also **anointed by His God**, affirming His dependence. The Son's throne is real and eternal—but it is given, not inherent.

### The Enthroned Son and the Restoration of God's Rule

The New Testament does not stop at identifying Yeshua with preexistent divine agents—it proclaims His enthronement as the ultimate validation of

His identity and mission. This exaltation is not a departure from Jewish monolatry, but its climactic expression: YHWH restores His kingdom by enthroning the one He has appointed to bear His Name and reign on His behalf.

Psalm 110:1 remains the central scripture for understanding this exaltation:

*"The Lord says to my Lord: 'Sit at My right hand until I make Your enemies a footstool for Your feet.'" (NASB 1995)*

This verse is quoted or alluded to more than any other Old Testament passage in the New Testament. It provides the theological backbone for apostolic teaching on Yeshua's exalted status. Peter's Pentecost sermon explicitly interprets the resurrection and ascension of Yeshua as the fulfillment of this enthronement:

*"Therefore let all the house of Israel know for certain that God has made Him both Lord and Messiah—this Yeshua whom you crucified." (Acts 2:36, NASB 1995)*

To be enthroned at the right hand of God is not to become a second deity but to be installed as God's messianic agent—Lord by appointment, not by independent nature. This role is consistent with Second Temple Jewish expectations of a heavenly vice-regent who would administer divine rule.

Paul echoes this framework in 1 Corinthians 15:24–28:

*"Then comes the end, when He hands over the kingdom to the God and*

## KEY NT PASSAGES SHOWING SUBORDINATION WITHIN MONOLATRY

*Father... For He must reign until He has put all His enemies under His feet... The Son Himself also will be subjected to the One who subjected all things to Him, so that God may be all in all." (NASB 1995)*

This passage makes two points clear:

1. **Yeshua's reign is real and divinely authorized.**
2. **Yeshua's reign is ultimately temporary and derivative.**

He does not seek glory apart from the Father, but reigns as a faithful Son until all things are brought under divine order. His final act of kingship is to return the kingdom to God, reaffirming the Father's unrivaled supremacy.

### John 1:18 – The "Only Begotten God," Highlighting Derived Divinity

One of the most profound Christological statements in the New Testament appears in John 1:18, which describes Yeshua as the "only begotten God" (μονογενὴς θεὸς, *monogenēs theos*), who reveals the unseen Father:

*"No one has ever seen God; the only begotten God, who is in the bosom of the Father, He has explained Him." (John 1:18, NASB95)*

This verse encapsulates both the **divine status** of Yeshua and His **subordination** to the Father. He is called "God," affirming His genuine divinity, but He is also "begotten," meaning His divine identity is **derived** from the Father, not self-originated.

## MONOLATRY

## 1. Textual Variants and Their Significance

There are two major textual traditions for this verse:

- Some manuscripts read **"only begotten Son"** (*monogenēs huios*).
- Others, including the earliest and most reliable (P66, P75, Codex Sinaiticus, Codex Vaticanus), read **"only begotten God"** (*monogenēs theos*).

The latter, though theologically more challenging, is almost certainly the original. It reflects an elevated view of Yeshua as divine, yet not as an independent or co-equal deity. Instead, this phrase highlights a **unique derivation**: He is the only one who shares in God's nature because He comes from God in a way no other being does.[39]

---

[39] The reading "only begotten God" (*monogenēs theos*) is widely accepted by modern textual critics as the original wording of John 1:18, as it is found in the earliest and most reliable manuscripts (including 𝔓66, 𝔓75, Codex Sinaiticus, and Codex Vaticanus). This scholarly consensus is affirmed across the theological spectrum. Bart D. Ehrman, for example, argues that this phrasing reflects an early, pre-Nicene Christology where the Son is a distinct divine being subordinate to the Father.

Critically, this view is also championed by leading conservative evangelical scholars. **Daniel B. Wallace**, a foremost expert on New Testament textual criticism, has argued extensively that the evidence strongly supports "only begotten God" as the authentic reading. He concludes that this phrasing is a powerful and intentional declaration by the apostle John, emphasizing that the Son has the very same nature as the Father because He is uniquely derived from Him. For Wallace, this construction is how John can "state that the Word was God and yet was distinct from the Father."

See: Bart D. Ehrman, *The Orthodox Corruption of Scripture* (New York: Oxford University Press, 1993), 78-82. See also: Daniel B. Wallace, "The Text and Grammar of John 1:18," in *Revisiting the Corruption of the New Testament* (Grand Rapids, MI: Kregel Publications, 2011).

KEY NT PASSAGES SHOWING SUBORDINATION WITHIN MONOLATRY

## 2. Yeshua Reveals the Unseen God

The first clause of the verse affirms a foundational truth: "No one has ever seen God." This aligns with Exodus 33:20, where YHWH tells Moses, "You cannot see My face, for no man can see Me and live." God's full essence remains veiled, inaccessible to human perception.

But Yeshua, the **only begotten God**, "has explained Him." The Greek word *exēgēsato* implies not just verbal explanation, but **interpretation** and **revelation**—a bringing forth of what was previously hidden. Yeshua becomes the lens through which the invisible God is seen, known, and encountered.

## 3. Continuity with Jewish Divine Agency Traditions

In this role, Yeshua fulfills the function attributed to the *Memra* in the Targums and the *Logos* in Philo's writings: a divine-but-subordinate intermediary who makes God known. But the connection is deeper still. He does not just *mirror* the Angel of YHWH; He *is* that Angel—the visible, personal presence of the invisible God throughout Israel's history. This identification is the very key that unlocks the profound statement in John 1:18: "No one has ever seen God at any time." If that is true, who did Abraham, Jacob, and Moses see? The verse itself provides the answer: "the only begotten God who is in the bosom of the Father, He has explained Him." They saw the Son.

This theological necessity was understood even before the time of Christ. Philo of Alexandria argued that the transcendent Father is too great to have an image in which mortal man could be made; therefore, man was made in the likeness of the "second God," the Logos. The Son is, and has always been, the image of the invisible God for the simple reason that the Father has no image but him. The Bible itself testifies that God is invisible (Colossians 1:15) and "dwells in unapproachable light, whom no one has ever seen or can see" (1 Timothy 6:16). This is not a metaphor; it is a statement of reality. **To receive light directly from the Father is impossible, because that very light is unapproachable.**

In the eternal logic of God's being, the Father's act of will to beget the Son is the very source of the Son's existence as the Image. But from the moment the Son was brought forth, he became the living solution to the problem of how an infinite, unseen God could reveal Himself to a finite creation. This is why those who "saw God" in the Old Testament lived: they were not seeing the unbegotten Source who dwells in unapproachable light, but the perfect, begotten Image who makes Him known. This very distinction between the seen and the unseen, the Image and the Source, is the essence of their subordinate relationship and the heart of Christian Monolatry.

Thus, John 1:18 is not a declaration of Trinitarian co-equality, but a **perfect summary of Christian Monolatry**: Yeshua is divine, but He derives that divinity from the Father. He is fully capable of revealing God because He shares in God's nature, yet He remains **dependent**, **sent**, and **submissive** to the One who begot Him.

### Hebrews 1:8–9 – Messiah is Called "God," but His God Anoints Him

Another deeply significant Christological text is found in Hebrews 1:8–9, where the Son is addressed directly and given divine titles, yet still presented in a **subordinate role**:

*"But of the Son He says, "Your throne, O God, is forever and ever, And the righteous scepter is the scepter of His kingdom. "You have loved righteousness and hated lawlessness; Therefore God, Your God, has anointed You With the oil of gladness*

## KEY NT PASSAGES SHOWING SUBORDINATION WITHIN MONOLATRY

*above Your companions.*"'" (Hebrews 1:8–9, NASB95)

This passage quotes from **Psalm 45:6–7**, a royal enthronement psalm originally applied to a Davidic king. The author of Hebrews reapplies it to Messiah, affirming His exalted status, while also preserving His **derived authority**.[40]

## 1. *Messiah Addressed as "God"*

The opening declaration—"Your throne, God, is forever and ever"—grants the Son the divine title "God." This shows that He is not merely a prophet or messianic figure; He reigns with a throne and a kingdom that are **eternal**. The Son, therefore, partakes in the **divine identity** and is worthy of supreme honor.

Yet this exaltation does not contradict monolatry, because the passage immediately clarifies the **source** of that exaltation.

---

[40] The quotation from Psalm 45 in Hebrews 1:8-9 is a key Christological text. The author of Hebrews applies the title "God" (*Theos*) to the Son, affirming his divine status. However, in the very next verse, he affirms that this "God" has a God over him ("Therefore God, Your God, has anointed You"). This juxtaposition of divine title with clear subordination is a perfect example of the monolatrous framework, where a divine agent is exalted without being made equal to the ultimate source of his anointing.

For a detailed analysis of the grammar and theology of this passage, see: Harold W. Attridge, *The Epistle to the Hebrews, Hermeneia—A Critical and Historical Commentary on the Bible* (Philadelphia: Fortress Press, 1989), 58-63.

## 2. "God, Your God, Has Anointed You"

In the very next breath, the author declares, "Therefore God, Your God, has anointed You…" This confirms that the Son, though divine, is still in a **relationship of subordination** to the Father. He has a God—**"Your God"**—who anoints Him, who grants Him His throne, and who elevates Him above all others.

This dual affirmation (divinity and dependence) is critical:

- The Son is called "God," showing He shares the divine nature.
- Yet He has a **God above Him**, affirming that His divinity is not autonomous but **granted**.

## 3. A Perfect Summary of New Testament Monolatry

Hebrews 1:8–9 captures the heart of Christian monolatry: the **Son is exalted**, enthroned, and divine—but **He is not unbegotten**. His authority and status derive from the Father, who remains the ultimate God. This relationship preserves the unity and singularity of God while allowing space for an exalted Son who acts as God's supreme emissary.

## KEY NT PASSAGES SHOWING SUBORDINATION WITHIN MONOLATRY

### *Yeshua Has a God: Explicit Statements of Subordination*

Beyond the theological implications drawn from poetic or prophetic texts, the New Testament offers **direct and explicit declarations** from Yeshua Himself—statements in which He openly identifies the Father as **His God**. These affirmations, especially in post-resurrection contexts, are vital for understanding the ongoing **subordination** of the Son, even in His exalted state.

### A. John 20:17 – "I Am Ascending... to My God and Your God"

After His resurrection, Yeshua says to Mary Magdalene:

> "Jesus said to her, 'Stop clinging to Me, for I have not yet ascended to the Father; but go to My brothers and say to them, '**I am ascending to My Father and your Father, and My God and your God.**'"
> (John 20:17, NASB95)

This statement is **remarkable** in its clarity. Even after conquering death and standing glorified, Yeshua refers to **the Father as "My God."** This indicates that His dependence and relational subordination to the Father did not end with the resurrection but **continues in His exaltation**.

### B. Revelation 3:12 – "The Name of My God"

Speaking to the church in Philadelphia, the glorified Yeshua makes another unmistakable declaration:

> *"The one who overcomes, I will make him a pillar in the temple of **My God**, and he will not go out from it anymore; and I will write on him **the name of My God**, and the name of the city of **My God**, the new Jerusalem, which comes down out of heaven from **My God**, and My new name."*
> (Revelation 3:12, NASB95)

Here, **four times in a single verse**, Yeshua calls the Father **"My God."** This is not poetic ambiguity—it is a repeated and deliberate confession of relational hierarchy.

## A Theology of Dependence, Not Inferiority

These verses underscore a consistent pattern:

- Yeshua is honored, glorified, and enthroned.
- Yet He still acknowledges that **the Father is His God.**

This affirms that divine **exaltation does not eliminate subordination**. It is precisely because Yeshua is the faithful Son that He honors the Father as His God—even in glory.

# KEY NT PASSAGES SHOWING SUBORDINATION WITHIN MONOLATRY

## *A Key Component of Christian Monolatry*

Rather than undermining Yeshua's divinity, these affirmations clarify its **origin and structure**:

- Yeshua shares in the divine nature because He is the **begotten Son**, not the unbegotten Source.
- The Father remains the one **supreme God**, and Yeshua's exaltation flows from Him.

These explicit declarations are indispensable for any Christology that wishes to remain **biblically grounded** and **monolatrous**.

# 12

# God Granted Yeshua Revelation, Throne, and Authority

A core affirmation of Christian Monolatry is that Yeshua's divine status is not self-generated—it is given by the Father. The New Testament consistently depicts the Son as the recipient of revelation, power, and enthronement. These are not signs of inferiority but of derived authority: Yeshua reigns because God wills it, not by independent right.

**A. Revelation 1:1 – "The Revelation... Which God Gave Him"**

*"The Revelation of Jesus Christ,* **which God gave Him** *to show to His bond-servants, the things which must soon take place..."*
(Revelation 1:1, NASB95)

This verse opens the final book of the Bible by stating that **even the**

**apocalyptic revelation Yeshua delivers was granted by God.** Yeshua is the conduit of divine knowledge—but the **source is the Father**. This reflects a monolatrous hierarchy: all authority and insight flow **from the One God to the Son**, and then to the Church.

## B. Revelation 3:21 – "I Also Conquered and Sat Down with My Father"

In one of the most powerful Christological statements in all of Scripture, the glorified Yeshua makes a stunning promise:

> *"The one who overcomes, I will grant to him to sit with Me on My throne, **as I also overcame and sat with My Father on His throne.**" (Revelation 3:21, NASB95)*

This single verse reveals both the Son's ultimate exaltation and His continued subordination. First, it affirms that His enthronement was not His by default, but was a reward **granted** by the Father for His victorious obedience. He "overcame" and *then* He "sat." This preserves the monolatrous framework: the Father, as the ultimate source of authority, is the one who bestows this honor.

But the verse reveals something far more profound. The throne Yeshua is granted to sit upon is not merely his messianic throne, the throne of David. It is the Father's *own* throne—the ultimate seat of cosmic authority. This is an honor of an entirely different magnitude. For the Son to share the very throne of the one supreme God is the highest possible exaltation and is a primary reason why He is rightly called "God" and receives such profound honor and reverence (Revelation 5:12-13).

Even in this ultimate display of glory, the hierarchy remains perfectly clear. The Son sits *with* the Father, not *in place of* the Father. This co-regency is a specific, mediatorial role for the current age. As the Apostle Paul explains, this mediatorial reign will conclude when the Son, having put all enemies under his feet, hands the kingdom back to God the Father. At that point, the Son himself **"will also be subjected to the One who subjected all things to Him, so that God may be all in all"** (1 Corinthians 15:24-28).

The Bible does not give us enough information to know precisely what this future state of "subjection" will look like, but it is not a removal from glory. The Son's own messianic reign on the throne of David is eternal (Luke 1:32-33). Rather, this final act affirms the foundational principle of monolatry: all authority originates from the Father and ultimately returns to Him. It is from this position of ultimate, delegated authority that the Son is fully empowered to act as God's designated judge. The entire divine arrangement is the ultimate display of trust. It reveals a Father so confident in the love and loyalty of His Son that He can grant him a share in His own throne, knowing that this perfect Son will faithfully complete his mission and willingly affirm his glorious subjection to the one who sent him.

## C. Revelation 5:7 – "The Lamb Approached the One on the Throne"

*"And He came and took the scroll out of the right hand of Him **who sat on the throne.**"*
(Revelation 5:7, NASB95)

This vision highlights a decisive moment: **Yeshua (the Lamb) receives divine authority not autonomously, but from the One seated on the throne**—a clear representation of the Father.

- Yeshua does not begin **on the throne**; He approaches it.
- He does not **seize** the scroll; it is **given**.

## GOD GRANTED YESHUA REVELATION, THRONE, AND AUTHORITY

- He does not act by **personal right**, but by **heavenly commission**.

*Derived Authority, Not Independent Sovereignty*

These three passages combine to establish a consistent message:

1. Yeshua receives **revelation** from God.
2. Yeshua shares in **enthronement** through obedience.
3. Yeshua executes **judgment and redemption** by commission.

This pattern reflects **functional subordination**, not ontological inequality. The Father remains the supreme initiator; the Son, the obedient and glorified agent.[41]

---

[41] The Book of Revelation consistently portrays the Son's authority as delegated by the Father. Scholars of Revelation note that the book's Christology, while exceptionally high, is framed within a a clear theocentric and hierarchical structure. The vision begins with a revelation that God "gave" to Jesus (Rev 1:1), shows that Jesus's place on the throne was a reward for having "overcome" (Rev 3:21), and climaxes with the Lamb approaching the throne to *receive* the scroll of authority from the One seated upon it (Rev 5:7). This consistent pattern of bestowal is central to the book's theology.

See: Richard Bauckham, *The Theology of the Book of Revelation* (Cambridge: Cambridge University Press, 1993), 54-65. Bauckham emphasizes that while Christ is worthy of worship, his sovereignty is always exercised in subordination to God the Father.

## *Yeshua Declares the Father as the "Only True God" (John 17:3)*

A pivotal moment in Yeshua's high priestly prayer occurs in **John 17:3**, where He makes one of the clearest Christological statements in all the New Testament:

> *"And this is eternal life, that they may know **You**, the **only true God**, and **Jesus Christ** whom You have sent."*
> (John 17:3, NASB95)

This verse encapsulates the **monolatrous framework** of the New Testament. The Father is explicitly identified as "the only true God," and Yeshua is recognized not as a coequal partner, but as the **one sent** by that true God.[42]

### 1. The Shema Affirmed, Not Undermined

By calling the Father "the only true God," Yeshua reaffirms the Jewish Shema

---

[42] John 17:3 is one of the most explicit statements of monolatrous hierarchy in the New Testament. New Testament scholar C.K. Barrett, in his renowned commentary on John, notes that the language here is stark and clear: "The Father is designated as 'the only true God,' and this supreme claim is not made for Jesus." While later theology would find ways to harmonize this with a co-equal Trinity, the plain sense of the text, as acknowledged by grammarians and exegetes, establishes a clear distinction between the Father as the "only true God" and Jesus Christ as the one whom He has "sent."
See: C.K. Barrett, *The Gospel According to St. John: An Introduction with Commentary and Notes on the Greek Text*, 2nd ed. (Philadelphia: Westminster Press, 1978), 505-507.

(Deuteronomy 6:4):

*"Hear, O Israel! The LORD is our God, the LORD is one."*

He does not contradict this central Jewish confession. Instead, He affirms it—**while also clarifying His own identity as the one sent to reveal that one God.**

## 2. Yeshua as the Mediator of Eternal Life

The verse also reveals **how eternal life is accessed**:

- It comes from **knowing** the only true God.
- And from **knowing the one sent by Him**, Yeshua Messiah.

Thus, while the Father remains the sole God, **Yeshua is the authorized path** through whom that God is known and encountered. This is the essence of **Christian Monolatry**—God is one, but His agency is revealed and mediated through His Son.

## 3. Identity and Mission, Not Equality

Importantly, Yeshua distinguishes between Himself and the Father:

- **The Father** is "the only true God."
- **Yeshua** is the one whom that God has **sent**.

This reaffirms the hierarchy seen throughout the Gospels: **Yeshua is divine, but not the Supreme Deity.** He is **begotten**, not unbegotten; **sent**, not self-appointed.

In sum, **John 17:3** reinforces the theology of the entire New Testament:

- There is **one true God**—the Father.
- Yeshua is **the Son**, divinely appointed to reveal and glorify Him.

This verse alone dismantles any notion that early Christianity equated Yeshua with the Father in a Nicene or coequal sense. Instead, it upholds a **monolatrous relationship** between Sender and Sent, God and Messiah.

## Acts and Gospels: Yeshua Appearing as He Did Before?

The Gospels and the Book of Acts include several narratives where the risen Yeshua appears in ways that **strongly echo Old Testament** theophanies—dramatic encounters where God (or His angelic representative) visibly interacts with humans. These post-resurrection appearances reinforce the early Christian belief that **Yeshua was the same divine agent who had acted throughout Israel's history**, now fully revealed.

### A. Acts 9 (with Parallels in Acts 22 and 26) – The Blinding Light

In Acts 9, Saul (Paul) encounters Yeshua on the road to Damascus:

> *"Suddenly a light from heaven flashed around him... 'I am Jesus, whom you are persecuting.'"* (Acts 9:3–5, NASB95)

This account:

- **Resembles Old Testament theophanies** (e.g., Exodus 3, Ezekiel 1),
- Echoes the appearance of the **Angel of YHWH** or the **glory of YHWH**, and
- Presents Yeshua in **radiant, heavenly form**—consistent with divine manifestations seen in Jewish Scripture.

Repeated twice more (Acts 22 and 26), this moment anchors Paul's authority in a direct encounter with the **same figure** who spoke to the prophets.

## B. The Transfiguration – Yeshua in Glory with Moses and Elijah

In the Synoptic Gospels, Yeshua is transfigured before His disciples:

> *"His face shone like the sun, and His garments became white as light... And behold, Moses and Elijah appeared to them, talking with Him."*
> (Matthew 17:2–3, NASB95)

This moment parallels:

- The divine **radiance of Moses** after meeting God (Exodus 34:29),
- The **heavenly glory** of YHWH's presence, and
- Reinforces that Yeshua **participates in the divine radiance**.

By appearing with Moses (the Law) and Elijah (the Prophets), Yeshua is shown to be **the fulfillment of all prior revelation**, confirming His role as the **climactic divine agent**.

## C. Continuity with the Old Testament Messenger

Though the New Testament does not explicitly state "Yeshua was the Angel of the Lord in the Old Testament," these appearances heavily imply **continuity** with the figure who:

- Spoke with divine authority,
- Appeared in radiant light or cloud,
- Interacted personally with patriarchs and prophets,
- Forgave sins, and
- Carried the divine Name.

The early Christian view held that **Yeshua was not merely a new messenger**, but **the same one who had always revealed the Father**—now fully incarnate and glorified.

## Conclusion: Upholding Monolatry While Exalting Yeshua

Through the lens of divine agency, the New Testament presents **Yeshua as the apex of a long-established Jewish tradition**: the exalted agent who reveals, enacts, and represents the will of YHWH. His identity fulfills—not contradicts—the core tenets of **Jewish monolatry**, which always distinguished between the Most High God and those through whom He operated.

### 1. Yeshua Shares in God's Authority

The New Testament affirms that Yeshua:

- **Performs miracles**, heals, and casts out demons by the Holy Spirit
- **Forgives sins**—a divine prerogative previously exercised only by God or His angel (cf. Zechariah 3:4).
- **Receives homage** from followers, angels, and even creation itself.
- **Reveals God's will**, being the ultimate prophet, priest, and king.

All of this indicates a **real participation in divine prerogatives**, but always as **a derived and appointed agent**, not an independent deity.

**2. Yeshua Remains Subordinate to the Father**

At every point, the New Testament maintains **a hierarchical relationship**:

- Yeshua refers to the Father as **"my God"** (John 20:17; Revelation 3:12).
- He **receives revelation, authority, and enthronement** from God (Revelation 1:1; 3:21; 5:7).
- He **gives the kingdom back to the Father** at the end (1 Corinthians 15:24–28).
- He explicitly states: **"the Father is greater than I"** (John 14:28).

This affirms that **divine sonship is not the same as divine equality**. The Son shares in the Father's nature and glory because the Father has **willed it to be so**.

## 3. Yeshua Fulfills All Jewish Categories of Divine Agency

The New Testament identifies Yeshua with:

- The **Angel of YHWH** – the bearer of God's Name and authority.
- The **Logos** – God's eternal Word through whom all was made.
- The **Memra** – the visible expression of the invisible God in the Targums.
- The **Son of Man** – exalted and enthroned beside the Ancient of Days.
- The **Messenger of the Covenant** – the long-anticipated purifier and judge.

Each role reflects a **subordinate yet divine function**, one that sits perfectly within Second Temple Jewish thought prior to its post-70 CE consolidation under stricter monotheism.

## *Monolatry Preserved, Not Broken*

At no point does the New Testament suggest **two independent gods**. Instead, it proclaims **one supreme God—the Father—who acts through one ultimate Agent—the Son**. The Son is divine, not because He is co-equal in origin, but because the Father has **begotten, sent, and exalted Him**.

*"The Father... is greater than I."*
   (John 14:28, NASB95)

*"That all will honor the Son just as they honor the Father... The one who does not honor the Son does not honor the Father who sent Him."*
   (John 5:23, NASB95)

*"...to the glory of God the Father."*
   (Philippians 2:11, NASB95)


These passages demonstrate that **worship directed to the Son** is always meant to **glorify the Father**, not to create a competing object of devotion.

# 13

# Messianic Jews After Yeshua – Maintaining Jewish Traditions and Welcoming the Gentiles

What did it look like for first-century Jews to follow Yeshua while remaining faithful to their ancestral traditions? This question remains central for many Jewish believers today, especially when reading the New Testament texts that seem to differentiate between Jewish and Gentile obligations concerning the Torah.

The early followers of Yeshua—including the Apostles—did not see themselves as abandoning Judaism. On the contrary, they lived as observant Jews, honoring the Sabbath, celebrating the appointed feasts, maintaining ritual purity, and participating in Temple worship. At the same time, the inclusion of Gentiles into the people of God did not require those Gentiles to take on the full weight of Jewish covenant obligations. Instead, the Apostles affirmed a vision of unity that preserved Jewish identity while making space for Gentile inclusion—each group honoring God within its own covenantal framework.

This chapter explores how Messianic Jews in the first century embodied a faithful Jewish life in the light of Yeshua's messianic mission, while also helping define a place for Gentiles in God's covenant community without imposing full Torah observance upon them.

## *Yeshua and the Apostles as Observant Jews*

**Living Jewish Observance in Daily Life**

Jewish life in the first century was shaped by far more than sacrificial worship at the Temple. It included Sabbath rest (Luke 4:16), dietary laws (Mark 7:1–13; Acts 10:14), ritual garments such as tzitzit (Matthew 9:20; Numbers 15:37–41), and the regular observance of festivals like Passover, Shavuot (Pentecost), and Sukkot. These daily and seasonal rhythms expressed covenant faithfulness to God. For Yeshua and His earliest followers—who were all Jewish—there was no reason to discard these practices. On the contrary, the New Testament presents them continuing in these customs unless they were directly reoriented by the Messiah's instruction.

The Gospel accounts and the book of Acts reveal a Judaism alive with expectation, tradition, and Torah commitment—even as it opened to a transformative revelation in Yeshua.

## Yeshua's Faithful Observance

From His earliest years, Yeshua's life was marked by covenantal faithfulness to the Torah. He was raised in a devout Jewish household and participated fully in the practices of His people. The Gospels show Him attending pilgrimage festivals in Jerusalem, teaching in synagogues, honoring the Sabbath, and engaging in ritual observance.

He kept Passover with His disciples (Luke 22:7–13), read from the scroll in the synagogue on the Sabbath (Luke 4:16–21), and instructed others to keep even the "least" of the commandments (Matthew 5:17–19). Yeshua did not set Himself against the Law of Moses but revealed its full intent. His teachings repeatedly deepened, clarified, and elevated the meaning of the commandments, drawing attention to the heart and spirit behind the Law rather than mere ritual compliance.

Far from undermining Jewish law, Yeshua's ministry reaffirmed its holiness—while also fulfilling its prophetic direction. He condemned hypocrisy, not observance; He challenged the misuse of tradition, not tradition itself. His message was one of continuity and fulfillment, showing that loyalty to the Torah and allegiance to the Messiah were never meant to be in conflict.

## The Apostles After Yeshua's Death and Resurrection

After Yeshua's resurrection and ascension, His closest followers continued to live as Torah-observant Jews. Far from abandoning Jewish life, they participated actively in Temple worship, honored traditional practices, and maintained a visible Jewish identity within their communities.

## 1. Temple Worship and Daily Jewish Life

The Book of Acts records that the early believers, including the Apostles, were "continually in the temple, praising God" (Luke 24:53) and "day by day, continuing with one mind in the temple" (Acts 2:46). This ongoing presence in the Temple underscores their commitment to the central place of Jewish worship. They did not consider faith in Yeshua as reason to withdraw from the spiritual heart of Israel's religious life.

## 2. James the Just – A Pillar of Jewish Fidelity

James (Ya'akov), the brother of Yeshua, became the leading figure in the Jerusalem assembly. Early historical sources, including Hegesippus and Josephus, describe him as a righteous man known for his prayers, adherence to Jewish law, and frequent presence in the Temple. He was respected even among non-believing Jews for his piety. His eventual martyrdom—being thrown from the Temple—testifies to his uncompromising commitment to Jewish life even while proclaiming Yeshua as Messiah.[43]

## 3. Peter and Dietary Laws

---

[43] The portrait of James as a deeply pious and Torah-observant figure is one of the strongest historical traditions of the early church. The second-century Jewish-Christian writer Hegesippus, whose work is preserved by the historian Eusebius, describes James's righteousness and constant presence at the Temple in detail. The first-century Jewish historian Josephus also corroborates James's identity as "the brother of Jesus, who was called Christ" and his martyrdom at the hands of the high priest. These extra-biblical sources confirm the New Testament's picture of a Jerusalem church that remained deeply embedded in Jewish life.
See: Eusebius, *Ecclesiastical History*, Book 2, Chapter 23 (preserving Hegesippus). See also Flavius Josephus, *Antiquities of the Jews*, Book 20, Chapter 9.

In Acts 10, Peter's vision of unclean animals is often misunderstood as canceling kosher food laws. However, Peter's own interpretation contradicts this. When the vision ends, he says, "By no means, Lord, for I have never eaten anything unholy and unclean" (Acts 10:14, NASB95). The Spirit immediately clarifies that the vision concerns the inclusion of Gentiles, not food. Peter remains Torah-observant, and the point is about removing barriers to Gentile fellowship—not changing dietary requirements for Jews.

**4. Paul's Observance and Nazirite Vow**

Paul—often misunderstood as a Torah-breaker—publicly demonstrated his own fidelity to Jewish law. In Acts 21:20–26, Paul is urged by James and the elders in Jerusalem to accompany men who had taken a Nazirite vow and to purify himself in the Temple to prove he still "walks orderly, keeping the Law." Paul agrees without protest, revealing that he did not view Torah observance as contrary to faith in Yeshua.

## *Paul's Jewish Identity*

Among the Apostles, no figure has sparked more debate regarding Torah observance than Paul. Often mischaracterized as the one who "freed" believers from the Law, Paul in fact affirms his Jewish identity and Torah fidelity multiple times throughout his ministry. His mission to the Gentiles did not entail a rejection of Jewish customs for Jews, but rather a distinction of roles within the broader covenant family of God.

**1. A Pharisee by Training and Conviction**

Paul declares in Acts 23:6, "I am a Pharisee, a son of Pharisees." Even after coming to faith in Yeshua, he does not renounce this heritage. In Acts 22:3, he emphasizes that he was "brought up in this city, educated under Gamaliel, strictly according to the Law of our fathers." His training placed him in the heart of Jewish tradition, and he retained great respect for that tradition—even as he redirected its fulfillment toward Yeshua.

**2. Loyalty to the Traditions of His Fathers**

Paul affirms in Galatians 1:14 that he was "advancing in Judaism beyond many of my contemporaries," being "more extremely zealous for my ancestral traditions." While his zeal was initially misapplied, leading to persecution of believers, his conversion redirected that passion toward proclaiming Yeshua—not discarding Jewish observance.

**3. The Nazirite Vow in Jerusalem**

Paul's participation in purification rites in Acts 21 shows his active Torah observance. To calm concerns among the Jewish believers that he was teaching Jews to forsake Moses, James and the elders urge him to accompany men completing a Nazirite vow. Paul not only agrees but pays for their sacrifices—an act requiring Temple participation and strict adherence to Numbers 6. This public act proves his continued identification with Jewish law and community.

**4. Circumcision of Timothy, but Not Titus**

Paul circumcises Timothy (Acts 16:3), whose mother was Jewish, to honor his Jewish heritage and avoid offense in Jewish regions. Conversely, he refuses to circumcise Titus, a Gentile (Galatians 2:3), because doing so would have implied that Gentiles must adopt Jewish identity to be saved. These actions demonstrate Paul's nuanced approach: preserving Jewish identity for Jews, while rejecting legal compulsion for Gentiles.[44]

## *Distinguishing Jewish and Gentile Believers*

### 1. The Jerusalem Council (Acts 15)

The earliest followers of Yeshua lived in a world where Jewish and Gentile identities were distinct, and the Apostles maintained that distinction within the body of Messiah. This did not signal division or hierarchy but recognized differing covenantal roles within God's unified people, a reality Paul himself describes when he speaks of his calling as the "apostle to the Gentiles" and Peter's as the "apostle to the circumcision" (Galatians 2:7-8). This distinction is the very key to understanding why Paul was so often misunderstood.

This is why the Jerusalem Council in Acts 15 was so pivotal. When Jewish believers insisted that Gentiles must be circumcised and obey the Law of Moses to be saved (Acts 15:1, 5), they were not being arbitrary. They understood that full participation in the covenant life of Israel was impossible without circumcision; for example, an uncircumcised man was

---

[44] Paul's actions regarding Timothy (a man of Jewish heritage whom he circumcised) and Titus (a Gentile whom he refused to have circumcised) are often seen by scholars as the key to understanding his complex theology of the Law. His approach was not one of abolition, but of differentiation. Circumcision remained a valid sign of covenant identity for Jews like Timothy, but it was not a requirement for salvation for Gentiles like Titus. This demonstrates Paul's principle of maintaining distinct Jewish and Gentile identities within a unified body of believers.

For a detailed analysis of this *"differentiated"* Pauline view, see: *E.P. Sanders, Paul and Palestinian Judaism*(Philadelphia: Fortress Press, 1977). See also *James D.G. Dunn, The Partings of the Ways: Between Christianity and Judaism and their Significance for the Character of Christianity* (London: SCM Press, 1991).

forbidden from partaking in the Passover (Exodus 12:48).

However, the apostles, led by Peter and James, discerned a new work of God. Peter's powerful testimony confirmed that God had already accepted the Gentiles through faith alone, evidenced by the ultimate sign of His approval: they had received the Holy Spirit apart from any Torah observance (Acts 15:7–9). This was the undeniable proof that God had a path for Gentiles that did not require them to become Jews.

This stunning turn of events was something Yeshua himself had foretold. In the parable of the wedding feast, the king's invited guests—his own people—were too busy and refused to come. In response, the king declared that they were not worthy and sent his servants to the main roads to invite **"everyone they found, both evil and good"** (Matthew 22:1-14). These new guests were not held to the same standard of relationship as the original invitees; their only requirement was to be properly dressed for the wedding, a symbol of a righteous life. In the same way, because many in Israel rejected the Messiah, the invitation was extended to the Gentiles with a different set of requirements.

The Apostle Paul builds on this with his allegory of the olive tree in Romans 11. He explains that some of the natural branches (Israel) were broken off because of unbelief, making room for wild branches (the Gentiles) to be grafted in. This grafting is a pure act of grace; the wild branches should never become arrogant toward the root that supports them, for their inclusion was only made possible by the rejection of the natural branches.

Crucially, Paul explains that this hardening of Israel is both partial and temporary. It serves a specific, redemptive purpose in God's plan: it remains in effect "until the fullness of the Gentiles has come in" (Romans 11:25). This means the current age is a special period of grace where the gospel is extended to the nations. But this period will come to an end. Paul promises that once this "fullness" is achieved, the hardening will be removed, and "all Israel will be saved" (Romans 11:26), leading to a time of widespread acceptance of the Messiah among the Jewish people.

This context explains the constant confusion that followed Paul. When Jewish believers heard his message of freedom for the Gentiles, they failed to see it through the lens of these parables. They wrongly concluded that he was teaching Jews "to forsake Moses" (Acts 21:21), when in fact he was simply living out the new reality that God had ordained: a path for Gentiles to enter the covenant with fewer requirements, because they were the unexpected guests at a feast their original hosts had refused.

The Council's decision was both bold and measured:

> *"For it seemed good to the Holy Spirit and to us to lay upon you no greater burden than these essentials: that you abstain from things sacrificed to idols, from blood, from things strangled, and from sexual immorality..."*
> (Acts 15:28 29, NASB95)

These four requirements—moral and ritual—likely reflected the Noahide laws, a known Jewish paradigm for righteous Gentile conduct. Notably, the Council did not require circumcision or full Torah adherence from Gentiles. At the same time, it did not declare Torah obsolete for Jews.[45]

## 2. Paul's Defense of Distinction

Paul's letters affirm this same distinction. He tells the Galatians that circumcision adds nothing to their salvation (Galatians 5:2–4), and even

---

[45] The Jerusalem Council of Acts 15 is a pivotal moment in the history of the early Church. Scholars widely agree that its decision to not impose circumcision or the full weight of the Mosaic Law on Gentile converts was a landmark ruling. The four requirements that were imposed (abstaining from things offered to idols, from blood, from things strangled, and from sexual immorality) are often understood as a version of the "Noahide Laws," a traditional Jewish legal category for righteous Gentiles, demonstrating that the council was working within an existing Jewish legal and theological framework.

See: James D.G. Dunn, *The Acts of the Apostles* (Grand Rapids, MI: Eerdmans, 1996), 200-209.

endangers it if pursued as a requirement. Yet he circumcises Timothy (Acts 16:3), affirming the continued covenantal identity of Jews. This was not contradiction, but contextual faithfulness.

### 3. Clarifying Common Misinterpretations

- **Jews misunderstood Paul** to be abolishing Torah entirely, especially because of his advocacy for Gentile freedom. Acts 21:21–24 records the accusation that Paul taught Jews "to forsake Moses," which Paul actively refutes by participating in Temple rituals.
- **Gentiles misunderstood Paul** to mean that the Law was obsolete for everyone. Yet Paul writes in Romans 3:31:

*"Do we then nullify the Law through faith? Far from it! On the contrary, we establish the Law."* (NASB95)

Paul's gospel invited Gentiles into God's family by faith, not conversion to Judaism. Yet he never erased the unique role of Jewish covenantal observance.

### 4. One People, Distinct Roles

Jewish believers retained their identity within the Law; Gentile believers entered through grace without adopting Jewish ethnicity or ritual. This model—unity without uniformity—is foundational for Christian Monolatry: one God, one Messiah, one people, but distinct roles within God's redemptive design.

## Paul's Letters to Gentile Audiences

Paul, as the "apostle to the Gentiles" (Romans 11:13), writes his letters primarily to non-Jewish believers navigating their new life in Messiah. A consistent theme emerges: Gentiles are full members of God's people without becoming Jews or submitting to the full weight of Mosaic Law.

**1. Salvation by Faith, Not Works of the Law**

Paul vigorously defends the gospel of grace. In Galatians, he warns Gentile believers that pursuing justification through Torah observance—particularly circumcision—undermines Messiah's work:

> *"If you receive circumcision, Messiah will be of no benefit to you."* (Galatians 5:2, NASB95)

This does not mean Torah is bad. Rather, it emphasizes that the Law was never the pathway to salvation for Gentiles. Paul distinguishes between righteousness by faith and attempts to attain righteousness through legal observance.

**2. Gentile Freedom and Jewish Responsibility**

Paul maintains that Jewish believers retain their covenantal identity. In Romans 3:1–2, he affirms that Jews have a special advantage:

> *"They were entrusted with the oracles of God."* (NASB95)

But this privilege does not create two separate salvations—it reflects different covenantal responsibilities. In 1 Corinthians 7:18–20, Paul advises both Jews and Gentiles to remain in the calling they were in when they came to Messiah. A Jew should not seek to erase his Jewish identity, and a Gentile need not adopt Jewish markers like circumcision.

### 3. Titus and Timothy: Case Studies in Context

- **Titus** was a Gentile. Paul refused to circumcise him (Galatians 2:3), recognizing that doing so would send the wrong message: that Gentiles must become Jews to be saved.
- **Timothy**, on the other hand, had a Jewish mother. Paul circumcised him (Acts 16:1–3) to affirm his Jewish heritage and facilitate ministry among Jews. These actions reinforce Paul's guiding principle: faith does not erase ethnic identity, nor does it impose a uniform code of ritual behavior.

### 4. Torah's Ongoing Value

Paul affirms the Torah's holiness and usefulness:

> *"So then, the Law is holy, and the commandment is holy and righteous and good."*
> (Romans 7:12, NASB95)

But this praise is contextual. The Law is holy—for those under it. Gentiles, having been grafted into Israel's spiritual blessings (Romans 11:17), are not under the same covenantal obligations. Their inclusion is by grace, not legal adoption.

This section of Paul's letters reflects the theological foundation of early Messianic faith: salvation unites Jews and Gentiles in one body, yet it does not collapse their God-given distinctions. Christian Monolatry upholds this diversity—honoring the Torah's role for Jewish believers while affirming Gentile believers' freedom in Messiah.

## *The Balanced Position: Torah and the Unified People of God*

The early Messianic movement did not promote uniformity but unity. Both Paul's writings and the Acts of the Apostles reflect a deep concern for preserving the distinct callings of Jews and Gentiles—without dividing them spiritually.

**1. Jews Keep the Torah; Gentiles Are Not Obligated**

Paul never taught Jews to abandon Torah. His own observance—including taking a Nazirite vow (Acts 21:23–26) and celebrating Jewish festivals (Acts 18:21)—testifies to his enduring commitment. He states clearly:

> *"Are they descendants of Abraham? So am I."*
> (2 Corinthians 11:22, NASB95)

He urges Jewish believers to remain faithful to their calling, even while proclaiming freedom to Gentiles:

> *"Was anyone called when he was already circumcised? He is not to become uncircumcised. Has anyone been called in uncircumcision? He is not to be circumcised. Circumcision is nothing, and uncircumcision is nothing, but what matters is the keeping of the commandments of God."*
>
> (1 Corinthians 7:18–19, NASB95)

Paul's view affirms that the Torah still applies to Jewish believers—not as a means of salvation, but as an expression of covenant fidelity. At the same time, Gentiles, justified by faith, are not expected to take on those same covenant signs.

## 2. Unity Through Yeshua, Not Uniform Law

The Jerusalem Council (Acts 15) embodied this unity-in-diversity. It did not cancel the Torah for Jews, nor did it impose the full weight of Mosaic Law on Gentiles. Instead, it provided a practical and theological model: both Jew and Gentile come to God through Yeshua, yet they live out that relationship within their distinct identities.

Christian Monolatry sustains this balance: one God, one Messiah, one Spirit—yet two covenantal callings. This reflects not a divided Church, but a diversified body, rooted in God's original promises to Israel and extended by grace to the nations.

## 3. Avoiding Two Extremes

This framework guards against two enduring errors:

- **Legalism:** That Gentiles must become Jews and take on the entire yoke of Torah for salvation or spiritual maturity.
- **Supersessionism:** That Jewish believers must abandon their heritage because faith in Yeshua "replaces" Torah.

Instead, it calls for respect, mutual honor, and theological humility. God's family contains both circumcised and uncircumcised, each reflecting His glory in distinct yet complementary ways.

## *Historical Witness: Evidence of Continued Torah Observance Among Jewish Believers*

One of the clearest indicators that early Jewish believers in Yeshua continued observing Torah comes from historical records, both Christian and non-Christian.

### 1. Accounts from Eusebius and Hegesippus

Eusebius, quoting the earlier Jewish-Christian historian Hegesippus, records that **James (Ya'akov) the Just**, the brother of Yeshua and leader of the Jerusalem assembly, was highly esteemed for his righteousness and Torah faithfulness. He was described as one who **prayed regularly in the Temple**, followed purity laws, and adhered to Jewish practices until his martyrdom in Jerusalem. That James, as a prominent follower of Yeshua, could gain such respect in a Jewish context highlights that **faith in Messiah** did not mean abandoning Torah.

## 2. Josephus's Mentions of James and Jesus

The first-century Jewish historian **Josephus** also mentions James in *Antiquities of the Jews* (Book 20), calling him "the brother of Jesus, who was called Christ," and describing his death at the hands of the high priest. While Josephus does not affirm the messiahship of Yeshua, his neutral historical account provides further evidence of **Jewish believers being present and known in the Jewish world**, even decades after the resurrection.

## 3. Early Rabbinic Responses (Tosefta, b. Sanhedrin)

Another compelling line of evidence comes from **early rabbinic texts**, particularly the *Tosefta* and *Babylonian Talmud* (e.g., *Sanhedrin* 43a, 90a). These sources often use the term **minim** ("heretics") to refer to **Jewish followers of Yeshua**. Their presence is not treated as external, but as internal threats within the Jewish community. This response only makes sense if these believers were **still practicing Jews**—attending synagogue, participating in Jewish life, and honoring Torah commandments. The rabbis found it necessary to argue against them and, in some cases, **excommunicate** them. Such actions demonstrate that Yeshua-believing Jews were **not viewed as pagans** or outsiders, but as fellow Jews whose faith in Messiah had to be contested from within the framework of Jewish discourse.⁴⁶

## 4. Continuity Until the Temple's Destruction

There is strong evidence that **Jewish believers continued practicing Temple-based worship** until the destruction of the Second Temple in 70 CE. As seen in Acts and corroborated by early historical sources, believers such as James and Paul **frequented the Temple**, offered sacrifices, and engaged in ritual purification. Even after the Temple's destruction, Jewish followers of Yeshua **continued to observe Torah**, adapting where necessary, but not abandoning their covenantal identity.

## *The Future Temple, Messiah's Priesthood, and Historical Parallels*

### The Third Temple and Future Observance

Prophecies in Ezekiel (chapters 40–48) describe a restored Temple and renewed Torah observance during the reign of the Messiah. This prophetic

---

⁴⁶ The rabbinic references to *minim* ("heretics") are a key source for understanding the early relationship between Rabbinic Judaism and Jewish followers of Jesus. Scholars like Alan F. Segal argue that the polemics against the *minim* in texts like the Tosefta and the Babylonian Talmud are often directed at Jewish Christians. The fact that they were seen as an *internal* threat to be debated and excommunicated, rather than as outsiders, confirms that these early believers were still participating in Jewish life and seen by the rabbis as fellow Jews, albeit ones with a dangerous and contested theology.

See: Alan F. Segal, *Two Powers in Heaven: Early Rabbinic Reports about Christianity and Gnosticism* (Leiden: Brill, 1977). See also Daniel Boyarin, "The Gospel of the Memra: Jewish Binitarianism and the Prologue to John," *Harvard Theological Review* 94, no. 3 (2001).

vision affirms that the commandments given to Israel are not temporary, but enduring. In the Messianic age, these practices will not be discarded but reestablished in proper order and holiness—centered around the presence of the Messiah Himself.

This vision affirms the continuity of Jewish identity and practice, even after Yeshua's atoning work. Torah observance under the Messiah's rule will reflect not legalism, but covenantal fulfillment—God's people living in alignment with His original intent.

**Yeshua's Priesthood: Melchizedek and the Aaronic Order**

Hebrews 7 teaches that Yeshua is a High Priest according to the order of Melchizedek—a priesthood not based on lineage or temple service, but on divine appointment and heavenly authority. As Hebrews 8:4 (NASB95) states: "Now if He were on earth, He would not be a priest at all, since there are those who offer the gifts according to the Law."

This implies that the Aaronic priesthood remains valid on earth while the Temple stands. Yeshua's priesthood operates in the heavenly sanctuary, interceding directly before God, while the Levitical system continues to serve Israel in its earthly calling. These two priesthoods are not at odds—one is heavenly and eternal, the other earthly and temporal, both instituted by God for their respective purposes.

**Isaac, Abraham, and the Sacrifice Fulfilled**

In Genesis 22, when God asked Abraham to offer Isaac, Abraham obeyed—but God ultimately provided a ram instead. Abraham's prophetic words, "God will provide for Himself the lamb" (Genesis 22:8, NASB95), looked forward to Yeshua, the Lamb of God, who was sacrificed in place of Israel and the nations.

This moment of substitution foreshadows the cross: the Son, loved by the Father, offered as a sacrifice—but this time, not withheld. It anchors the gospel in Jewish expectation and points to the fulfillment of covenant promises.

**Parallels with Joseph**

*Parallels with Joseph: The Rejected Brother and the Path to Redemption*

The story of Joseph, preserved in the final chapters of Genesis, is more than just a historical account; it is a profound, living parable of the Messiah. It is a drama that unfolds in two acts, mirroring with stunning precision the journey of Yeshua, His rejection by Israel, and His eventual embrace by the Gentile world.

First came the rejection by his own brothers. Joseph, the beloved son, shared his God-given dreams of future leadership, and for this, he earned their hatred. In their envy, they conspired against him, threw him into a pit, and sold him into the hands of foreigners. To cover their crime, they deceived their father, Jacob, presenting a goat's-blood-stained coat as "evidence" that Joseph was dead. For all intents and purposes, to the house of Israel, Joseph was gone—killed and erased from the story.

So too, Yeshua, the beloved Son, came to His own, and His own did not receive Him. He spoke of His kingdom, and for this, His brothers conspired against Him. They delivered Him into the hands of the Gentiles to be crucified. And when God raised Him from the dead, they orchestrated a second deception. The leaders of Israel paid the Roman guards to spread a lie—that the disciples had stolen the body—ensuring that to the nation, Yeshua would remain dead and gone.

Then came the second act: the journey through the Gentile world. Like Joseph, who was falsely accused and thrown into an Egyptian prison, the early followers of Yeshua were persecuted by the Roman world. But what began in suffering ended in exaltation. Joseph, through divine wisdom, was raised from the dungeon to sit at the right hand of Pharaoh, the Egyptian god-king. He became the sole administrator of the known world, so powerful that all of Egypt bowed to him.

So too, Yeshua, through His resurrection, was exalted. The Gentile world, after a period of persecution, eventually embraced Him with a fierce devotion. And in their zeal to honor their savior, they elevated Him to the highest possible place. Mistaking the Son for the Father, they declared Him co-equal with the one true God—a theological over-correction born of profound reverence. Just as Joseph was not a god, but was treated as one by the Egyptians, so Yeshua was exalted by the Gentile church to a status that, while well-intentioned, obscured His true, subordinate relationship to His Father.

And yet, all of this—the betrayal, the false death, the suffering in a foreign land, and the ultimate exaltation—served a single, breathtaking purpose. Joseph's rise to power was not for his own sake, but for the salvation of the very brothers who had rejected him. When famine finally brought them, broken and starving, to his feet, he revealed himself not as a vengeful prince, but as their brother, their deliverer. In that moment of recognition, he spoke words that echo through eternity:

> *"You meant evil against me, but God meant it for good in order to bring about this present result, to preserve many people alive." (Genesis 50:20, NASB95)*

This is the drama that is still playing out. Yeshua has been embraced by the Gentile world and, in their theology, has been given a foreign identity that makes Him unrecognizable to His Jewish brethren. But the day is coming when the famine will be great in the land, and His brothers will come seeking bread. In that day, they will see Him not as the co-equal God of a Gentile religion, but as their brother, the Messiah of Israel. And in that moment of recognition, the floodgates will open. Perhaps the recovery of this ancient, Jewish, monolatrous understanding of Yeshua is the very path God will use to allow Israel to finally see the one they pierced, and to welcome their long-lost brother home.

# *Implications for Today*

## If the Temple Were Rebuilt

If a future Temple is constructed, many Messianic Jews would likely participate in its life—not to replace Yeshua's atonement, but to express covenant faithfulness. As seen in Acts 21:20–26, Paul supported four men in completing Nazirite vows, including sacrifices and purification rites, to demonstrate that he remained "zealous for the Law." These acts were not in conflict with belief in Yeshua but complemented it.

Temple sacrifices in such a setting would not serve for salvation but as ritual expressions of holiness, remembrance, and covenant continuity. They would function much like the Torah festivals do today for many observant Messianic Jews—signposts pointing to Messiah's redemptive work and affirming identity within Israel's story.

## Jewish and Gentile Believers Together

The model of Acts 15 still applies: Jewish believers may continue to walk in the Torah as their covenantal heritage, while Gentiles are not obligated to do the same. Both are united by faith in Yeshua, with different roles under one Lord. This diversity does not divide; it honors God's multifaceted plan for His people.

### Recognizing Historical Roots

Restoring the early, Jewish context of the New Testament helps modern believers appreciate that the earliest Yeshua-followers upheld the Torah. They did not invent a new religion, but proclaimed the fulfillment of the promises made to Israel. Honoring the Torah and trusting in Yeshua were not opposing ideas—they were one and the same for the first community of believers.

## Conclusion

Far from severing Jewish believers from their ancestral traditions, Yeshua and the Apostles affirmed the enduring value of the Torah. They demonstrated that Jewish identity and observance could thrive alongside faith in Yeshua as Messiah. The New Testament presents a united community of Jews and Gentiles—both honoring God within their respective covenant roles.

- **Jewish believers** remained faithful to the Torah as a God-given expression of their national and spiritual calling.
- **Gentile believers** were welcomed into the covenant people through faith in Yeshua, without the burden of adopting full Mosaic observance.

This model creates unity without demanding uniformity. It reflects a divine pattern: Israel's faithfulness continues, and the nations are grafted in—not by becoming Jews, but by being joined to Israel's Messiah.

For today's Messianic believers, this offers clarity and purpose. Jewish disciples can embrace Yeshua while honoring the Torah. Gentiles can follow Yeshua wholeheartedly without assuming Israel's national obligations. Together, they form one body, distinct yet united, reflecting the beauty of God's covenantal faithfulness.

Having explored how the earliest Jewish followers of Yeshua maintained fidelity to the Torah while embracing His identity as the exalted but subordinate Son, we now turn to the generation that followed—the Apostolic Fathers. These early Christian leaders inherited not only the teachings of the apostles but also the foundational Jewish worldview that shaped their theology. Far from inventing new doctrines, they continued to articulate Yeshua's role as the divine intermediary in harmony with the long-standing Jewish tradition of monolatry. Their writings—produced in the critical decades following the New Testament period—bear witness to a unified vision: that the one uncreated God reveals Himself through subordinate, divine agents, a framework consistently affirmed in the Targums, Philo, and the Gospel of John. In tracing how these post-apostolic voices handled the identity of the Son, we uncover a robust and coherent theology—one deeply rooted in the past, yet profoundly shaping the future of the faith. Before this we will momentarily look and the Jewish rejection of monolatry and acceptance of strict monotheism.

# 14

# The "Two Powers" Controversy and the Jewish-Christian Divide

The controversy over the "Two Powers in Heaven" provides a critical window into the transformation of Jewish theology in the aftermath of the Second Temple's destruction. This shift—from a flexible monolatry that could accommodate divine intermediaries to a rigid, uncompromising monotheism—was not merely the result of gradual doctrinal evolution. Instead, it emerged as a reactionary recalibration, driven by historical and cultural forces. In this context, the label "Two Powers" became a polemical tool used by emerging rabbinic authorities to delineate the boundaries of acceptable belief, specifically targeting early Christian claims about Yeshua's divine status. **For any reader who wishes to understand this pivotal moment in theological history, Alan F. Segal's book *Two Powers in Heaven* is the most important and comprehensive study ever written on the subject.**[47]

## Pre-70 CE Jewish Theology: An Openness to Divine Intermediaries

Before 70 CE, Jewish theology operated within a monolatrous framework, where YHWH alone was worshiped, yet divine intermediaries played active roles. Several key figures supported this structured divine hierarchy: The Angel of YHWH, the Memra (Word) and Wisdom, the Son of Man, Metatron, and Philo's Logos. These figures all functioned under YHWH, preserving monolatry, yet their exalted status left room for interpretation. This theological flexibility would later become a problem in post-70 CE Judaism.

## The New Testament's Use of "Two Powers" Motifs

Rather than affirming a solitary, undifferentiated God, the New Testament proclaims two distinct figures—the Father and the Son—who share divine titles and authority while maintaining the Son's subordination. The early Christian identification of Yeshua with exalted figures from Jewish Scripture provided the structure for this claim: Yeshua as the Son of Man (Daniel 7), the exalted Lord (Psalm 110:1), and the embodiment of the Angel of YHWH motif.

## The Post-70 CE Rabbinic Reaction

As Christian theology developed, early believers in Yeshua used these Jewish

---

[47] The seminal academic work on this topic is Alan F. Segal's *Two Powers in Heaven*. Segal meticulously documents how the rabbinic concept of the "Two Powers" heresy emerged as a polemical tool to create boundaries for a new, normative Rabbinic Judaism in the centuries following the Temple's destruction. He argues it was used to reject various Jewish traditions, including early Christian claims about Jesus, which had previously existed within a more theologically diverse Judaism. See: **Alan F. Segal, *Two Powers in Heaven: Early Rabbinic Reports about Christianity and Gnosticism*(Leiden: Brill, 1977).**

texts to argue for his divine role. To counter these interpretations, rabbinic authorities redefined monotheism, condemning any belief that could imply divine plurality.

### Rabbinic Statements Rejecting the Two Powers Doctrine

The rabbinic literature records vivid and often contentious debates where sages confronted interpretations of scripture that seemed to suggest a second divine power. A heretic (*min*), often understood to be a Jewish-Christian, would point to a biblical text, and a rabbi would offer a counter-exegesis to neutralize the claim.

- **Genesis 1:26 - "Let Us Make Man":** The plural language in the creation account was a key point of debate. The Babylonian Talmud records this exchange:

    *A certain heretic said to Rabbi Meir: "When it says, 'Let us make man in our image,' who was God speaking to?" Rabbi Meir replied… "God was speaking to the angels." (Babylonian Talmud,* Sanhedrin 38b)

- **The Exalted Angel Metatron:** The vision of an enthroned angelic figure caused deep anxiety. The Talmud recounts a story where a sage witnesses the high angel Metatron seated in heaven (a privilege normally reserved for God) and immediately suspects heresy:

    *It has been taught: Rabbi Akiba said: "Aher mutilated the shoots [became a heretic] when he saw that permission was granted to Metatron to sit and write down the merits of Israel. He said: 'It is taught as a tradition that on high there is no sitting… perhaps there are—God forbid!—**two powers**.'" (Babylonian Talmud,* Hagigah 15a)

In the story, Metatron is punished with fiery lashes to prove his subordinate, angelic status and to demonstrate that he is not a second, independent power. These narratives reveal how sensitive rabbinic authorities were to any theology that could be interpreted as compromising God's unique singularity.⁴⁸

## Scriptural Reinterpretations and Textual Modifications

Beyond direct debate, the rabbinic response also involved a systematic reinterpretation of key biblical texts and, in some cases, the preservation of textual traditions that minimized divine plurality.

- **Psalm 110:1:** Where early Christians saw the "second Lord" as the exalted Messiah, rabbinic exegesis later redirected the title to a human figure like Abraham or David.
- **Daniel 7:13–14:** The divine "Son of Man" was reinterpreted not as a personal messianic figure, but as a corporate symbol for the nation of Israel.
- **Deuteronomy 32:8:** The original reading, "sons of God," found in the Dead Sea Scrolls and the Septuagint, was changed in the later Masoretic Text to "sons of Israel," erasing an explicit reference to the divine council.⁴⁹

---

⁴⁸ These specific rabbinic passages are the primary evidence used by scholars to reconstruct the "Two Powers" controversy. Each text is analyzed in detail by Segal, who shows how the rabbis actively worked to counter interpretations of Scripture that could imply a second divine figure, whether that figure was an exalted angel like Metatron or the Christian conception of the Son. See: **Alan F. Segal, *Two Powers in Heaven*, for analysis of *b. Sanhedrin 38b* (p. 60-64), *b. Ḥagigah 15a* (p. 84-89), and other related texts.**

⁴⁹ The argument that post-Christian rabbinic interpretation involved a deliberate "rewriting" of scripture and tradition to counter Christian claims is advanced by several scholars. Daniel Boyarin argues that what later became "heresy" was once a common form of Jewish belief. The alteration of Deuteronomy 32:8 from "sons of God" to "sons of Israel" in the Masoretic textual tradition is a well-documented example of a later scribal change that erased an explicit reference to the divine council. See: Daniel Boyarin, "The Gospel of the Memra: Jewish Binitarianism and the Prologue to John," *Harvard Theological Review* 94, no. 3 (2001): 243–284. For the textual criticism of Deuteronomy 32:8, see Michael S. Heiser, *The Unseen Realm* (Bellingham, WA: Lexham Press, 2015), 113-116.

## Conclusion: The Loss of the Monolatrous Framework

By appealing to exalted intermediaries, the New Testament remains deeply embedded in Second Temple Jewish theology. But by identifying Yeshua as the fulfillment of these figures, it triggered a sharp theological divergence. Post-70 CE Judaism responded by narrowing acceptable views of monotheism—redefining Jewish theology to exclude the very intermediaries that had once flourished in its own sacred literature. The "Two Powers in Heaven" controversy, therefore, did not arise from a novel heresy but reflects a reactive theological transformation by rabbinic authorities. Its polemical use marked a turning point—away from the rich and complex hierarchy of divine beings found in earlier Jewish tradition and toward an exclusive monotheism forged in the crucible of cultural and religious conflict.

# 15

# The Apostolic Fathers and Early Christian Diversity

Following the close of the New Testament era, the early Christian movement entered a crucial period of theological reflection and consolidation. Contrary to the popular notion that Christian doctrine slowly evolved into higher Christological claims, the writings of the Apostolic Fathers reveal a different story: one of continuity, not innovation. Their theology stands firmly in line with Jewish *monolatry*, affirming the supremacy of the one uncreated God—**the Father**—while also exalting **Yeshua** as the *divine but subordinate mediator* of God's will.

The early believers did not possess a vague or uncertain Christology awaiting later clarification. Rather, they affirmed a robust and clear theological framework inherited from both the Hebrew Scriptures and Jewish interpretive traditions such as the **Memra** in the Targums and **Philo's Logos**. This framework—what we now identify as **Christian Monolatry**—maintained that God reveals Himself through divine intermediaries without compromising His ultimate singularity or supremacy.

In this model, **the Father alone possesses underived essence**—He is unbegotten, unoriginated, and the source of all divine activity. The **Son**, while fully divine in function and nature, possesses **a derived essence**—His existence, power, and role flow from the will of the Father. This distinction is not a diminishing of the Son's dignity but a clarification of the hierarchy within divine mediation: **the Father is supreme**, and the Son, as Logos, is **begotten** and empowered to act as His visible agent.

## *Rejecting the Later Narrative*

The modern tendency to frame the early church as marching steadily toward a fully co-equal Trinity imposes later theological categories—especially those cemented at **Nicaea (325 AD)** and **Constantinople (381 AD)**—onto writers who operated from a fundamentally different paradigm. The Apostolic Fathers did not struggle to define Christ's divinity; rather, they assumed that divine mediation had always been part of the story of Israel and now continued, climactically, in **Yeshua**.

Writers such as **Clement of Rome, Ignatius of Antioch**, and **Polycarp of Smyrna** reflect a unified voice: the Son is exalted, preexistent, and divine— but **always in relational subordination to the Father**, never claiming underived divinity. Their theology affirms the **Christian Monolatrous** vision: that **YHWH alone** is unbegotten and worthy of ultimate worship, and that **Yeshua**, as His Son and Logos, is honored and obeyed as the divine mediator appointed to carry out His will.

# THE APOSTOLIC FATHERS AND EARLY CHRISTIAN DIVERSITY

## *Introducing the Key Distinctions*

Throughout this chapter, we will trace how the early post-apostolic writers upheld this pattern of divine agency:

- **Derived vs. Underived Essence**: The Son is divine, but His divinity is received. Only the Father exists independently—He is the origin of all that is divine.
- **Mediator, Not Equal Source**: The Son reveals the Father, but does not replace Him as the ultimate object of worship.
- **Consistent with Jewish Monolatry**: Like the Angel of the Lord or the Memra, the Son acts as God without being a second, independent deity.
- **Pre-Nicene Clarity**: Before the theological upheavals introduced by Athanasius, early Christians did not view begetting as a timeless necessity but as a **willed act**—what would later be clarified as **dynamic eternity**.

This chapter will examine the writings of the Apostolic Fathers and early Christian texts like the **Didache, Epistle of Barnabas**, and **Shepherd of Hermas** to demonstrate that **Christian Monolatry**, not Trinitarian co-equality, was the shared foundation of the early faith. This continuity of thought not only preserves the supremacy of the Father but also explains why the later shift was not a continuation but a **disruption** of the earlier tradition.

## Clement of Rome — Divine Order and Apostolic Continuity

Writing near the end of the first century, **Clement of Rome** stands as one of the earliest and most respected voices of post-apostolic Christianity. His letter to the Corinthians (1 Clement), composed around 96 AD, reveals a community deeply rooted in both Jewish reverence for the one true God and the apostolic confession of **Yeshua** as the appointed divine mediator.

Clement's theology reflects **a clear hierarchical structure** of divine revelation. He does not speculate about metaphysical sameness or eternal co-equality. Instead, he affirms the pattern of transmission already familiar from Scripture: **the Father sends the Son, and the Son commissions the Apostles.**

> *"The apostles received the Gospel for us from the Lord Yeshua Messiah; Yeshua Messiah was sent forth from God. So then Messiah is from God, and the apostles are from Messiah."*
> (1 Clement 42:1–2)

This threefold chain underscores a **monolatrous structure**: all divine revelation flows **from the Father** as the supreme, unbegotten source. Messiah is **not a rival deity** nor an independently divine being, but **the agent through whom God's will is revealed**—*divine in function and origin*, yet always **derived**.

Elsewhere, Clement reflects on the redemptive work of Messiah:

> *"Let us look steadfastly to the blood of Messiah and see how precious*

> *his blood is to God, which having been shed for our salvation, brought the grace of repentance to all the world."*
> (1 Clement 7:4)

Even here, Clement emphasizes **Messiah's obedience** and the Father's initiative. The Son's sacrificial role is deeply honored, but the **glory belongs to God**, who ordained and accepted the offering. This language never suggests that Yeshua is **equal in underived essence** with the Father; rather, His mission flows from the Father's will and is **precious to Him** precisely because it fulfills the divine purpose.

Clement's vision is not speculative or philosophical—it is deeply practical and reverent. He is concerned with obedience, order, and fidelity to what the apostles received. In that order, **the Father remains the unoriginated God**, and **Yeshua the divine but subordinate Son**, exalted not by nature alone, but by **appointment and obedience**.

This reflects a theology **already deeply rooted in Jewish tradition**: God remains supreme, and His agent is exalted not to co-equality, but to **visible mediation**. Clement's language—clear, scriptural, and faithful—affirms that the earliest Christians saw no contradiction between **honoring the Son as divine** and maintaining **exclusive worship of the Father** as the one true God.[50]

---

[50] J.N.D. Kelly, a leading patristic scholar, notes that Clement of Rome's theology is characterized by its emphasis on order and apostolic succession. Clement's Christology is robust but remains within a clear hierarchical framework. As Kelly states, "The Son is the Father's agent, high-priest and ambassador... but the Father is the ultimate reality, the God of Jesus Christ as of all men." This confirms that the earliest post-apostolic witness maintained a clear distinction and subordination.
See: J.N.D. Kelly, *Early Christian Doctrines*, 5th ed. (London: A&C Black, 1977), 95-97.

## Ignatius of Antioch — Exalting Messiah, Upholding Divine Order

**Ignatius of Antioch**, writing in the early second century while en route to his martyrdom, offers one of the most vivid portrayals of Yeshua's exalted status. Yet even as he glorifies the Son with striking titles, Ignatius never loses sight of the **divine order** rooted in the Father's supremacy.

Ignatius speaks of Yeshua as:

> "...both flesh and spirit, born and unborn, God in man, true life in death, both from Mary and from God."
> (Ephesians 7:2)

Here, he reflects the **mystery of incarnation**: the divine Logos taking on flesh. Yet this exaltation is **not a metaphysical equalizing** of Father and Son. Instead, Ignatius consistently maintains the **priority of the Father**—Yeshua is **from God**, sent by the Father, and remains obedient to His will.

In his letter to the **Magnesians**, he writes:

> "Jesus Messiah, who was with the Father before the ages and appeared at the end of time for our sake."
> (Magnesians 6:1)

This language affirms the **preexistence** of the Son, but frames it within **dependence**: the Son's presence "with the Father" before time speaks not of co-equality in unbegotten essence, but of **derived origin—a divine status that flows from the Father's will,** not eternal necessity.

Ignatius also models divine hierarchy in his exhortation to the Church:

> *"See that you all follow the bishop,* **as Jesus Christ follows the Father,** *and the presbytery as you would the apostles..."*
>   (Smyrneans 8:1)

His concern for order in the Church mirrors his theology: **just as Messiah submits to the Father**, the Church submits to Messiah and His appointed leaders. Reverence is directed through the Son, but ultimately **toward the Father**, the **underived source** of all.

Even where Ignatius uses the title "God" of Messiah, his writings never assert **ontological parity**. Instead, they fit within the **monolatrous tradition**: the one supreme God reveals Himself through His Son, who is fully divine in role and status, but **subordinate in origin and authority**. This is not a contradiction, but a **faithful continuation** of the ancient biblical pattern—where God's Word, Wisdom, and Angel speak and act on God's behalf without threatening His unique supremacy.

In Ignatius, we see a profound devotion to Yeshua—not as a second deity or abstract "Person" of a metaphysical Trinity—but as the **visible, obedient agent** through whom the Father redeems, guides, and gathers His people. This early Christian monolatry remains saturated in **worship, awe, and theological order**—where the Son is honored **because** He reflects the will and glory of the One who sent Him.[51]


## *Polycarp of Smyrna — Faithful Witness to Apostolic Order*

**Polycarp**, a disciple of John and a revered bishop in Smyrna, serves as a living bridge between the apostles and the next generation of believers. His writings—though brief—are rich with theological clarity. Like Ignatius and Clement, Polycarp consistently upholds a **hierarchical view of divine mediation** that centers on the Father's supremacy and the Son's obedient agency.

In his letter to the Philippians, he writes:

> *"May the God and Father of our Lord Yeshua Messiah, and Yeshua Messiah Himself, who is the Son of God, bless you..."*
> (Philippians 12:2)

This blessing preserves the same order seen throughout early Christian texts:

---

[51] While Ignatius of Antioch uses exalted language for Jesus, even referring to him as "God," scholars like Larry W. Hurtado place this within the context of early Christian devotional practice. For Ignatius, the Son is the one through whom the silent Father has spoken, and his divinity is understood in relational and functional terms. The Father remains the ultimate source, and the Son is His unique agent. Ignatius's framework is one of divine agency, not of later metaphysical co-equality.

See: Larry W. Hurtado, *Lord Jesus Christ: Devotion to Jesus in Earliest Christianity* (Grand Rapids, MI: Eerdmans, 2003), 257-280.

- The **Father is supreme**, the "God and Father of our Lord."
- The **Son is divine**, but not independently so—He is God's Son, not God Almighty.

Polycarp's prayer life and theology mirror the language of the New Testament itself, where God is "the God and Father of our Lord Yeshua Messiah" (e.g., 2 Corinthians 1:3). These expressions are not accidental—they reflect a **deep conviction** that the Father is **the unbegotten source**, and the Son is **His begotten mediator**.

Crucially, Polycarp never collapses their roles or attributes. He does not blur the Father and Son into a single essence. Instead, he faithfully preserves the early model of **Christian monolatry**:

- The Son is honored, invoked, obeyed, and trusted—because He was **sent by the Father** and perfectly enacts His will.
- The Father remains **the one uncreated, underived God**—the source of all.

This is not subordinationism in the later, pejorative sense. It is **biblical order**, upheld with reverence and clarity. Polycarp's entire life, culminating in martyrdom, modeled this faithful allegiance to the Father through the Son. As recorded in *The Martyrdom of Polycarp*, his dying prayer begins:

> "O Lord God Almighty, the Father of Your beloved and blessed Son Yeshua Messiah... I bless You because You have counted me worthy of this day and hour..."

Even in death, Polycarp's worship remains directed to the **Father**, in the **name and mediation of the Son**. There is no theological confusion, no tension between honoring Messiah and upholding the supremacy of God. In Polycarp, we find not a proto-Trinitarian formula, but a continuation of the **relational, representational structure** of Scripture.

He stands as a testimony that the **earliest Christian theology was rooted not in metaphysical speculation, but in covenantal faithfulness**:

- YHWH is one.
- Messiah is His exalted, obedient Son.
- Honor of the Son is not a breach of monolatry, but its rightful fulfillment—because it flows from and returns to the Father.[52]

## *Synthesizing the Apostolic Fathers: A Clear Theology of Derived Divinity*

The writings of **Clement**, **Ignatius**, and **Polycarp** form a remarkably consistent witness. These early leaders, trained by the apostles or their immediate disciples, reflect a theological confidence that **did not arise from speculative philosophy**, but from fidelity to the teachings of Yeshua,

---

[52] Polycarp's dying prayer in *The Martyrdom of Polycarp* is a powerful example of early Christian worship. As scholars note, the prayer is explicitly directed "to the Father, through the Son, in the Holy Spirit." This ordered, hierarchical structure of worship was typical of the second century. The Father is the ultimate recipient of praise, while the Son is the mediator through whom that praise is offered. This is not a Trinitarian formula of co-equal persons, but a clear expression of a subordinationist devotional pattern.
See: J.N.D. Kelly, *Early Christian Doctrines*, 5th ed. (London: A&C Black, 1977), 99-101.

the Scriptures, and the apostolic proclamation.

Across their works, several key convictions emerge:

1. **The Father is the One Supreme, Unbegotten God**

Every writer explicitly refers to God as the *Father*—the uncreated, underived source of all, including the Son. Worship begins with Him, and all divine authority originates from Him.

1. **The Son is Divine, Yet Always From the Father** Yeshua is exalted, honored, and even called "God" in certain high-context passages. Yet never is He presented as equal to the Father in **origin** or **authority**. Instead, His divinity is **derived**—not in the sense of creation, but of being begotten, appointed, and empowered by the will of the Father.
2. **No Ontological Collapse** None of the Apostolic Fathers merge the Father and the Son into a shared, undifferentiated essence. They speak in **relational terms**—the Son sent by the Father, obedient to Him, and glorified by Him. This reveals a **hierarchy of source and agent**, not of worth or value, but of order and function.
3. **A Monolatrous Framework** These early Christians preserved the Shema's confession: "YHWH is one." Yet they honor the Father *through* the Son, recognizing in Messiah the **divine mediator**—the visible expression of the invisible God. This is **monolatry refined**, not replaced.
4. **No Language of Consubstantiality.** Terms like *homoousios* ("of the same essence")—which would later become central to post-Nicene theology—are completely absent. The Apostolic Fathers were not groping toward metaphysical formulations. They were **confidently transmitting** the theology they had received: that of the **one God** who acts through His **only begotten mediator**.

This is the heart of **Christian Monolatry**—not a lesser view of Yeshua, but a **rightly ordered** one. Messiah is the Logos, the Memra, the visible Angel of YHWH. He bears divine authority, not as an equal source of being, but as the **perfect image** and **obedient Son** of the one true God.

As we move into later texts like the *Epistle of Barnabas*, the *Didache*, and the *Shepherd of Hermas*, we will see this same theological structure reinforced. Far from being an "undeveloped" prelude to later formulations, this early theology was **mature, deliberate, and deeply rooted in Scripture**. Only much later do we find efforts to **redefine these relationships** using different metaphysical assumptions—a shift we will address in due time.

For now, what matters most is this:

The earliest followers of Yeshua **knew exactly who He was**—the divine Son, from the Father, through whom all things are revealed. And in honoring Him, they did not abandon the oneness of God; they **embodied it** more fully.

# The Epistle of Barnabas, the Didache, and the Shepherd of Hermas

### Preserving the Framework of Christian Monolatry

The early Christian writings that followed the New Testament were not theological improvisations. Rather, they **continued and clarified** the already robust monolatrous framework passed down through the apostles. In these texts—**Barnabas**, the **Didache**, and the **Shepherd of Hermas**—we see no rupture in theology, no drift toward consubstantial Trinitarianism. Instead, we find writers **grounded in the same tradition** of a supreme

Father and a subordinate, yet divine, Son who mediates God's will to humanity.

## 1. The Epistle of Barnabas: Messiah as the Agent of Creation and Covenant

Likely written between 70–135 AD by an anonymous Christian teacher in Alexandria, the *Epistle of Barnabas* is a theological exposition that interprets the Torah allegorically to show how the Hebrew Scriptures point to the Messiah. Though some early church fathers attributed it to Paul's companion, the scholarly consensus is that the biblical Barnabas was not its author. Understanding this is key to grasping the epistle's intensely polemical tone, which sought to create a sharp separation between Christianity and the Jewish traditions from which it sprang.

The importance of this work to the early church, however, cannot be overstated. In a stunning testament to the authority it once held, the *Epistle of Barnabas* is included in one of the world's most important and ancient biblical manuscripts, the **Codex Sinaiticus**. In that fourth-century codex, it is placed at the very end of the New Testament, right after the Book of Revelation and is followed by another key text from this era, the *Shepherd of Hermas*. While these books were ultimately not included in the final canon, their presence in this foundational manuscript demonstrates the immense respect they commanded in the early Christian world.

> "The Lord submitted to suffer for our souls, although He is the Lord of all the earth, to whom God said at the foundation of the world: 'Let us make man in our image and likeness.'"

(Barnabas 5:5)

This statement presents Messiah as the **pre-existent agent** of creation—the one through whom God made man. The echo of Genesis 1:26 is clear. Yet even here, Barnabas does not treat Messiah as the **source** of creation but as the **instrument** through whom the Father's will is carried out.

What's notably absent is any suggestion of **ontological equality**. The Son is glorified and Lordly, but always **dependent** on the will and initiation of God the Father. This aligns perfectly with Christian Monolatry: **one supreme God**, and **one divine mediator**, begotten for His purpose.

## 2. The Didache: Practical Piety Within a Triadic Structure

The *Didache*, composed roughly between 90–120 AD, reads more like a **church manual** than a theological treatise. But its triadic baptismal formula shows an early pattern that could be misunderstood without context:

> *"Baptize in the name of the Father, and of the Son, and of the Holy Spirit."*
> (Didache 7:1)

Some modern readers view this as a proto-Trinitarian statement, but the **structure does not imply co-equality or shared essence**. The Didache never elaborates metaphysical definitions. It offers **practical liturgy**, in which the **Father is the object of worship**, and the **Son and Spirit** function as **extensions of divine activity**, just as the Logos and the Memra did in earlier Jewish traditions.

Crucially, there is **no confusion of persons, no merging of substance**. The roles are preserved, and the hierarchy remains: **the Father initiates, the Son mediates, and the Spirit empowers**.

## 3. The Shepherd of Hermas: Preexistent Son, Divine Adviser

The *Shepherd of Hermas*—a visionary text written between 100–150 AD and widely read in early Christianity—contains one of the most striking affirmations of derived divinity:

> *"The Son of God is older than all His creation, so that He became the Father's adviser in His creation."*
> (Hermas, Similitude 9:12)

Here, the Son is both **pre-existent** and exalted. But his position is clearly **derivative**: He is "older than all creation," but not **equal to the Father**. He becomes the Father's "adviser"—not His peer or twin. This language reflects the same **hierarchical pattern**: exalted agency, but never ontological parity.

This vision is not an aberration. It reinforces what early believers had always known: **God acts through an appointed, divine Son,** who is "God" in a functional, glorified sense, but whose **being is from the Father**, not alongside Him as an independent, co-equal Person.

## *A Theological Constant, Not an Evolution*

Together, Barnabas, the Didache, and Hermas show a coherent continuation of the theology preserved by Clement, Ignatius, and Polycarp. At no point is there any confusion between:

- **Unbegotten and begotten essence**
- **Source and agent**
- **Worship of the one God and reverence for His appointed mediator**

Instead, we see a full embrace of **Christian Monolatry**—a theology in which the Father remains the supreme source of all, and the Son functions as His visible, empowered, divine Word.

Next, we'll draw these threads together in a synthesis that shows just how consistent this theology remained before later innovations attempted to reshape it.[53]

## Synthesizing the Early Witness: A Consistent Monolatrous Theology

Far from revealing theological confusion or evolution, the writings of Barnabas, the Didache, and the Shepherd of Hermas reflect a coherent **monolatrous vision** shared with earlier voices like Clement, Ignatius, and Polycarp. These authors, diverse in geography and style, all affirm the same core truth:

**God the Father is the one supreme, unbegotten source of all divine activity. Messiah, though pre-existent and glorified, is always subordinate—God's divine but derived agent.**

---

[53] The Christology of these other second-century texts remains firmly within the subordinationist framework. *The Shepherd of Hermas*, in particular, presents the Son as the pre-existent "adviser" to the Father in creation, a position of supreme honor but clear subordination. The baptismal formula in the *Didache*, while triadic, does not imply co-equality and was understood within the same hierarchical structure of worship (to the Father, through the Son). None of these texts contain the language or metaphysics of later Nicene orthodoxy.

See: Jaroslav Pelikan, *The Christian Tradition: A History of the Development of Doctrine, Vol. 1: The Emergence of the Catholic Tradition (100-600)* (Chicago: University of Chicago Press, 1971), 182-184.

## Key Themes Reaffirmed Across the Texts

**1. Preexistence Without Co-Equality**

From Barnabas to Hermas, Messiah is acknowledged as pre-existent—present at creation, older than all things—but never presented as the **source** of creation. Instead, He is God's agent, echoing the Logos of John and the Memra of Jewish tradition. He is divine by **appointment and function**, not by **underived essence**.

**2. Derived but Divine**

The Son is never called "unbegotten." Rather, He is **begotten of the Father's will**, emphasizing a **derived essence**—gloriously divine, but contingent upon the Father. This terminology avoids the implications of Anomean Arian "createdness," while also clearly resisting the later Nicene insistence on ontological co-equality.

**3. Subordination Without Diminishment**

Each text preserves a consistent hierarchy: the Father initiates, the Son mediates, and the Spirit empowers or sanctifies. This order is not one of inferiority but of **functional distinction**, deeply rooted in Jewish monolatry. In Christian Monolatry, to exalt the Son is not to rival the Father—it is to glorify the One who sent Him.

**4. No Philosophical Speculation**

These writings offer **pastoral and worshipful theology**, not metaphysical formulas. There is no use of terms like *homoousios*, no philosophical musings about essence or nature. The emphasis remains relational, covenantal, and mission-focused: Who sent whom? Who represents whom? Who acts on behalf of whom?

## The Picture That Emerges

The earliest post-apostolic literature confirms a **living continuity** with the New Testament and with Second Temple Jewish theology. The divine hierarchy is preserved, the worship of the Father remains supreme, and the identity of the Son as God's unique, empowered mediator is proclaimed without hesitation or confusion.

This vision is not "proto-Trinitarian" in the later Nicene sense. It is instead **a fully developed, confident articulation of divine mediation**—what we rightly call **Christian Monolatry**.

In this framework:

- **Yeshua is the preexistent Logos**, the "Lord of all the earth" (Barnabas), the "adviser" of the Father (Hermas), and the agent through whom God creates and redeems.
- **Yet He is always from God**, begotten of His will, functioning under His authority, and never merged with the Father into one undivided essence.

This, not Trinitarian metaphysics, was the **default assumption** of early Christian faith.

# 16

# From Jewish Monolatry to Christian Monolatry

In the preceding chapters, we explored how both Jewish and early Christian thought embraced a monolatrous framework—a view that acknowledged the existence of multiple divine beings while insisting on the exclusive worship of one supreme God. This background is crucial for understanding the later theological debates. As the Christian movement expanded beyond the New Testament era into the turbulent second and third centuries, its adherents encountered new challenges. They were pressed to articulate their faith in a context where critics—both pagan and Jewish—queried the consistency of worshiping Yeshua alongside the absolute primacy of the Father.

The question of "one God yet multiple divine beings" thus emerged as a central concern, forcing early apologists to reexamine and redefine their understanding of divine unity and hierarchy.

This chapter examines how key second- and third-century Christian writers—among them Justin Martyr, Tertullian, Athenagoras, Theophilus, and Origen—navigated this tension. These apologists were tasked with defending the faith before a skeptical public and imperial authorities, while also addressing internal theological debates. They argued that Messiah, as the Logos or "second God," served as the divinely appointed mediator through whom the supreme God (the Father) enacted His creative and redemptive will. Importantly, they maintained that although Messiah was divine, His authority was always derived from and subordinate to the Father. This subordinationist approach allowed them to safeguard the worship of one God even as they affirmed the genuine divinity of the Son.

Several interrelated themes underpin their thought. First, the concept of the Logos—deeply influenced by the works of Philo of Alexandria—provided a vocabulary for expressing how Yeshua, as the divine Word, was both an agent of creation and revelation, yet not an independent source of divinity. Parallel to this were traditions found in the Jewish Targums, where the Memra functioned as God's spoken word or presence, reinforcing the idea that any divine agency ultimately points back to the one true God. Finally, the incorporation of Greek philosophical terminology—terms such as *essence, substance,* and *hypostasis*—enabled these early apologists to articulate a complex and nuanced picture of the divine structure. This lexicon later paved the way for the full-fledged Trinitarian formulations of the fourth century, even as the early apologists remained firmly committed to a monolatrous vision.

In sum, this chapter aims to show that the early development of Logos theology was not a departure from Jewish monolatry but rather an extension of it. By emphasizing Christ's role as the subordinate yet fully divine mediator, these apologists provided a framework that defended exclusive worship of the Father while also affirming the unique divine status of the Son.

## Historical Context: Growth, Diversity, and Controversy

By the second century, Christianity had expanded well beyond its Jewish roots, spreading across the Roman Empire and forming diverse communities in cities like Rome, Alexandria, and Antioch. This period of growth brought with it new theological challenges. As Christian communities encountered an array of cultural and philosophical influences, they found themselves needing to clarify and defend their core beliefs—particularly their understanding of divine unity and the nature of Messiah.

A central tension faced by early believers was how to affirm the worship of one supreme God while also honoring Yeshua as divine. This question became especially urgent in the face of criticism from both Jewish and pagan voices. Jewish critics, grounded in the Shema ("Hear, O Israel: the Lord our God, the Lord is one"), accused Christians of introducing a second deity by venerating Yeshua. Pagan observers, meanwhile, often misunderstood Christian worship practices—some accusing Christians of atheism for rejecting the Roman pantheon, while others suspected polytheism due to Christian reverence for both the Father and the Son.

Internally, the Christian movement was far from monolithic. Alternative theological systems arose that pushed the boundaries of traditional monolatry. The Marcionites, for instance, rejected the Hebrew Scriptures and portrayed the God of the Old Testament as inferior to the Father of Yeshua. Gnostic groups introduced complex cosmologies involving multiple divine beings and secret knowledge, often diluting the uniqueness of the one supreme God. These teachings posed significant challenges to the unity and simplicity of early Christian monolatry.

In response, a group of thinkers that would later be identified as "proto-orthodox" emerged to articulate a cohesive vision of divine order. They insisted that while Yeshua was indeed divine, His divinity was derived from—and subordinate to—the Father. This subordinationist stance allowed them to maintain the integrity of Jewish monolatry while also affirming the revelatory role of the Son.

These early defenders developed a theological vocabulary that helped clarify their position. Drawing on Jewish traditions like the Memra and the Angel of the Lord, as well as on Greek philosophical concepts, they articulated a model in which divine mediation did not violate the oneness of God. The Son could be honored and even worshiped—not as an independent deity, but as the appointed agent of the one unbegotten Father.

This historical and intellectual context set the stage for the emergence of Logos theology—a doctrine that sought to explain the relationship between the Father and the Son without collapsing them into a single person or elevating the Son to an equal source of divinity. In the sections that follow, we will explore how figures like Justin Martyr, Tertullian, and Origen refined and developed this theological model.

## *Justin Martyr: The Logos as Mediator of the One God*

Justin Martyr stands as a pivotal figure in the development of early Christian theology. Writing in the second century, he offered one of the first sustained philosophical defenses of the Christian faith. His engagement with both Greco-Roman philosophy and Jewish Scripture enabled him to construct a model of divine mediation that honored the uniqueness of Yeshua as the Logos while carefully preserving the absolute supremacy of God the Father.

## Justin's Background and Theological Aims

A former Platonist, Justin converted to Christianity and redirected his philosophical training toward defending the faith. In his *First Apology*, *Second Apology*, and *Dialogue with Trypho*, he argued that Christianity was not a novel superstition but the fulfillment of both philosophical reason and prophetic revelation. Central to this defense was the figure of the Logos—identified with Yeshua—not as a rival deity, but as the personal, obedient expression of the one uncreated God.

Justin's goal was to demonstrate that the Christian belief in Messiah did not compromise the unity of God. Rather, it affirmed the longstanding pattern—familiar from Jewish sources—of divine agency working through a subordinate yet exalted mediator.

## The Logos as Divine Agent, Not Independent Deity

While modern theology often treats the divine titles in Scripture as separate and sometimes conflicting concepts, the early Church saw a unified reality. For them, the various mediators who appeared throughout Israel's history—the Angel of YHWH, the personified Wisdom, the creative Word—were not different beings, but different facets of a single, glorious Person: the Son of God.

No one articulated this with more stunning clarity than Justin Martyr. Writing in the mid-second century, he confronts this very issue head-on. In a breathtaking summary that validates the entire framework of Christian Monolatry, Justin explains that the one whom God begot from His own being before all creation is known by a cascade of divine titles. He states that these are the names **given to the Son *in Scripture* (which is inspired by the Holy Spirit)**:

## FROM JEWISH MONOLATRY TO CHRISTIAN MONOLATRY

> *"I shall give you another testimony... that God begot before all creatures a **Beginning**... who is called by the Holy Spirit, now the Glory of the Lord, now the **Son**, again **Wisdom**, again an **Angel**, then **God**, and then Lord and **Logos**."* (Justin Martyr, Dialogue with Trypho, Chapter 61)

This is not a modern theory; it is an ancient testimony. Here, a central figure of the early Church, writing just a generation after the apostles, explicitly confirms that all these divine, mediatorial roles converge in one Person. The titles of "Beginning," "Angel," "Logos," and even "God" are scriptural designations for the Son, testifying to his various functions as the Father's agent. Justin is making the very connections this book has sought to recover. His words are a powerful confirmation that the monolatrous framework—a supreme Father who acts through a single, subordinate, and multi-titled divine Son—was not a later invention, but the foundational theology of the pre-Nicene faith.

Justin Martyr refers to the Logos as "another God," a phrase that can seem shocking if detached from its context. However, Justin immediately clarifies that this "other God" is not a rival or an equal, but a subordinate agent. He explains his meaning with stunning clarity in his *Dialogue with Trypho*, leaving no room for ambiguity:

> *"I shall attempt to persuade you... that there is, and that there is said to be, **another God and Lord subject to the Maker of all things**; who is also called an Angel, because He announces to men whatsoever the Maker of all things—**above whom there is no other God**—wishes to announce to Him."* (Justin Martyr, Dialogue with Trypho, Chapter 56)

In this single, remarkable statement, Justin lays out the entire framework of Christian Monolatry. He makes two crucial points that define the divine hierarchy. First, he establishes that this second divine figure is explicitly "**subject to the Maker of all things**." Second, he affirms that the Father is the one "**above whom there is no other God**."

This is the exact same theological structure we see in the Epistle to the Hebrews. In Hebrews 1:8-9, the Son is addressed with the divine title, "Your throne, O God, is forever and ever." Yet, in the very next sentence, His subordination is made equally clear: "Therefore God, **Your God**, has anointed You." In both Justin's apology and the apostolic witness of Hebrews, we see the same pattern: the Son is truly called God, but He has a God over Him.

This demonstrates that for early Christians, the Son's divinity and His subordination were not contradictory ideas; they were two sides of the same coin. He is divine *because* he is the begotten of the Father, but his subjection to the Father is what preserves the ultimate truth that there is only one supreme God, the "Maker of all things."

In Justin's theology, the Logos is divine only by delegation. He is not unbegotten or self-existent. His identity, power, and function all flow from the initiative of the Father. In this, Justin closely aligns with the mediatory logic of Jewish tradition, where figures such as the Angel of the Lord or the Memra (Aramaic: "Word") serve as divine agents without ever eclipsing the singular worship of YHWH.

Thus, when Justin describes the Logos as the one through whom God created the world, appeared to Moses, or communicated with humanity, he does so to illustrate divine transcendence—not to imply an equal, second godhead. The Logos acts representatively, not autonomously.[54]

---

[54] Justin Martyr's reference to the Logos as "another God" is a classic example of pre-Nicene subordinationism. Patristic scholar J.N.D. Kelly explains that for Justin, the Son is "a second God," but only in a secondary sense. The Father is the ultimate, unoriginated source, while the Son is the personal agent He brought forth by an act of will before creation. This affirms a clear hierarchy of origin and authority.
See: J.N.D. Kelly, *Early Christian Doctrines*, 5th ed. (London: A&C Black, 1977), 95-97.

## Clarifying Worship: Representational Honor, Not Rival Devotion

While Justin acknowledges that Christians show reverence toward Messiah, this honor is never detached from the Father. The Son is honored precisely because He represents the Father and enacts His will. Worship, in the strict sense—prayer, adoration, and final devotion—is reserved for the Father alone, whom Justin consistently names as "the one unbegotten God" (*First Apology* 13).

Any language of honoring the Son is always subordinate and representational. Just as honoring a king's envoy honors the king who sent him, so too in Justin's model, reverence toward the Logos glorifies the one who begot and sent Him. At no point does Justin advocate for worship that terminates in the Son apart from the Father. This distinction safeguards Christian monolatry and ensures fidelity to the Shema: "The Lord our God, the Lord is one."

## Continuity with Jewish Mediatory Patterns

Justin's model draws heavily on Jewish traditions of divine mediation. In the Targums, the Memra is often described as the voice, presence, or manifestation of God—appearing in narratives such as the burning bush or the giving of the Torah. While the Memra acts with divine authority, it is never an object of worship independent of God.

Similarly, Justin presents the Logos as the visible and personal expression of the Father—one who speaks, appears, and acts, yet never rivals the Father in origin or authority. His divinity is entirely derived, and his identity is inseparable from the mission he fulfills on behalf of the one true God.

### Preserving the Structure of Monolatry

The theological structure Justin outlines affirms both the uniqueness of Messiah and the inviolable supremacy of the Father. This is not a compromised or transitional theology; it is a carefully balanced vision rooted in both Scripture and tradition. It upholds the integrity of Christian monolatry by insisting that all divine power flows from the unbegotten Father, and that all mediation, even when exalted, points back to Him alone.

In Justin's system, there is no ontological rivalry, no duality of uncreated gods, and no confusion in worship. The Logos is divine by participation and obedience, not by equality or self-existence. He serves, reveals, and glorifies the Father—never displacing Him as the exclusive recipient of worship.

## *Tertullian, Athenagoras, and Theophilus: Triadic Language and the Supremacy of the Father*

While Justin Martyr was one of the first to articulate a Logos theology that balanced divine mediation with monolatry, he was not alone. Other early apologists—Tertullian of Carthage, Athenagoras of Athens, and Theophilus of Antioch—further refined this theological structure, using language that acknowledged a triadic reality within the divine order while preserving the Father's sole supremacy. Their formulations, while often later appropriated by Trinitarian frameworks, were rooted in a fundamentally monolatrous logic: **only the Father is unbegotten, only He is the ultimate source, and only He receives worship as the supreme God.**

## A. Tertullian: A Structured Economy of Divine Activity

Tertullian was the first known Christian writer to use the Latin term *Trinitas* (Trinity). However, his use of this term must not be confused with later, co-equal Trinitarianism. Tertullian's thought was structured around the concept of the "divine economy" (*oikonomia*)—a hierarchical arrangement of divine operations flowing from the Father, through the Son, and by the Spirit.

In *Against Praxeas*, Tertullian insists: "The Father is the whole substance, while the Son is a derivation and portion of the whole." This statement makes clear that Tertullian viewed the Son not as a co-equal divine peer, but as an extension or projection of the Father's will. He uses metaphors like fire and flame, fountain and stream, sun and ray—to illustrate the Son's complete dependence on the Father's essence and authority.

Tertullian affirms the Son's divinity, but always within the boundaries of subordination. The Son is "God" insofar as He is generated from the Father, not in the sense of independent or equal origin. In this "economic" view, divine action is structured, sequential, and ordered. Worship is directed to the Father, through the Son, not equally or interchangeably. The honor given to Messiah reflects His role as the Father's emissary—never as an autonomous recipient of ultimate worship.[55]

---

[55] Although Tertullian was the first to use the Latin term *Trinitas*, his conception was explicitly hierarchical. He described a "divine economy" (*oikonomia*) in which the Father, as the sole source, extends His substance to the Son, and through the Son to the Spirit. As Jaroslav Pelikan notes, Tertullian's analogies (fountain/stream, sun/ray) were meant to show that the Son is "of one substance" with the Father by derivation, but not co-equal in status or origin. The Father remains the ultimate source, and the Son and Spirit are subordinate in rank.

See: Jaroslav Pelikan, *The Christian Tradition: A History of the Development of Doctrine, Vol. 1: The Emergence of the Catholic Tradition (100-600)* (Chicago: University of Chicago Press, 1971), 199-204.

## B. Athenagoras: The Logos as the Father's Rational Power

At first glance, the language of the second-century apologist Athenagoras can sound strikingly similar to later Trinitarian formulas, but a closer look reveals a fundamentally different and staunchly hierarchical framework.[56] In his *Plea for the Christians*, while refuting charges of atheism, he describes Christians as those who, when speaking of the Father and His Son, "declare both their power in union and their distinction in order." While the phrase "power in union" might suggest co-equality to modern ears, in its second-century context it refers to a perfect unity of purpose and will—the Father and His Logos act in complete harmony, as a single force in creation and revelation.

However, this unity is immediately qualified by the crucial phrase "distinction in order." The Greek word for "order" here is *taxis* (τάξις), a term signifying a fixed arrangement, rank, and hierarchy, often used to describe the ordered ranks of soldiers. It explicitly denies equality and instead points to an ordered structure with clear levels of authority. Therefore, Athenagoras is describing a divine command structure, not a metaphysical equality. To use a simple analogy, a supreme king and his perfectly loyal general are "united in power" on the battlefield, acting with a single will to achieve victory, yet they remain absolutely "distinct in order" of rank and authority. The general's power is derived from the king and is always subordinate to him. Far from anticipating the co-equality of Nicaea, Athenagoras's formula is a precise articulation of Christian Monolatry: a supreme God the Father who acts in perfect unity with His divine, yet

---

[56] Athenagoras, *A Plea for the Christians*, Ch. 10: "We acknowledge one God, uncreated, eternal...by whom the universe has been framed through His Logos...the Son of God is the Logos of the Father, in idea and in operation...the Father and the Son being one. The Son being in the Father and the Father in the Son, in oneness and power of spirit...Who, then, would not be astonished to hear men called atheists who speak of God the Father, and of God the Son, and of the Holy Spirit, and who declare both their power in union and their distinction in order?"

subordinate, Son.[57]

## C. Theophilus of Antioch: The Triad and the Divine Voice

Theophilus, bishop of Antioch in the late second century, adds another layer to this tradition. In *Ad Autolycum*, he is the earliest known writer to use the term *triados* (triad) to describe the divine structure. But Theophilus does not present the Father, Son, and Spirit as ontologically equal. He describes the Logos as the "voice" or "expression" of the Father—eternally with Him, yet always flowing from Him.

He writes: "God... having His Logos within His own heart, begat Him along with His Wisdom before all things." This image echoes the Memra tradition in the Jewish Targums, where the Word is the communicative extension of God—not a second object of worship, but the presence by which God acts in the world.

Theophilus's triad is not co-equal; it is functional and ordered. He affirms that Messiah is divine because He is the Father's agent, not because He possesses an underived essence. The Son is glorified as the vehicle through whom the Father reveals Himself. Thus, Theophilus maintains the Shema's vision of one God by ensuring that worship flows upward—to the one underived source, the Father.

---

[57] The Greek word for "order" used by Athenagoras is *taxis*, a term signifying a fixed arrangement, rank, and hierarchy, often used to describe the ordered ranks of soldiers. As scholars of the period affirm, this language clearly subordinates the Son to the Father in origin and authority, even while asserting a perfect unity of will. It describes a divine command structure, not a metaphysical co-equality.

See: R.P.C. Hanson, *The Search for the Christian Doctrine of God: The Arian Controversy 318-381* (Edinburgh: T&T Clark, 1988), 61-62.

## Sabelianism: The Challenge of Undifferentiated Unity

As early Christian thinkers carefully worked to articulate a vision of divine hierarchy that preserved the exclusive worship of the Father while acknowledging the divinity of the Son and Spirit, a competing model emerged that sought to simplify this complexity by removing distinction altogether. This perspective, known as **Sabelianism** (or **Modalism**), proposed that the Father, Son, and Spirit were not distinct persons or agents, but simply different *modes* or *manifestations* of a single divine person. While motivated by a desire to uphold monotheism, this view inadvertently introduced new problems—chief among them, the **collapse of divine mediation** into a flat, indistinct unity.

Sabellius and others in his line of thought argued that the one God expressed Himself in different roles across time: as Father in creation, as Son in redemption, and as Spirit in sanctification. According to this model, these are not distinct agents within a divine order, but successive operations of one undifferentiated being. This idea sought to protect divine unity by denying any real distinction or hierarchy among the expressions of God.

However, early apologists had already laid a theological groundwork that rejected this approach. Figures such as **Tertullian**, **Origen**, and **Justin Martyr** had emphasized that while the Son and Spirit were subordinate, their distinction from the Father was real and essential to maintaining the biblical witness. Passages where the Son prays to the Father (e.g., John 17), or is sent by the Father (e.g., John 5:30), and even dialogues in Genesis featuring the "Angel of the Lord," all present real interpersonal dynamics within the divine order. The early church recognized that collapsing these distinctions would not clarify theology—it would obscure Scripture and undermine the structure of divine revelation.

Tertullian, in particular, responded directly to Sabelianism in his work *Against Praxeas*, where he defended a structured "economy" (*oikonomia*) in which the Father, Son, and Spirit are truly distinct, yet united in will and purpose. He was concerned that modalism erased the Father-Son relationship altogether, turning divine interactions into mere illusions and robbing the Gospel of its depth. "The Father is not the Son," he argued, "nor is the Son the Father." For Tertullian and others, this distinction was not optional—it was essential to preserving both **divine unity** and **revelatory order**.

The problem with Sabelianism was not just its theological compression, but its impact on worship. If the Father, Son, and Spirit are merely masks worn by a single person, then the relational dynamics of prayer, obedience, and mediation are rendered meaningless. The Son is no longer the Father's agent; He becomes the Father Himself under a different name. This undermines the pattern of Christian worship attested in Scripture and practiced in the earliest communities: worship directed *to the Father, through the Son*, and *by the Spirit*.

Moreover, early church councils were wary of the implications that modalism had for Christ's suffering and incarnation. The notion that "the Father suffered" (a view sometimes called **Patripassianism**) blurred the distinction between the divine nature and the human experience of Yeshua. This conflation risked confusing the impassibility of the uncreated God with the temporal suffering of the incarnate Son.

Thus, the rejection of Sabelianism in early Christian discourse was not merely reactionary; it was theological and pastoral. The apologists were committed to safeguarding both the transcendence of the one God and the genuine, functional distinction of His mediators. They did not yet speak in the later language of "persons of one essence," but they recognized that divine unity did not require modal identity. On the contrary, true unity was preserved by a **hierarchical order** in which the Son and Spirit are genuinely divine and truly distinct, yet always subordinate to the Father.

In this way, the early church preserved the integrity of **Christian monolatry**—the exclusive worship of the Father—while upholding the real and relational divinity of the Son and Spirit. The rejection of Sabelianism protected this balance, ensuring that the dynamic relationship within the divine economy could still reflect the full scope of scriptural testimony.

**Origen and Eusebius: The Apex of Pre-Nicene Monolatry**

Among the early Christian thinkers, Origen of Alexandria stands as one of the most influential and systematic. His work represents not an innovation, but a profound synthesis of the biblical, Jewish, and philosophical traditions that preceded him. At the heart of his theology is the doctrine of "eternal generation," a concept that, when properly understood, is a cornerstone of Christian Monolatry and its framework of dynamic eternity.

To understand Origen's original thought, we can turn to his most dedicated defenders: Pamphilus of Caesarea and his student, Eusebius. Together they authored the Apology for Origen, a work designed to prove his orthodoxy against his critics. Crucially, this defense itself has been filtered through the lens of a later controversy. It survives only in a Latin translation by Rufinus, who admitted to altering controversial texts to make them more acceptable to a post-Nicene audience. Therefore, the "defended Origen" we read is likely a version already softened, yet even in this form, his hierarchical and monolatrous framework is unmistakable.

For Origen, the term "eternally begotten" was a direct affirmation of the Son's **eternal dependence**. To be *begotten* was to have one's origin in another, and to be *eternally* begotten meant this relationship of dependence was itself perpetual and without beginning. This was not a static, metaphysical necessity, but a continuous, willed act. The Father eternally *wills* to generate the Son, just as a light eternally and actively emits its radiance. The Son's existence, therefore, is perpetually and eternally *derived from* the Father. [58] This framework allowed Origen to affirm the Son's pre-existence while unambiguously stating that the Father alone is unbegotten (*agennetos*) and the sole "fount of divinity."

This legacy was carried forward by Origen's most prominent intellectual heir, **Eusebius of Caesarea**. Eusebius clarifies that this eternal dependence results in a clear and enduring hierarchy. Using language directly from Origen, Eusebius confirms that while the Son is divine, the Father is necessarily **prior**—not in time, but in origin, rank, and supremacy. He quotes Origen to make the hierarchy explicit:

> "We say that the Saviour and the Holy Spirit are without comparison and are incalculably superior to all things that are made, but also that **the Father is incalculably superior to them.**" (Origen, quoted by Eusebius in Praeparatio Evangelica, VII, 15)

In the theology of Origen and Eusebius, the Son could **never be considered equal** to the Father in ultimate authority. His divinity is real because he is born "of the Father's essence," but it is a derived divinity. Philosophically, Origen's use of terms like *hypostasis* (individual existence) and *ousia* (essence) provided a precise language for distinguishing these roles. But even as he employed Greek metaphysics, he remained grounded in the biblical narrative of a God who sends and a Son who is sent in loving obedience.

While later debates would misread or repurpose his formulations, Origen's work should not be judged by post-Nicene categories. He was not

---

[58] Origen, On First Principles: "For if the Son does what the Father does, then, in virtue of the fact that the Son does all things as the Father does them, is the image of the Father created. But in our view, God is the Father, who is unbegotten... And the Son, being less than the Father, is subordinate to him..." (cf. Book 1, Ch. 3, Sec. 5). Elsewhere he clarifies the Son's eternal nature: "This effulgence... is generated eternally and without ceasing... For he is not a Son by adoption... but a Son by nature." (Book 1, Ch. 2, Sec. 2).

concerned with proving ontological co-equality, but with safeguarding the mediatorial structure affirmed by tradition. In sum, his legacy—faithfully articulated by Eusebius—is a theological hierarchy that upholds Christian Monolatry: one supreme God (the Father), and one exalted, divine Son who derives his being from Him to mediate His will to the world.[59]

## Transition: From Hierarchical Mediation to the Mystery of Dynamic Eternity

The early Christian apologists presented a clear theological structure in which the Father alone is unbegotten and supreme, and the Son—though fully divine—is always subordinate, functioning as His agent and mediator. This vision preserved the exclusive worship of one God, consistent with the monolatrous pattern rooted in Scripture and Jewish tradition. In figures like Justin Martyr, Tertullian, and Origen, we see that the Son's divinity was always understood in relation to the Father's will—a derived, empowered reality rather than a co-equal, co-ultimate one.

But a deeper question increasingly pressed upon the early Church: *When was the Son begotten, and what kind of reality is His generation?*

The earliest sources speak of the Son as begotten "before the ages," but

---

[59] Origen's doctrine of "eternal generation" was his systematic attempt to affirm the Son's true divinity (as being eternally from the Father's own nature) while simultaneously preserving the Father's unique status as the sole uncaused source. As R.P.C. Hanson explains, for Origen, the Son is a "perfect creature who is not a creature," a divine but subordinate intermediary. His entire system is one of a clear hierarchy, with the Father as the "fount of divinity" and the Son as eternally dependent upon Him.
See: R.P.C. Hanson, *The Search for the Christian Doctrine of God*, 137-142.

without the metaphysical rigidity that would later define Nicene theology. Their view of divine generation was relational and volitional—*dynamic* rather than static. The Son's origin was not an impersonal necessity, but an intentional act of the Father's will, establishing a divine relationship that existed before time but not apart from divine choice.

This is the heart of what we now call **dynamic eternity**: a vision of divine generation that is **eternal in scope**, yet always **relational and deliberate**—a generation **before** time, but never **independent** of the Father's initiative.

# 17

# The Apex of Christian Monolatry: The Theology of Eusebius of Caesarea

To understand the authentic, mainstream theology of the Church leading into the Council of Nicaea, there is no better witness than Eusebius of Caesarea. As a student of the Origenist tradition through his teacher Pamphilus, and as a leading bishop at the council itself, Eusebius provides a clear window into the pre-Athanasian worldview. His work *On Ecclesiastical Theology*, a direct refutation of his contemporary Marcellus of Ancyra, is not merely a polemic; it is a masterclass in the framework we identify as Christian Monolatry. In it, he meticulously defends a divine hierarchy that upholds the Father's unique supremacy while affirming the Son's true, derived divinity.

## 1. Defending Hierarchy Against Modalism

One of the clearest expressions of Eusebius's monolatrous framework comes at the very beginning of his work, where he refutes the teachings of Marcellus. Marcellus, who advocated for a theology that strongly unified the Son with the Father, argued that the Word was not a truly distinct person but was "one and the same with God."[60]

Eusebius immediately identifies this position as a revival of the older heresy of Sabellianism. He powerfully argues that if the Word is identical to the supreme God, then one is forced into a blasphemous conclusion. He writes:

> *"For if [the Word] is not something other than God... then it is plain that God himself, according to this godless heresy, was born of the Virgin... This idea the Church of God has long ago rejected."* (cf. Eusebius, On Ecclesiastical Theology, Book 1, Chapter 1)

For Eusebius, the distinction was non-negotiable. The supreme God—the Father—was not born and did not become flesh. It was His divine Son, the Word, who was born. This separation of roles and persons is foundational to his theology.

## 2. The "One God" is the Father; The Son is Divine by Derivation

Building on this, Eusebius explains that the unique revelation given to the Church was the understanding that the "one God" confessed by the Jews is also a Father. He meticulously clarifies that the Son's divinity is entirely derived from and dependent on the Father. Using a powerful metaphor, he explains that the Son is divine:

> *"...by participating in the paternal Divinity itself,* **which flows into him as a fountain.***"* (cf. Eusebius, On Ecclesiastical Theology, Book

---

[60] This argument comes from the opening of Eusebius's direct refutation of Marcellus. He immediately frames Marcellus's theology as a revival of Sabellianism, which he considers a "godless heresy" for its failure to distinguish between the Father and the Son.
 See: Eusebius of Caesarea, On Ecclesiastical Theology 1.1, in *Eusebius of Caesarea: Against Marcellus and on Ecclesiastical Theology*, trans. Kelley McCarthy Spoerl, The Fathers of the Church, vol. 135 (Washington, DC: The Catholic University of America Press, 2017), 119-120.

1, Chapter 2)⁶¹

This "fountain" analogy is a perfect illustration of derived divinity. The Father is the singular, uncaused source—the fountainhead. The Son is truly divine because He is eternally filled by that fountain, not because He is a second, independent source. Eusebius concludes that the Church rightly proclaims **"one God... and there is no other besides him,"** because that one God is the Father, and simultaneously proclaims the **"one only begotten Son of God"** who, because he is the unique descendent of the Father, **"is God."**

### 3. The Reality of Fatherhood and the Priority of the Father

Eusebius then exposes the central absurdity of collapsing the Father and Son into a single being: it makes the titles meaningless. He argues that a real Son requires a real Father who existed **prior** to him—not in time, but in origin and rank. He writes:

> *"For of whom will the Father be Father, if no Son subsists? And of whom will the Son be Son, if the one who has begotten him has not existed **prior** to him?"* (cf. Eusebius, On Ecclesiastical Theology, Book 1, Chapter 4)⁶²

---

[61] Eusebius uses the metaphor of a fountain to explain that the Son's divinity is not His own but flows entirely from the "paternal divinity." This reinforces the Father's role as the singular, uncaused source, which is a central theme of his theology.
   See: Eusebius, *On Ecclesiastical Theology* 1.2, in *Fathers of the Church* 135, trans. Spoerl, 120.

[62] Eusebius's argument here is one of logical necessity based on relational language. For him, the very titles "Father" and "Son" require a distinction in order and origin. He argues that if there is no Son who subsists as a distinct entity, the Father cannot truly be a Father, making the relational language of the Gospel meaningless.
   See: Eusebius, *On Ecclesiastical Theology* 1.4, in *Fathers of the Church* 135, trans. Spoerl, 122.

This argument demonstrates Eusebius's unwavering commitment to the monolatrous hierarchy. The Father's priority is non-negotiable. He is the supreme, unbegotten God who truly begets a real, distinct, and subordinate Son.

## 4. The Uniqueness of the Begotten Son vs. Creatures

Eusebius confronts the Arian error by establishing the absolute distinction between the Son's origin and the origin of everything else. The Son is unique because He is the only one who **derives His being directly from the Father**. All other things in existence were created *through* the Son. This places the Son in a category entirely His own. He explains that to define the Son as a creature "out of nothing" is to "unwittingly grant only the name to him, but deny that he is truly the Son." The title becomes hollow, and the relationship is reduced to one of adoption, not true, natural begetting.[63]

## 5. The Giver and the Receiver of Life

Perhaps Eusebius's most profound point concerns the Son's own life. He cites Jesus's words to show that the Father is the source of the Son's very existence:

> *"'For as the Father has life in Himself, so also* **He has given to the Son to have life in Himself.'** *Therefore, the one has given, the other has received."* (cf. Eusebius, On Ecclesiastical Theology, *quoting John*

---

[63] A cornerstone of Eusebius's anti-Arian argument was that the Son, as the *only begotten*, could not be a creature. He argues that to define the Son as a creature made "out of nothing" is to deny that He is a true Son by nature, reducing his sonship to a mere title.
See: Eusebius, On Ecclesiastical Theology 1.9, in Fathers of the Church 135, trans. Spoerl, 129-130.

*5:26)*[64]

His argument is a masterstroke. He affirms that the Son possesses self-sustaining life, just like the Father—a quality that elevates Him far above any creature. However, this divine attribute was not something He inherently had; it was **given** to Him by the Father. This eternal gift of life establishes the ultimate dependence of the Son.

## 6. The Distinct Persons of the Son and the Spirit

Finally, in Book 3, Eusebius solidifies his case by arguing for the real, distinct existence (*hypostasis*) of both the Son and the Spirit. He uses Proverbs 8 ("I was present with him") to prove the Son must be a distinct person to be "with" the Father. He then applies the same logic to the Holy Spirit, proving He is a distinct person by citing Jesus's words that the Spirit is **"another counselor"** and that He **"will take what is mine."** For Eusebius, "that which takes from another is thought to be other than the one who gives," proving the Spirit and Son are not the same being.[65]

## Conclusion: The Coherent Vision of Eusebius's Monolatry

---

[64] Eusebius's exegesis of John 5:26 is a masterstroke of his subordinationist theology. He affirms that the Son possesses self-sustaining life, a divine attribute, but emphasizes that this attribute was *given* to Him by the Father. This eternal gift of life, for Eusebius, establishes the ultimate dependence of the Son while simultaneously confirming his divine nature as the Father's perfect image.
See: Eusebius, *On Ecclesiastical Theology 1.20,* in *Fathers of the Church 135,* trans. Spoerl, *169-170.*

[65] In his third book, Eusebius argues forcefully against any theology that would conflate the Father, Son, and Holy Spirit into a single being. His reasoning, based on Jesus's own words in the Gospel of John, is that the Spirit is called "another counselor" and "takes from" what is the Son's, proving they are distinct persons in a clear hierarchy of purpose and action.
See: Eusebius, *On Ecclesiastical Theology 3.5,* in *Fathers of the Church 135,* trans. Spoerl, *258-261.*

The testimony of Eusebius of Caesarea is a comprehensive defense of Christian Monolatry. He meticulously argues for a divine hierarchy:

1. **One supreme, uncaused God, the Father.**
2. **One truly distinct, divine, and subordinate Son,** begotten by the Father's will.
3. **One distinct, personal Holy Spirit,** sent by the Father through the Son.

His entire theological project was to defend this ordered, relational model against any theology that would either diminish the Son to a mere creature or collapse the divine persons into an undifferentiated, static unity.

# 18

# "How the Bible Reveals an Eternal God Who Acts, Begets, and Transforms Across the Ages"

Having explored the theological frameworks of the early apologists and Origen, we now arrive at a foundational issue that continues to shape Christian theology: How should we understand the begetting of the Son in relation to God's eternal nature and the act of creation? Is the generation of the Son an abstract, timeless necessity—or a willed, dynamic act within the eternal life of God?

This chapter seeks to recover the early monolatrous assumptions that preceded later metaphysical developments. In this early framework, there is no tension between God's transcendence and His capacity to initiate relational acts—such as begetting the Son or creating through the Logos. The Word (Logos), the Memra, and Wisdom all functioned in Jewish and Christian thought as mediating agents—divine but subordinate, expressive of God's will yet never equated with the unbegotten nature of the Father.

This chapter will:

- Contrast fixed and dynamic models of eternity, showing how each one leads to different readings of Scripture and doctrinal conclusions.
- Re-examine key biblical and Second Temple texts—particularly those referring to Wisdom and the Word—noting how they imply a dynamic act of begetting or expression, rather than a metaphysical co-equality.
- Rethink the meaning of "the beginning" in Genesis and John's Gospel, considering whether it refers to a point in time or to a first principle, agent, or act within God's eternal will.
- Frame the fourth-century controversies (Arian, Nicene, Semi-Arian) in light of these competing paradigms—arguing that the confusion often stemmed from unspoken assumptions about what it means for something to be "eternal."

By drawing together these themes, we argue that the dynamic view of eternity better preserves the biblical pattern: a singular, supreme God who acts relationally and decisively—begetting, creating, and revealing—not in timeless stasis but in dynamic eternal initiative. The Son's generation is not a passive, metaphysical reality that simply always was, but an eternal act of will—before time yet still truly "from" the Father, in a way that preserves both divine freedom and hierarchical monolatry.

## Fixed Eternity vs. Dynamic Eternity — A Brief Revisit

To move forward with clarity, we must revisit a foundational distinction: how different theological systems understand the nature of God's eternity. This distinction frames the entire discussion around the Son's begetting and God's creative will.

## 1. Fixed Eternity

The **fixed eternity** model portrays God's nature as entirely static—eternally unchanging not only in essence but also in expression. Within this framework:

- **All divine actions** (begetting, creating, relating) are viewed as timelessly existent, never truly "occurring" or initiated—even outside of chronological time.
- **The begetting of the Son** is reinterpreted as an eternal necessity, not a decision or act of divine will. This makes the Son's existence and relationship to the Father metaphysically automatic and ontologically equal.
- **Concerns about divine perfection** drive this view: if God truly "acts" or "begets" in any sense, He must have changed or lacked something before acting—something the fixed model rejects entirely.

As a result, any hint of development, distinction, or decision within the divine life is viewed as compromising God's absolute simplicity and timeless perfection.

## 2. Dynamic Eternity

In contrast, the **dynamic eternity** model maintains that God's essence is unchanging, yet His internal life includes relational and expressive acts that are not temporally bound but are truly willed.

- **God can act**—beget, create, reveal—without undergoing change in essence.
- **The generation of the Son** is seen as a genuine, eternal act of the Father's will. It is "before time," but it is still a real begetting—relational, intentional, and expressive.
- **Creation itself** is not merely an eternal disclosure but a free, dynamic act. God initiates, not out of necessity, but out of volition and love.

In this model, eternity is not frozen. God remains transcendent and immutable in essence, yet capable of initiating new realities from within His eternal life. The Son, then, is begotten in a way that reflects this dynamic—not as an eternal co-equal by necessity, but as a true expression of the Father's will and purpose, prior to all temporal creation.

**Summary of the Tension**

The heart of the tension lies here:

- **Fixed eternity** denies any real "before and after" even in God's eternal life, insisting that all divine relations are static and unchanging.
- **Dynamic eternity** affirms that, while time as we know it does not exist before creation, God's relational expressions (such as begetting the Son) can still be real, decisive, and ordered—even if not temporal.

This distinction helps explain why later theological developments—especially at Nicaea—struggled to reconcile begetting with subordination. Fixed eternity leads naturally to consubstantial equality; dynamic eternity allows for real derivation without undermining divine unity or transcendence.[66]

## Early Monolatrous Assumptions: The Memra, Wisdom, and Creation

To rightly understand how early Jewish and Christian thought conceived of divine mediation, we must explore the figures of the **Memra** and **Wisdom**, and how these relate to creation. What emerges is a pattern of **relational hierarchy** and **dynamic begetting**—a framework utterly foreign to later Nicene metaphysics, yet thoroughly consistent with biblical and Second Temple assumptions.

---

[66] The contrast between a dynamic, relational understanding of God's inner life and a more static, metaphysical one is a key theme in the history of doctrine. Patristic scholar R.P.C. Hanson notes that many pre-Nicene theologians, like Origen, understood the Son's generation as a matter of the Father's will, an eternal act. This "volitional" model stands in contrast to the later Athanasian view, where the Son's existence is a necessity of the Father's essence, a timeless and unchanging fact of being, which aligns with what is here termed a "fixed" view of eternity.

See: R.P.C. Hanson, *The Search for the Christian Doctrine of God: The Arian Controversy 318-381* (Edinburgh: T&T Clark, 1988), 191-198, 871-872.

## A. The Memra and Logos as Functional, Not Ontological Equals

In Aramaic Targums, the **Memra** (Word) appears regularly as the agent through whom YHWH acts—especially in creation, revelation, and covenant-making. Likewise, early Christians adopted **Logos** language to describe Yeshua as the one through whom the Father creates and speaks.

Crucially, however:

- **Neither tradition suggests the Memra/Logos is ontologically identical** to YHWH. Rather, the Memra/Logos **represents** YHWH—functionally divine, but always **derived**, always **subordinate**.
- This is evident in **John 1:3**, where "all things came into being through Him," and yet the Word is "with God" in a relational sense—not simply identical with God's essence in a Nicene manner.
- **No Targumic source or early apologist equates the Word with an unbegotten, co-equal Godhead.** Instead, the Word proceeds from God—sent, commissioned, begotten—not eternal alongside the Father in any abstract or metaphysical way.

Thus, from a monolatrous standpoint, the use of the Memra or Logos as God's creative agent was never intended to collapse the distinction between the one true God and His emissary. This makes the **dynamic model of eternity** a more faithful fit, where the begetting of the Son is a relational, volitional act—not a timeless ontological necessity.

## B. Wisdom as "The First of His Works"

The personification of **Wisdom** in **Proverbs 8** serves as another crucial witness to the early model of divine mediation.

1. **Wisdom as Pre-Creation Agent** Proverbs 8:22 reads, "YHWH created (or acquired) me as the beginning of His way, the first of His works of old." Whether we translate this as "created," "possessed," or "brought forth," the sense is unmistakable: Wisdom precedes all else but is still **established by God**.
2. **Relational, Not Ontological, Origin** Wisdom speaks: "I was brought forth" (vv. 24–25). The language is strikingly generative—expressing an act, not an eternal condition. This begetting precedes time but is still **a willful, relational initiation by God**, not an eternal co-existence.
3. **Early Christian Echoes** Church Fathers, including Origen, often linked this Wisdom with the Logos and the Son. But later metaphysical assumptions sometimes obscured the original implication: that this **Wisdom is first in order, not equal in essence.** The relational begetting becomes abstracted into a timeless state of shared being.

In the **dynamic model**, however, God's act of bringing forth Wisdom—or the Logos—is both relational and decisive. It reflects His creative intent without compromising His sovereignty or introducing any co-equal second deity.

Jewish monolatry and early Christian Monolatry both reflect a pattern: God acts through a **begotten, commissioned**, and **subordinate** agent—

whether called the Memra, Logos, or Wisdom. These figures are divine in role, not in essence. They mediate the Father's will without diluting His supremacy.

This framework makes no demand for timeless co-equality. Instead, it affirms that **God can beget and commission within eternity**, in ways that are relational, not temporal—and certainly not ontologically identical. This opens the door to a truly **dynamic eternity**, in which God acts decisively from eternity past, not by necessity but by volitional expression.[67]

## *"In the Beginning": Not the Beginning of Time?*

An essential point of confusion arises from the phrase "In the beginning" (Hebrew: *bereshit*) in Genesis 1:1. Commonly interpreted as the absolute start of time, this expression is often overlaid with fixed eternity assumptions. In such a reading, God exists in a changeless state until the temporal universe begins, and anything "begotten" must have either always existed or else be merely created in time.

Yet within a **dynamic eternity** perspective, "the beginning" can be read less as a timestamp and more as a title—one that refers to God's first

---

[67] The personification of Wisdom in Proverbs 8, particularly the language of being "brought forth" or "possessed" by Yahweh "at the beginning of His way," is central to the Second Temple understanding of divine mediation. Scholars affirm that this text depicts Wisdom as the first and highest of God's acts, subordinate to Him yet the agent through whom creation is ordered. This relational begetting, an act of divine will before time, serves as a crucial Old Testament precedent for the New Testament's Logos Christology.

See: Richard J. Clifford, *The Wisdom Literature, Interpreting Biblical Texts* (Nashville: Abingdon Press, 1998), 45-51.

relational act or principle. This opens the way for a more faithful and nuanced interpretation of both Genesis 1 and John 1.

## "Beginning" as Firstborn or Primary Agent

In dynamic readings, "beginning" aligns closely with concepts like "chief," "firstborn," or "foremost." Certain Jewish traditions interpret *bereshit* as "By means of the First [God created...]," understanding the "first" as God's chosen agent. This first principle is the divine Logos—the Word—who proceeds from God and functions as the foundation for all subsequent creation.

Thus, *Genesis 1:1* may not be marking the onset of linear time but rather referencing **God's first relational act**: the begetting of the Logos as mediator. This fits the ancient view that God's "first" act was not impersonal or abstract, but relational—the generation of the one through whom He would create all things.

## Creation Without Time

Accepting that created time itself begins with the cosmos, then "in the beginning" must refer to something *prior to time*—an act or identity not bounded by sequence, yet distinct from timeless stasis. This aligns perfectly with dynamic eternity: God begets the Logos as a genuine event—relational, volitional—outside of time, yet not reducible to eternal sameness.

Under the fixed model, "in the beginning" becomes merely symbolic—a pointer to a logical order within God's unchanging being. But in the dynamic model, it can be a **real act**—the Father expressing Himself by begetting the Logos as the first principle of creation, even before "time" exists.

**A More Coherent Reading of John 1**

This same dynamic insight illuminates **John 1:1–3**:

> "In the beginning was the Word, and the Word was with God, and the Word was God.
> He was in the beginning with God. All things came into being through Him..."

We often read this linearly, but the sequence is deeply theological:

*"In the beginning was the Word"* — This identifies the Word as the Beginning itself—*the principle through whom creation begins, just as Wisdom is described as "the beginning of [God's] works" in Proverbs 8:22.*

*"The Word was with God"* — This describes the pre-temporal relational distinction. Crucially, it establishes that the Logos is a distinct entity from the God He is with. This is not merely a statement that the Son is not the Father, a claim with which a Trinitarian would agree. It is a more fundamental distinction: the Logos is not the very God whom He was with. *This preserves a clear hierarchy between the unbegotten God and His begotten Word.*

*"The Word was God"* — *A statement of divine status, expressing that the Logos participates in the divine nature as God's derived, mediating agent, but not as the unbegotten God He is "with."*

## MONOLATRY

Only *after* these theological realities are affirmed do we hear:

*"All things came into being through Him."*

This sequence makes clear that the Logos already exists with God—already divine in function—**before** creation begins. And so, the second reference—"He was in the beginning with God"—takes on a temporal nuance, while the first—"In the beginning was the Word"—is better understood as **identifying** the Beginning as the Logos Himself.

In this sense, John's Gospel may be echoing Genesis not only by referencing *when* God created, but by clarifying **through whom** God created. The "Beginning" is not a point in time—it is the **person of the Logos**. Creation unfolds through this first divine act: God's begetting of His Word.

This fits naturally within the dynamic eternity framework. The begetting of the Son is not an unchanging metaphysical state, but a volitional, relational expression of the Father's will—**an act that precedes time but still happens**, in the truest theological sense.[68]

---

[68] The interpretation of "the beginning" (*arche* in Greek) in John 1:1 as referring not just to a temporal start but to the *person* of the Logos was a significant theme in early Christian exegesis. **Origen, in his first homily on Genesis, makes this connection explicit. When commenting on Genesis 1:1, he asks, "What is the beginning of all things except our Lord and 'Savior of all,' Jesus Christ, 'the firstborn of every creature'? In this beginning, therefore, that is, in his Word, 'God made heaven and earth.'"** This reading has deep roots in Jewish interpretive traditions where Genesis 1:1 (*bereshit*) was sometimes understood as "by means of the First/Beginning," with "the Beginning" being a divine agent like Wisdom. This very interpretation later became a point of contention in the "Two Powers in Heaven" controversy, as rabbinic authorities saw it as a dangerous theological move that supported the Christian claim of a second, divine figure alongside God.

## *Why the Dynamic View Suits the Earlier Framework*

Having examined how biblical and Second Temple texts present creation, wisdom, and the divine Word, we now ask: why does a dynamic view of eternity—and not a fixed one—best match the theological assumptions of early Jewish and Christian monolatry?

**1. Harmony with Jewish Monolatry**

Early Jewish thought—especially as reflected in the Targums, apocalyptic literature, and Philo—consistently affirmed that YHWH alone is supreme, yet allowed for divine agents who executed His will. Angels, the Memra, and Wisdom were all exalted figures, but none were ever regarded as ontologically identical to the Most High. In this context, the Son can be dynamically begotten without violating monolatry. A subordinate divine agent acting at the behest of the supreme God was familiar and acceptable. The idea that the Son could be "the firstborn of all creation" (Colossians 1:15) or "the beginning of God's creation" (Revelation 3:14) fits comfortably in this worldview.

**2. Consistency with Second Temple Texts**

Second Temple writings such as 1 Enoch or the Wisdom of Solomon depict divine intermediaries who serve on God's behalf with tremendous authority, yet never share His ontological uniqueness. Philo's Logos theology illustrates how the Word is God's instrument, radiating divine reason but not co-equal in essence. These works do not present the Logos or Wisdom as co-eternal "persons" in the later Trinitarian sense.

---

*For Origen's exegesis, see: Origen, Homilies on Genesis and Exodus, trans. Ronald E. Heine, The Fathers of the Church, vol. 71 (Washington, DC: The Catholic University of America Press, 1982), 47. For the Jewish background of the Logos as the "Beginning," see: Daniel Boyarin, "The Gospel of the Memra: Jewish Binitarianism and the Prologue to John," Harvard Theological Review 94, no. 3 (2001): 258-262.*

Instead, they emphasize derived origin, functional subordination, and divine commission—elements best explained by a dynamic view of divine relationship.

### 3. Biblical Allusions to Real Events

Scripture is filled with references to divine action, relational developments, and new initiatives—covenants, callings, anointings, even begettings. God speaks, acts, creates, chooses, and reveals in sequence. Though these acts originate from the eternal, transcendent God, they are consistently described as **real events**, not timeless states. This includes the Son's begetting, enthronement, or being sent. The dynamic framework accommodates this language naturally, allowing divine acts to occur outside chronological time yet remain genuine expressions of God's will.

### 4. Clarifies Historical Theological Disputes

The Arian and Semi-Arian resistance to Nicene co-equality was not born from ignorance but from a different metaphysical framework. They understood generation as a real, willed event—a relational act between Father and Son. By contrast, Nicene defenders approached the question through the lens of fixed eternity, where the Son's generation was not an event but an unchanging state of being. These two models speak past one another because they are rooted in different assumptions. Recognizing this allows us to make better sense of why the debates persisted and why both sides saw themselves as defending orthodoxy.

### Time in the New Creation: A Final Witness to Dynamic Eternity

Some theologians insist that "eternity" must be timeless—that once creation ends, history dissolves into an unchanging present. But Scripture does not support this view. Instead, the Bible affirms a continuing reality that unfolds from age to age, even into the new creation. The biblical vision is not of a motionless eternity but of ongoing divine rulership through structured time, both now and in what is to come.

### 1. A New Creation Means a New Timeline

Scripture does not teach that the eternal realm is timeless and unchanging. Instead, it teaches that the current heaven and earth will be destroyed, and a new heaven and new earth will be created:

> *"Then I saw a new heaven and a new earth; for the first heaven and the first earth passed away..."* (Revelation 21:1, LSB)

> *"But according to His promise we are looking for new heavens and a new earth, in which righteousness dwells."* (2 Peter 3:13, LSB)

> *"For behold, I am creating new heavens and a new earth; and the former things will not be remembered or come upon the heart."* (Isaiah 65:17, LSB)

The language is explicit: the old creation passes away. In cosmic terms, the current timeline ends, and a new one begins. This is not a reformatting of the same world; it is a new platform of existence, a new age with new structure, order, and perception.

### 2. Time Exists in the New Creation

Even within the New Jerusalem, measurable time continues. The clearest evidence appears in the final chapter of Revelation:

> *"...On either side of the river was the tree of life, bearing twelve kinds of fruit, yielding its fruit every month..."* (Revelation 22:2, LSB)

This detail is critical. The tree of life produces fruit "every month"—a term that only has meaning in relation to temporal sequence. The twelvefold cycle echoes the twelve months of Israel's calendar, showing that duration and rhythm persist in redeemed creation. Time is not abolished—it is made anew.[69]

### 3. From Age to Age — Two Timelines in View

*The Bible repeatedly speaks of God reigning from age to age:*
*"Your kingdom is an everlasting kingdom, and Your dominion endures throughout all generations." (Psalm 145:13, LSB)*

*"But You are the same, and Your years will not come to an end." (Psalm 102:27, LSB)*

These verses do not eliminate time—they declare that God remains unchanged across the transitions between ages. In other words, He is not bound by any timeline, but acts within each as He wills. The old timeline ends; the new begins. But YHWH remains supreme, active, and consistent across both.

From the perspective of those within the new heaven and earth, the prior age will have "passed away." It will be like a deleted world—its timeline closed. But from God's perspective, these successive ages are expressions of His ongoing will. He acts in one age, then acts again in the next. The static model cannot accommodate this. But dynamic eternity explains it: God causes real change without being changed, initiating new creations while remaining eternally Himself.

From the standpoint of someone living within the new creation, the previous creation no longer exists. And yet, it once did. The paradox arises for those holding to static eternity within the new creation: if the new

---

[69] The depiction of the tree of life yielding fruit "every month" in Revelation 22:2 is a significant detail for eschatology. Scholars of Revelation note that this language implies a continuation of sequence and ordered time, even in the eternal state. This biblical vision stands in contrast to later philosophical concepts of a purely static, timeless eternity, suggesting instead a renewed and redeemed temporality.

See: *G.K. Beale, The Book of Revelation: A Commentary on the Greek Text, New International Greek Testament Commentary (Grand Rapids, MI: Eerdmans, 1999), 1104-1105.*

creation is considered current time, then how could something (the old creation) truly have existed and cease to exist before the new temporal state began? In a static model, what is not present in the current temporal state must either have never existed or be eternally present. But this is contradicted by Scripture:

> *"Therefore if anyone is in Christ, he is a new creation; the old things passed away; behold, new things have come." (2 Corinthians 5:17, LSB)*

And again:

> *"Behold, I am making all things new." (Revelation 21:5, LSB)*

These are not just moral or personal renewals; they are cosmological declarations. The **old creation**, and with it its **time**, has **passed away**. **All things** includes **the structure of time itself**, which will be recreated in a new form. Static eternity cannot account for this transition. But in a dynamic eternity, **God is not bound by the sequence of ages**. He can begin and end timelines, establish one, close it, and initiate another—all while remaining consistent and unchanged in essence. This provides the only coherent explanation for how something could truly exist, end, and then no longer be found within the experience of a new age.

Dynamic eternity explains how God can act across ages, and why the inhabitants of the new creation experience true novelty, not illusion. Eternity is not a still frame but the theater of God's volitional acts, through which He renews, judges, and redeems.

### 4. Eternal, Yet Active — Not Frozen

Static eternity forces a dilemma: if something is "eternal," it must be unchanging. But that view misunderstands the biblical concept of eternity, which includes:

- Unchanging nature (God remains Himself),
- Unfolding initiative (God acts in stages),

- Sequential purpose (God works "from age to age").

Eternity is not the absence of time, but the divine transcendence of time. God is not trapped in one timeline. He creates them, sustains them, and ends them—without becoming temporal Himself.

Thus, the Father does not enter time, because to do so would make Him subject to it. Instead, He begets an Agent—the Son—who can enter creation, act within time, and represent the Eternal One to both men and angels.

**Crossing the Ages with the Begotten Son**

If time is structured in ages—each beginning and ending by the will of the Father—then only those who transcend time can move from one age to the next. Scripture reveals that Yeshua is begotten in eternity, not created in time. He is the firstborn of all creation, the one who existed with God before all ages, and the one through whom new creation begins.

This gives Him a unique ability: He can move across the ages. He was present in the old creation, entered into it through incarnation, and rose beyond it into the age to come. He is the bridge—the Ark—between the worlds.

**The Body of Christ as the Vehicle of Transition**

Those united to Him—who become His body, His bride, one flesh with Him—do not simply admire Him from afar. They are drawn into His eternal identity. Just as Noah's family entered the Ark and passed from one world into another, those in Messiah pass through the judgment of the old world and emerge into the new.

- He is the Ark — preserving the elect through divine judgment.
- He is the Red Sea path — opening a way between realities where none existed.
- He is the firstborn — and those who are His become part of that new humanity, fit for the world to come.

This is the mystery of union: "the two shall become one flesh." In communion, we symbolically partake of His body. But in resurrection, we are literally conformed to His likeness—no longer subject to sin, no longer bound to the dying world. Our identity is recast in Him, so that we might inhabit the age that is coming.

**Why This Matters for Dynamic Eternity**

Only if eternity is dynamic—capable of holding real action, transition, and begetting—can this vision make sense. If all is fixed, then no one moves. No one changes. No redemption occurs. But if eternity is the realm of divine initiative, then the Father can beget the Son, the Son can enter creation, and those in Him can be brought through the end of the age into a new heavens and new earth.

This is the hope of monolatrous faith:

- One God, supreme and unchanging,
- One Son, begotten and sent,
- One body, gathered from every nation,
- One new creation, prepared for those who love Him.

The current creation is like a sinking ship. But the Ark has already been prepared. The journey through the Red Sea has already begun. And the age to come awaits those who are in the Son—begotten from before the ages, alive forevermore.

# Conclusion

## A. Unifying Creation, Begetting, and Covenant

From Genesis to John, and from Proverbs to the early apologists, one theme remains consistent: God acts dynamically. He creates, speaks, chooses, covenants, and begets—not from necessity or unchanging abstraction, but from volitional love and purpose. The earliest frameworks for understanding the Logos or Memra never assumed that this agent was co-equal in being or indistinct in authority from the Father. Rather, Scripture and early tradition affirm that God brings forth a mediator—exalted, divine in function, but always subordinate in origin. In this, creation, begetting, and covenant all express God's freedom to act, not merely to manifest what has always been.

### B. Clarifying the Two Worldviews

We now see clearly the difference between the two lenses:

- Those who read eternity as **fixed** tend to flatten biblical events into metaphysical states. In this model, "begetting" becomes an eternal relation, never truly willed or initiated—thus necessitating co-equality.
- Those who affirm a **dynamic eternity** allow God to be eternally changeless in character yet genuinely capable of initiating new realities—begetting a Son, creating a world, establishing a covenant.

This distinction does not just explain divergent theological paths—it exposes the fundamental assumptions that created them.

### C. Affirming the Dynamic as the Early Monolatrous Lens

Early Jewish and Christian writers consistently held that:

- The Father alone is unbegotten, supreme, and the sole source of divine authority.
- The Word or Wisdom is divine because it comes from God—not because it is God's peer.
- Honor of the Son, when offered, is always ordered through and toward the Father, never as a second, co-equal deity.

This view affirms that the Son is "from God" in a real, relational, and event-like sense—not as an eternal abstraction. The Word is begotten—not from necessity, but from divine initiative. And just as God covenants, creates, and acts in Scripture, so too He begets in eternity—an act full of intention, meaning, and hierarchy.

**D. Looking Ahead**

In the chapters to come, we will explore how this dynamic view of eternity clashed with emerging theological trends in the fourth century. As church leaders sought to protect divine unity, they sometimes redefined generation into timeless sameness. The resulting creeds aimed to secure orthodoxy—but often at the cost of earlier nuance.

Understanding dynamic eternity does not merely correct a philosophical misstep. It reconnects us to a profoundly biblical and Jewish way of thinking about God—a God who is transcendent, yes, but also relational; who is immutable in essence, yet freely initiates; who begets the Son not as a static reflection but as a living expression of His will.

This is the foundation upon which the rest of this theological journey will build.

To understand how this shift occurred, we must now turn to the fourth-century crisis, where eternity was redefined, and divine hierarchy was flattened under the pressure of metaphysical abstraction.

# 19

# The Road to Nicaea (325 A.D.) Revisited with Balancing Perspectives

In the previous chapters, we have traced the development of what we now recognize as Christian Monolatry through the Old Testament, Second Temple Judaism, and into early Christianity. The consistent theme has been the understanding that the Father alone is the unbegotten God, and that the Son, identified with the Logos or Memra, is a subordinate yet exalted agent. This tradition maintained that while the Son was divine, He functioned as God's intermediary in creation and revelation, always under the authority of the Father.

However, by the time we arrive at the early fourth century, a seismic shift occurred with the theological challenge of Arius. What was once a stable framework for understanding the relationship between Father and Son was now being questioned in new ways. Arius's theology introduced ideas that would significantly disrupt the Christian Monolatrous tradition and spark a theological crisis that demanded resolution.

In this chapter, we will not simply recount the rise of Nicene orthodoxy. Instead, we seek to explore the novel challenge presented at Nicaea—the introduction of a completely new concept regarding the nature of the Son. While the early church had clearly maintained a subordinationist framework, Arius introduced a theory that shifted the focus from the Father's ultimate authority to an idea that conflated the divine with the created order in ways that the early church had not allowed. What became apparent in the aftermath of Arius's teachings was that the controversy wasn't just about the relationship between Father and Son; it was about redefining the very nature of Messiah—not as an intermediary agent of God, but as God Himself, co-equal and co-eternal.

## *Arius: Continuity with Christian Monolatry, but One Major Oversight*

Arius's theological framework was firmly rooted in the Christian Monolatrous tradition. His basic assertion—that the Son was divine, yet distinct and subordinate to the unbegotten Father—was consistent with the thinking of previous church fathers, including the Apostolic Fathers and the Apologists. The early church had always maintained a clear hierarchy, where God the Father held the supreme position, and the Son, though fully divine, acted as God's agent. This view was in line with the biblical narrative and the long-standing interpretation of Christ's relationship to the Father.

The Apologists—such as Justin Martyr, Tertullian, and Athenagoras—had all affirmed that the Father was the singular, ultimate God. They viewed the Son as pre-existent, co-eternal with the Father in a subordinate yet divine role. This framework allowed them to affirm both the unity and the distinctiveness of the divine persons without violating the biblical principle of exclusive worship. The Father alone was unbegotten and uncaused; the Son, though begotten before time, derived His divinity from the will of the

Father.

Arius, therefore, was not introducing a radically new framework; he was, in fact, continuing a tradition of subordinationism that had deep roots in Christian Monolatry. The novel aspect of his theology, however, lay in the way he articulated the Son's relationship to the Father and the specific claim he made about the Son's origin. In this way, Arius can be seen as one of the voice in the stream of Christian Monolatry—although his specific mistaken formulation of the Son's temporal origin would ultimately trigger the very metaphysical shift that displaced the tradition he was attempting to preserve.[70]

## *The Crucial Turn at Nicaea: From Dynamic Begetting to Static Ontology*

The Council of Nicaea was not merely a debate over Christological terminology—it marked a turning point in how divine eternity itself was understood. Beneath the doctrinal conflict lay two opposing conceptions of how God relates within Himself: one dynamic and relational, the other static and ontological. The Nicene formulation would ultimately solidify a metaphysical shift away from the earlier, volitional model of divine

---

[70] While Arius is often cast as a radical innovator, his core subordinationist framework was consistent with much of the pre-Nicene tradition. His crucial—and ultimately heretical—move was to insist that the Son's begetting implied a temporal beginning ("there was a time when He was not"), thereby making the Son a creature, albeit the highest of all creatures. This distinguished him from earlier theologians like Origen, who had argued for an *eternal* but still subordinate begetting.

See: Maurice F. Wiles, *Archetypal Heresy: Arianism through the Centuries* (Oxford: Oxford University Press, 1996), 25-48.

begetting toward a fixed conception of eternal relations.

This section will explore how the logic of *homoousios* gradually displaced the dynamic framework, reinterpreting the Son's begetting not as a divine act of eternal will but as a necessary state of eternal sameness. While the council's original intent may have been to safeguard the Son's divine status, the language it adopted obscured the relational hierarchy and eternal initiative so central to the earlier Christian Monolatrous tradition.

## Reframing the Controversy: Dynamic Eternity in Question

What was at stake at Nicaea was not merely whether the Son was "truly divine," but *how* that divinity was understood—*as derived through a dynamic, eternal act of the Father's will*, or *as an unchanging co-possessor of divine essence from all eternity*. The former aligned with dynamic eternity, where the begetting of the Son is a real, volitional act within God's eternal life. The latter reflected the emerging fixed eternity model, which eliminated all distinction of origin and function within the Godhead.

Arius erred by placing the Son within time, but his instinct—that the Son's begetting was a real act of the Father—was closer to the earlier dynamic framework. His failure was not in maintaining derivation, but in denying that the Father's act could be truly eternal without being temporal. By contrast, his opponents insisted on the Son's eternal nature but often did so by importing a metaphysical framework that denied the very possibility of dynamic eternal action.

## The Error of Arius: Misunderstanding Dynamic Eternity

Arius argued that:

- The Son was begotten, and thus had an origin.
- Therefore, there was a time when He was not.
- Only the Father is unbegotten and fully God in essence.

This view attempted to preserve monolatry but misunderstood how divine action could occur within eternity. By collapsing "eternal" into "temporal," Arius forced a false choice: either the Son always existed as an unbegotten equal, or He came into being in time as a creature. Arius chose the latter, rejecting fixed eternity but also failing to grasp the possibility of **dynamic eternity**—in which the Father can eternally beget the Son without implying a temporal beginning.

From the dynamic framework, the Son's begetting is not a process bound by time but a real, volitional expression of the Father's will. It happens "before all ages," but it still *happens*. It is not an eternal state of mutual essence, but a relational event within God's eternal life. Arius's failure was in denying this eternal act; yet his opponents, in affirming the Son's co-eternity, often obscured that this generation was truly *from* the Father.

**Nicaea's Response: Preserving Divinity, Flattening Distinction**

The Nicene solution—*homoousios*, or "of the same essence"—sought to correct Arius's error by affirming the Son's full divinity. Yet it did so by redefining divine generation in terms of shared substance rather than dynamic will. This marked a crucial departure:

- In Christian Monolatry, the Father begets the Son as an eternal act of will. The Son is divine by derivation.
- In Nicene metaphysics, the Son is of the same essence by necessity. Begetting becomes a metaphor for ontological sameness.

This change was subtle but profound. It signaled a shift from **dynamic relationality** to **static co-equality**, undermining the Father's monarchy as the sole fountain of divinity. Begetting ceased to be an eternal act and became a timeless condition—a "relation of origin" in name only, not in real expression.

### The Role of Philosophical Assumptions

Underlying this shift was a broader change in how eternity itself was imagined. Under dynamic eternity, God's internal life includes real acts: the begetting of the Son, the procession of the Spirit, the creation of the world. These acts are eternal, yet relational and willed. Under fixed eternity, by contrast, all divine relations must be statically present from all eternity as logical necessities.

This fixed model, drawn from Greek metaphysics, viewed change—even eternal initiative—as incompatible with divine perfection. To act was to imply need or development. Thus, the dynamic view of the Father choosing to beget the Son out of love was reinterpreted as a timeless relation of sameness. This redefinition, though unintentional by many council participants, would reshape Christian theology in the centuries to come.

### The Real Crisis—Eternity Itself

The real novelty at Nicaea was not the rejection of Arianism, but the redefinition of divine eternity in static terms. The biblical vision of a relational God, who begets, creates, and sends from eternity—not out of necessity but from volitional fullness—was eclipsed by a model that made eternal generation indistinguishable from eternal sameness.

Though some, like Eusebius, tried to preserve the older relational vision within the language of *homoousios*, the direction of post-Nicene theology would gradually close that door. What was once a dynamic, hierarchical framework rooted in Christian Monolatry began to give way to a static metaphysical model, built not on relational acts but on shared essence.

The Council of Nicaea, then, represents a decisive moment: not just in Christology, but in the Christian understanding of God's eternal life. It is the point at which dynamic eternity began to be overwritten—where divine relationship ceased to be an act and became an assumption, and where the monarchy of the Father was obscured in favor of abstract co-equality.

## *The Council's Agenda: Harmony, Not a Single Perspective*

The Council of Nicaea was convened in 325 A.D. under the patronage of Emperor Constantine—not primarily to resolve a theological puzzle, but to secure unity within a rapidly expanding and politically significant church. While the doctrinal crisis concerning the Son's nature was real, the deeper urgency was ecclesiastical and imperial: the fragmentation of Christian belief threatened the cohesion of both Church and empire.

Against this backdrop, the council's outcome was not a uniform imposition of fixed metaphysical doctrine, but a compromise—a theological middle ground negotiated by bishops who held divergent understandings of divine eternity, begetting, and authority. For many, the Nicene Creed provided a way to affirm the Son's divinity without fully relinquishing the dynamic relationality that had long defined the Christian Monolatrous tradition.

**Constantine's Role: Unity Over Clarity**

Emperor Constantine's interest in the Arian controversy was pragmatic. Recently converted and seeking to use Christianity as a unifying force, Constantine saw the ongoing disputes over the Son's nature as a threat to political stability. His goal was to forge a consensus, not to arbitrate theological nuance.

To achieve this, Constantine pushed for the inclusion of the term *homoousios*—"of the same essence"—believing it would silence division by affirming the Son's full divinity. However, he lacked the theological background to grasp the implications of that term, which had long been avoided by many bishops due to its associations with Sabellianism.[71]

---

[71] The term *homoousios* was not a biblical word, and its history made many bishops at the council deeply uncomfortable. The respected patristic scholar Christopher Stead, in his exhaustive study *Divine Substance*, traces the term's origins and demonstrates that it appears to have been introduced into theological discourse by second-century Gnostic Christians. Stead notes that the word is found in summaries of Gnostic teaching by Irenaeus and is attributed to the Gnostic teacher Ptolemy. He concludes that before its use by Christian theologians, "there is no trace at all of its existence" in pagan writers before Plotinus.

Crucially, Stead argues that its original meaning was simply "made of the same kind of stuff," often in a physical sense, and it was **not** originally used to express the Christian theology of the Trinity. For this reason, the term was viewed with suspicion and largely avoided by orthodox writers for over a century. Its sudden promotion by the Emperor at Nicaea was therefore seen by many as the introduction of a suspicious, non-scriptural, and philosophically loaded term into the creed.

See: *Christopher Stead, Divine Substance (Oxford: Clarendon Press, 1977), 190-191.*

Constantine was not motivated by a metaphysical agenda. He simply wanted peace in the Church. Ironically, the term he advocated would ignite decades of new debate, precisely because it was interpreted through different metaphysical lenses—some fixed, others dynamic.[72]

## A Diverse Assembly: Bishops with Different Ontologies

The bishops gathered at Nicaea were not of one mind. Many had emerged from a theological world where the Father was unquestionably the source of all divinity, and the Son, though eternally begotten, was begotten *from* the Father through a divine act of will. This preserved both the Son's exalted status and the Father's unshared supremacy.

These bishops—some now called Semi-Arian, others simply subordinationist—did not oppose affirming the Son's divinity. What they resisted was any formulation that erased the eternal relational structure that undergirded Christian Monolatry. For them:

- The Father alone is unbegotten.
- The Son is divine because He is begotten—not as a logical corollary, but by the Father's volitional, eternal act.
- Eternal begetting does not mean eternal sameness; it means relational

---

[72] Historians widely agree that Emperor Constantine's primary motivation for convening the Council of Nicaea was to secure political and ecclesiastical unity, not to settle fine points of theology, which he barely understood. His promotion of the term *homoousios* was a pragmatic move aimed at ending the debate. Ironically, the term itself, being non-scriptural and previously associated with the heresy of Sabellianism, ignited decades of further controversy.

See: Richard Rubenstein, *When Jesus Became God: The Struggle and Conflict over the Origins of Christianity in the Fourth Century* (New York: Harcourt Brace, 1999), 57-82.

derivation.

They were thus cautious about *homoousios*, fearing it implied a flattening of divine relations into metaphysical sameness. Yet after clarifications—particularly from Constantine and Eusebius of Caesarea—that the term was not meant to erase hierarchy or suggest modalism, many bishops accepted it as a safeguard against Arian reductionism, not a denial of the Father's monarchy.

**The Nicene Creed Through the Eyes of Eusebius**

The Nicene Creed of 325 A.D. is often presented as the definitive triumph of Trinitarian orthodoxy. However, a closer look at the historical context, guided by the eyewitness account of one of its most influential architects, Eusebius of Caesarea, reveals a profoundly different story. Was the Creed, as originally understood by its signatories, a declaration of a co-equal trinity, or was it a document that affirmed a hierarchical, monolatrous faith? Eusebius, a respected bishop who was initially a supporter of Arius, wrote a letter to his own church immediately after the council to explain what had happened and what the Creed meant, so that rumors and misrepresentations would not precede him. His account provides an invaluable window into how a key participant understood the council's decisions.

**One God, the Father Almighty**

The Creed begins with an unambiguous declaration that aligns perfectly with the monolatrous framework: **"We believe in one God, the Father Almighty."** This is a critical starting point. In a later Trinitarian creed, the "one God" would be identified as a multi-personal being. Here, in the original formulation of 325 A.D., the "one God" is explicitly and singularly identified as "the Father." The Creed then introduces a second figure, the "one Lord, Jesus Christ," as distinct from the one God.

**The Emperor and the Word *Homoousios***

According to Eusebius's letter, he first presented his own church's traditional creed, which was approved by Emperor Constantine and the council as "good and unexceptional." However, the Emperor then urged the addition of the single, non-biblical Greek word *homoousios* ("of one substance" or "one in essence").

This term caused significant concern among Eusebius and other bishops. They did not let it pass without inquiry and demanded clarification. Eusebius records the official explanation they were given, which convinced them to sign. The term did **not** mean:

*That the Son was a physical "part" of the Father, as if the Father's essence could be divided or severed.*

*That the Son and the Father were the same single person or being, which would be the heresy of Sabellianism.*

Instead, Eusebius explains that they accepted the term with the understanding that it meant the Son is truly *from* the Father and shares His divine nature (**like begets like**), bearing "no resemblance to the created creatures." It distinguishes the Son from all things that were *made*.

**The Anathemas: A Rejection of Strict Arianism**

The curses at the end of the Creed were aimed at the specific tenets of Arianism that the subordinationists like Eusebius also rejected. The Creed condemns those who say:

*"There was a time when he was not".*

*"Before being born he was not".*

*He came into existence "out of nothing".*

As Eusebius understood it, these curses rightly condemned the view that the Son was a temporal creature. He and others could agree to them because they believed the Son was eternally begotten *from* the Father's being, not created *in time from nothing*.

**The Silence on the Holy Spirit**

A final, crucial piece of evidence is the Creed's statement on the Holy Spirit. A Trinitarian document would define the Spirit's co-equal divinity. Instead, the Creed of 325 simply states, **"And in the Holy Spirit."** This minimalist affirmation does nothing to establish the Spirit as a co-equal person of a Trinity. The document is, at best, a statement about the Father and the Son, and even then, it affirms their relationship as hierarchical.

**Conclusion**

Based on the primary source testimony of Eusebius, the Nicene Creed of 325 A.D. was not the victory for Trinitarianism it is often claimed to be. It was a victory for the semi-Arian, or monolatrous, position. It successfully refuted the idea that the Son was a mere creature while carefully preserving the Father as the "one God Almighty" and the Son as His uniquely begotten, divine, but subordinate Lord.

**Interpreting Homoousios Dynamically**

For many signatories, *homoousios* was accepted not as a definitive metaphysical claim, but as a flexible affirmation of the Son's true divinity. Understood dynamically, the term could mean:

- The Son shares fully in divine nature, *because* He is begotten by the Father—not a lesser being, but one who receives divinity through eternal derivation.
- This begetting is eternal, yes—but it is also relational and volitional, not an abstract metaphysical necessity.
- The Father remains the sole source and fountainhead of divinity—the one "true God" (John 17:3)—while the Son reflects and embodies that divinity as His eternal emissary.

This interpretation preserved the framework of dynamic eternity, allowing for a divine hierarchy without denying the Son's divine status. It was a way to affirm the Logos as truly divine—without collapsing Him into the same ontological plane as the Father.[73]

## A Creed That Left Room for Monolatry

The Nicene Creed, then, did not immediately erase the dynamic model. For

---

[73] The account of Eusebius of Caesarea's own acceptance of the Creed is the primary evidence for this "dynamic" interpretation. He and many other bishops were deeply suspicious of *homoousios*, fearing it implied a Sabellian confusion of persons or a physical division of the Father's substance. They only consented after being reassured that the term was not meant to deny the Son's distinct personal existence or the Father's unique status as the unbegotten source. For them, "of one substance" meant the Son was truly *from* the Father's nature and not a creature, preserving a subordination of origin.

See: R.P.C. Hanson, *The Search for the Christian Doctrine of God: The Arian Controversy 318-381* (Edinburgh: T&T Clark, 1988), 163-172 a time, it functioned as a broad theological tent—room enough for both those leaning toward static co-equality and those maintaining a hierarchical, volitional framework. In fact, the lack of clarity on the Holy Spirit, and the minimal use of ontological language beyond *homoousios*, suggests that the creed was not the triumph of a metaphysical system, but a truce brokered amid theological diversity.

That truce, however, was fragile. While *Christian Monolatry* could still be articulated within the creed's language, later interpretations—especially those emphasizing fixed, immutable essence—would eventually dominate, marginalizing those who continued to affirm the dynamic view of divine relationship and causality.

## A Temporary Compromise, Not a Final Resolution

The Council of Nicaea must be understood not as a clean resolution of doctrinal tension, but as a transitional moment. It attempted to address a Christological question without first resolving a deeper metaphysical one. Beneath the debate over the Son's nature lay a more fundamental divide: between a **dynamic eternity**, in which God begets, sends, and acts with volitional freedom—and a **fixed eternity**, in which divine relations are reduced to timeless necessities.

For many bishops at Nicaea, the creed was acceptable so long as it preserved the monarchy of the Father and allowed the begetting of the Son to remain a true act—one that affirmed relational order without temporal sequence. In that sense, Nicaea did not yet close the door on Christian Monolatry. But the seeds of a metaphysical shift had been planted, and the decades to follow would determine which vision of eternity—dynamic and relational, or static and indivisible—would prevail.

## Focus on Christology, Less on the Holy Spirit

The Council of Nicaea gave detailed attention to the nature and origin of the Son, yet offered only a minimal reference to the Holy Spirit: "And in the Holy Spirit." This omission has often been treated as a gap to be filled by later Trinitarian creeds. However, from the perspective of **Christian Monolatry and dynamic eternity**, this restraint reveals a theological continuity with earlier biblical and patristic thinking—particularly as seen in the writings of **Eusebius of Caesarea**.

At this stage in doctrinal development, the Church was still thinking in terms of **ordered relationship and volitional causality**, not static co-equality. The Father was acknowledged as the uncaused source; the Son as the eternally begotten mediator; and the Spirit as the **ministering agent** who proceeds not directly as a third coequal person, but **from the Father through the Son**, subordinate in origin, role, and purpose.

### Christological Priority, Not Trinitarian Consensus

The central controversy at Nicaea was about the Son: whether He was a created being (as Arius claimed) or begotten before time and thus divine in origin. The Holy Spirit was not yet a doctrinal focal point because **the conceptual framework was not Trinitarian but hierarchically dyadic**, with the Spirit understood in functional and relational terms.

This silence was not a flaw—it reflected a coherent theological structure still preserved by many bishops. In this structure, the Spirit was personal, holy, and active, but not coequal with the Son or the Father. He did not require metaphysical explanation because He was not yet conceived as ontologically divine.

## Eusebius on the Spirit: Subordinate to the Son

Eusebius of Caesarea, the most prominent theological voice at Nicaea, offers the clearest articulation of this early view. In *On Ecclesiastical Theology*, he affirms:

- The Holy Spirit **proceeds from the Son**, and is **ministered by Him** in the divine economy.
- The Spirit is "not another god beside the Father and the Son," but a **ministering presence** who acts **at the Son's direction**.
- The Spirit is "the minister of [the Son's] works," subordinate in **order**, **authority**, and **origin**.

This view affirms both **personal agency** and **relational subordination**: the Spirit is not a mere impersonal force, but neither is He a coequal member of a divine triad. Instead, He functions within an eternal order of mediation, where divine action flows **from the Father, through the Son, by the Spirit**.[74]

---

[74] The Nicene Creed of 325 offers only a bare affirmation, "And in the Holy Spirit." As R.P.C. Hanson notes, this reflects the fact that the theology of the Holy Spirit was not a central point of the Arian controversy and remained largely undeveloped. The prevailing view among theologians like Eusebius was that the Spirit was a distinct but subordinate agent, ministered by the Son, and ranked third in the divine hierarchy. The Creed's brevity is not an oversight, but a reflection of the Church's pre-Trinitarian, hierarchical consensus at the time.
See: R.P.C. Hanson, *The Search for the Christian Doctrine of God*, 751-754.

## Dynamic Eternity and the Spirit's Role

In the model of **dynamic eternity**, the Spirit is eternally operative—not as a timeless equal, but as a **willed participant** in the divine mission:

- The Father initiates all things from His transcendent will.
- The Son, as "the Beginning" (arche), mediates all divine expression—including creation, revelation, and redemption.
- The Spirit proceeds as the **personal envoy of divine presence**, empowered by the Son, and active in the world.

This order is not temporal but **relational**. It reflects the eternal flow of divine purpose—without collapsing into metaphysical abstraction or fixed consubstantiality. The Spirit's role is real and pre-temporal, yet entirely **dependent on the will of the Father and the mediation of the Son**.

## Personal, Relational, and Subordinate

This view of the Holy Spirit, reflected in both Scripture and Eusebius, affirms that:

- The Spirit **personal in function**.
- He is **not begotten** like the Son, nor uncaused like the Father.
- He is **never worshiped, never addressed as "God"**, and **never depicted as initiating divine action**.
- He is the **Spirit of the Son**, proceeding at His direction, carrying out

the will of the Father in creation, sanctification, and glorification.

This aligns perfectly with the model of Christian Monolatry. The Spirit does not compete for divine status; rather, He enacts divine will. He glorifies the Son (John 16:14), who in turn glorifies the Father (John 17:1). He speaks, teaches, intercedes, and sanctifies—but always as **a dependent and obedient agent**.

**Preserved Order, Not Undeveloped Doctrine**

The Nicene Creed's brevity regarding the Spirit is not the result of theological immaturity, but of **doctrinal restraint consistent with a relational and volitional divine order**. In the framework of dynamic eternity, there was no theological pressure to define the Spirit as a third coequal person, because:

- The Father was already understood as the one true God.
- The Son was acknowledged as the begotten mediator of all divine action.
- The Spirit functioned within this ordered structure—not as a peer, but as an emissary.

Eusebius affirms what Nicaea leaves implicit: that the Spirit is **subordinate to the Son**, even as the Son is subordinate to the Father. This is not a diminishing of the Spirit's agency—it is a preservation of **divine order** and **monolatrous integrity**.

In later centuries, this framework would be eclipsed by the metaphysics of fixed eternity and coequal persons. But at Nicaea, and in Eusebius's theology, the Church still operated within the dynamic structure of Christian Monolatry. Here, the Spirit remains a living, personal, and holy presence—but eternally present in the outflow of God's will, **from the Father, through the Son, and by the Spirit.**

## Conclusion: A Balanced Step, Not a Final Settlement

The Council of Nicaea represents a decisive but transitional moment in the development of Christian doctrine. While often hailed as the cornerstone of Trinitarian orthodoxy, the council itself did not produce a full metaphysical system, nor did it resolve the underlying questions about divine eternity, hierarchy, and mediation. Instead, it issued a carefully worded creed that preserved theological ambiguity—allowing diverse views to coexist under a shared confession of the Son's divinity.

From the standpoint of **Christian Monolatry** and **dynamic eternity**, Nicaea did not close the door on relational theology. Rather, it preserved a space for those who affirmed:

- The **Father alone as uncaused and supreme,**
- The **Son as begotten—not created—but subordinate**, and
- The **Spirit as personal, active, and subordinate to the Son.**

This relational order reflects the biblical and early Christian witness far more faithfully than the later metaphysical formulations that would emerge at Constantinople and beyond.

## The Ambiguity of Homoousios

The term *homoousios* ("of the same essence") has often been read retroactively as a clear assertion of Trinitarian coequality. Yet at the time of the council, the term was fluid, controversial, and capable of multiple interpretations. For many bishops, its use did not imply an ontological collapse of Father and Son into one being, but a **functional affirmation** that the Son was truly divine—because He was begotten of the Father's own nature.

Understood through the lens of **dynamic eternity**, *homoousios* could be taken to mean that the Son shares in divinity **by derivation and volition**, not by timeless necessity or metaphysical identity. It preserved the Father's supremacy while affirming the Son's unique status as the firstborn over all creation (Col. 1:15), and the agent of divine action (John 1:3).

This dynamic reading allowed many to affirm the creed without embracing later Trinitarian metaphysics.

## Nicaea's Silence as Theological Integrity

The Nicene Creed's near silence on the Holy Spirit is often interpreted as a doctrinal gap later corrected by the Niceno-Constantinopolitan Creed. Yet from the standpoint of **Eusebius** and others within the monolatrous stream, this silence was **intentional theological restraint**.

At the time:

- The **Father** was understood as the only uncaused God.
- The **Son** was affirmed as divine by eternal begetting, not by coequality.
- The **Spirit** was regarded as a holy, personal agent—**proceeding from the Father, through the Son**, and subordinate in both function and status.

Eusebius clearly articulated this order, insisting that the Spirit is not "another god," but the **minister of the Son's works**, a servant of divine will who speaks and acts by delegation—not independently or as a coequal person.[75]

The Creed's brevity reflects a theology still rooted in **relational subordination**, not abstract unity.

**Preserving Dynamic Eternity**

Nicaea did not resolve the question of what it means for the Son to be "eternally begotten." It simply affirmed that He was—not made, but begotten "before all ages." The creed left open whether this begetting was a timeless metaphysical state (as later orthodoxy would assert) or an eternal, volitional

---

[75] Eusebius makes this argument in his direct refutation of any theology that would conflate the persons of the Godhead. He insists on a clear, three-tiered hierarchy of Father, Son, and Spirit. He writes: "And we have been taught of a third power as well... which holds the third rank... For just as the Son is other than the Father... so also the Holy Spirit is other than the Son... **He is the minister of [the Son's] works**, and on this account is not another god beside the Father and the Son, but since he too receives from what is the Son's, on this account he is to be honored along with the Father and the Son..."

See: Eusebius of Caesarea, *On Ecclesiastical Theology* 3.5, in *Eusebius of Caesarea: Against Marcellus and on Ecclesiastical Theology*, trans. Kelley McCarthy Spoerl, The Fathers of the Church, vol. 135 (Washington, DC: The Catholic University of America Press, 2017), 258-261.

act within the divine will.

This openness allowed many to maintain a view of **dynamic eternity**:

- Where God's eternal life includes real acts—not merely logical relations.
- Where the Son's begetting is an act of divine freedom, not a metaphysical necessity.
- Where divine hierarchy is not flattened, but preserved in eternal order and movement.

In this view, eternity is not frozen. The divine life is full of intention, relation, and structure—without temporality, but not without distinction.

**The Seeds of Change**

While the Nicene Creed did not demand Trinitarian orthodoxy as later defined, it planted the seeds of metaphysical reinterpretation. Over time, the ambiguities of *homoousios* would be resolved not in favor of relational hierarchy, but in favor of **ontological sameness**. The Spirit would be elevated to coequal status. The Father's role as the sole object of worship would be eclipsed by worship offered to a numerically singular divine essence shared among three persons.

These developments were not inevitable, nor were they present at Nicaea. They represent a shift—one that moved away from the dynamic, relational model seen in Scripture, early Christian writings, and thinkers like Eusebius.

## Reclaiming the Earlier Vision

By returning to the theological assumptions preserved at Nicaea—and made explicit in Eusebius—we recover a vision of God that is:

- **Relational, not metaphysical,**
- **Hierarchical, not coequal,**
- **Dynamic, not static.**

We affirm:

- **The Father alone is uncaused, supreme, and worthy of worship.**
- **The Son is divine by derivation, eternally begotten through the Father's volition.**
- **The Spirit is a personal, holy agent—subordinate to the Son, and ministering divine presence and power in the world.**

This model preserves biblical language, honors early Christian theology, and safeguards the singular worship of the one true God: the Father.

What the Council of Nicaea left open—intentionally or not—would soon become the battleground for one of the most radical shifts in Christian theology. The creed's ambiguity, particularly around the meaning of *homoousios* and the role of the Holy Spirit, preserved a degree of theological flexibility. Within this space, relational hierarchy, dynamic eternity, and

Christian Monolatry still had room to breathe.

But this openness would not last.

In the decades that followed, a single theological voice would rise to prominence—one that would reshape the framework of Christian thought and reconfigure the doctrine of God. That voice was **Athanasius of Alexandria**.

What Athanasius introduced was not merely a defense of the Son's divinity. It was a **fundamental redefinition** of divine ontology: collapsing hierarchy into coequality, transforming begetting into essence, and converting a dynamic, volitional eternity into a static, metaphysical unity. In doing so, he departed sharply from the earlier theological tradition shared by Jewish monolatry, Second Temple cosmology, and the early apologists.

The next chapter traces this turning point in detail—examining how Athanasius's theology moved beyond Nicaea, overturned prior assumptions, and laid the groundwork for the doctrinal settlement of 381 A.D. It is here, not with Arius, that we locate the true innovation—the moment Christian theology broke from its own foundations.

# 20

# The Athanasian Shift: Rewriting Christian Doctrine

For centuries, the theological narrative surrounding the Arian controversy has been framed as a conflict between orthodoxy and heresy—with Arius cast as the innovator, and Athanasius the heroic defender of apostolic truth. But this common framing masks the deeper theological reality: the true innovation did not come from Arius, but from Athanasius of Alexandria.

What Arius and many of his contemporaries defended was not a novel Christology, but a long-standing, biblically rooted framework—one that affirmed a singular, uncaused God (the Father), a begotten but subordinate Son, and a Spirit who proceeds in ordered relation. This theology had existed for centuries in Christian thought. Today, it is best and most accurately named **Christian Monolatry**.

Christian Monolatry affirms the one true God as the Father alone, while acknowledging the Son as divine by derivation and the Spirit as a subordinate, personal agent. It maintains both divine hierarchy and relational unity, grounded not in static metaphysics but in what we have called **dynamic eternity**—God's freedom to act relationally and volitionally before time.

# THE ATHANASIAN SHIFT: REWRITING CHRISTIAN DOCTRINE

This chapter will examine how Athanasius fundamentally redefined that theology. By rejecting dynamic eternity, collapsing divine agency into a single essence, and weaponizing the once-disputed term *homoousios*, Athanasius transformed Christian Monolatry into what would become the co-equal Trinitarian model formalized in 381 A.D. at the Council of Constantinople.

## *Pre-Nicene Theology: The World of Christian Monolatry*

Before the doctrinal upheavals of the fourth century, the dominant theological framework among Christians was not Trinitarianism as later defined, but what we now rightly recognize as **Christian Monolatry**. This model, deeply rooted in the monolatry of Second Temple Judaism and early Christian reflection, upheld the worship of one uncaused God—the Father—while affirming the divinity of the Son as derived and the activity of the Holy Spirit as subordinate.

Christian Monolatry understood God not as a static unity of essence shared among coequal persons, but as a **relational hierarchy** grounded in volition and mediation. The Father alone is uncaused, the source of all. The Son is begotten before time, not as an eternal necessity, but as a willed expression of the Father's initiative. The Holy Spirit is a personal, holy agent who proceeds from the Father through the Son, never worshiped as God but always functioning as an extension of divine will.

This framework preserved the biblical tension between divine transcendence and relational intimacy. It allowed early Christians to speak of divine persons without collapsing them into metaphysical sameness. Most importantly, it upheld monolatry—the singular worship of the Father

# MONOLATRY

alone—while giving full place to the Son and Spirit as distinct, ordered participants in the divine plan.

Jewish sources such as the Targums, the Wisdom literature, and the writings of Philo reveal a conceptual space for this theology. Figures like the **Memra**, **Wisdom**, and the **Angel of the Lord** acted with divine authority yet were never confused with YHWH Himself. In the New Testament, this logic continues: the Son is "from God" and "with God" (John 1:1), but never described as unbegotten or equal in authority. The Spirit is sent by the Son, glorifies the Son, and acts in perfect obedience—never as a second or third god, but as an agent of divine mission.

The earliest Christian theologians embraced this structure. Justin Martyr famously referred to the Son as "another God," yet subordinate to the Father. Irenaeus affirmed the Son's derivation and distinct role in the economy of salvation. Tertullian spoke of a divine order (*ordo*) in which the Father sends the Son and the Son sends the Spirit. None of these thinkers envisioned a coequal Trinity. What they articulated was **Christian Monolatry**: a theology of divine hierarchy, ordered action, and relational mediation.

Within this world, the idea of **dynamic eternity** naturally took shape. God's eternal life was not frozen or abstract. It was full of purpose, relationship, and initiative. The Son was begotten not within time, but before time—an eternal act of divine will. The Spirit proceeded as part of this same movement, not as a metaphysical person but as a personal emissary. This dynamic, volitional order allowed for eternal distinctions without denying God's transcendence.

This was the theological soil from which the Church grew. And it is this vision—Christian Monolatry—that would soon be redefined by a single figure whose interpretation of Nicaea would reshape Christian doctrine for centuries to come.

# THE ATHANASIAN SHIFT: REWRITING CHRISTIAN DOCTRINE

## *The Athanasian Reversal: Subversion of Monolatrous Theology*

The rise of Athanasius marks a pivotal rupture in the history of Christian theology. While earlier debates surrounding the Son's nature operated within the flexible boundaries of Christian Monolatry, Athanasius introduced a fundamentally new framework—one that dissolved relational hierarchy into metaphysical identity and recast divine generation as eternal necessity. In so doing, he replaced a volitional, dynamic God with a static co-eternal essence shared among indistinct persons.[76]

This shift was not merely exegetical; it was ontological. Athanasius departed from the longstanding model in which the Father alone is uncaused, the Son begotten by will, and the Spirit proceeding in functional subordination. He instead proposed that Father and Son are one not just in purpose or glory, but in *essence*—a move that erased the relational asymmetry at the heart of Christian Monolatry.

Athanasius was not content to affirm the Son's divinity in relational or participatory terms. He insisted that the Son must be fully and eternally consubstantial with the Father—sharing the same essence, without derivation or dependence.

---

[76] The scholarly consensus affirms that Athanasius's great contribution—and his break from his predecessors—was his insistence that the Son's divinity must be grounded in his eternal, essential unity with the Father, not in the Father's will. R.P.C. Hanson describes this as Athanasius's "major, and disastrous, contribution to the doctrine of God," because it removed the concept of volition from the act of begetting and made the Son a necessity of the Father's nature, thereby dissolving the clear subordination that had characterized nearly all pre-Nicene theology.
   See: R.P.C. Hanson, *The Search for the Christian Doctrine of God: The Arian Controversy 318-381* (Edinburgh: T&T Clark, 1988), 418-425.

This move transformed begetting from an eternal act of divine will into a timeless ontological fact: the Son simply always was, of necessity, not because the Father chose to beget Him.

This transformation is most evident in Athanasius's rejection of dynamic eternity. Whereas Origen and others had taught that the Son was begotten before all things as an expression of the Father's volition, Athanasius argued that any notion of divine will or sequence implied change in God—and was therefore unacceptable. By removing volition from divine begetting, he stripped the Father of His role as source and reduced the Son to an uncaused presence indistinct from the Father in nature.

Athanasius (Against the Arians, Discourse 1, ch. 4) declared:

*"The Son is not an act of the Father's will, but rather His essence itself."*[77]

In this statement, the distance between Athanasius and Christian Monolatry becomes clear. The Father no longer acts; He simply is. The Son no longer responds; He simply exists. The relationship is no longer dynamic or relational—it is metaphysical, necessary, and indistinguishable in being.

This redefinition extended beyond the Father and Son. Though Athanasius's early writings say little about the Holy Spirit, his later influence helped pave

---

[77] This statement encapsulates the core of Athanasius's argument against the Arians and the older subordinationist tradition. By denying that the Son is a product of the Father's will (*boulesis*), Athanasius sought to close any loophole that would allow the Son to be seen as a creature. However, in doing so, he also departed from the earlier, widely held view (articulated by theologians like Origen) that the Son's generation was a dynamic and eternal act of the Father's volition.

*This quote is a standard summary of Athanasius's position. For a direct discussion of this theme in his work, see: Athanasius, Against the Arians, Discourse 3, chapters 60-66.*

## THE ATHANASIAN SHIFT: REWRITING CHRISTIAN DOCTRINE

the way for the Spirit's elevation to co-equal status. The logic was consistent: if divine unity is essence rather than hierarchy, then the Spirit, too, must be included in that essence—or excluded from divinity altogether. Thus, the path was laid for the eventual formulation of the coequal, coeternal Trinity at Constantinople in 381.[78]

Athanasius's genius lay not just in his theological boldness but in his rhetorical strategy. He reframed the debate, turning older theological models into heresy by redefining the terms. Subordination became denial. Derivation became blasphemy. Christian Monolatry was no longer seen as the default framework of the faith, but as a dangerous innovation—when in fact it was Athanasius who introduced the conceptual rupture.

Where earlier theology had seen begetting as an act, Athanasius saw it as an identity. Where early Christians had maintained a hierarchy of persons and roles, Athanasius insisted on essential unity. The consequence was not clarification—it was the abandonment of a model that had harmonized biblical revelation with relational logic.

What Athanasius offered was something entirely different: a **static Trinity of indistinct persons**, grounded in essence rather than will, requiring belief in coequality rather than faith in divine order. Christian Monolatry—with its ordered, volitional, and worshipful hierarchy—was not clarified at Nicaea. It was overwritten.

---

[78] While Athanasius's early work focused primarily on the Son, his later writings, particularly his *Letters to Serapion*, applied the same metaphysical logic of *homoousios* to the Holy Spirit. He argued that if salvation is deification (becoming like God), and this is accomplished by the Spirit, then the Spirit must also share fully in the divine essence. This argument laid the essential groundwork for the final Trinitarian formulation at the Council of Constantinople in 381.

See: Jaroslav Pelikan, *The Christian Tradition: A History of the Development of Doctrine, Vol. 1: The Emergence of the Catholic Tradition (100-600)* (Chicago: University of Chicago Press, 1971), 213-215.

## MONOLATRY

### *The Political Triumph of Metaphysics*

The triumph of Athanasius's theology was not achieved solely through argument or exegesis. It was secured through the political machinery of the late Roman Empire. What began as a theological dispute became, over time, a doctrinal imposition—finalized not in open debate, but in imperial decree. The ascendancy of metaphysical Trinitarianism over Christian Monolatry was less a matter of theological consensus and more a result of ecclesiastical strategy and state enforcement.

In the years following the Council of Nicaea (325), the Church did not immediately settle into a fixed Trinitarian position. Many bishops continued to affirm relational subordination, preserving elements of Christian Monolatry. The so-called Semi-Arians, for example, confessed the Son as "like" (*homoiousios*) the Father in essence, but not identical. Their aim was to preserve divine hierarchy without denying the Son's preexistence or glory.

But Athanasius would not allow this middle ground. With increasing rhetorical force, he portrayed all forms of subordinationism—even moderate ones—as heretical. His theology, though initially controversial, gradually gained imperial favor, particularly under the reign of **Theodosius I**.

The decisive turning point came not in a council chamber, but in a law court. In **380 A.D.**, Theodosius issued the **Edict of Thessalonica**, declaring that only Nicene Christianity—defined by the consubstantial Trinity—was legally valid within the empire. All other positions, including those rooted in Christian Monolatry, were outlawed. Bishops who resisted were removed. Alternative theological schools were closed. Theological nuance became criminalized.

The following year, the **Council of Constantinople (381)** ratified this new orthodoxy. Though portrayed as a continuation of Nicaea, the council in fact enshrined **new elements**: not only the full consubstantiality of the Son, but the de facto deification of the Holy Spirit as the third coequal person of the Trinity. The relational hierarchy that had defined pre-Nicene theology was now gone. In its place stood a closed metaphysical system: one essence, three persons, coequal and coeternal, undivided and indistinct in glory.

Christian Monolatry had not been defeated by better arguments. It had been **displaced by imperial decree** and reclassified as heresy. Its adherents—once respected bishops and theologians—were retroactively labeled innovators or enemies of the faith. In truth, it was their theology that had more faithfully preserved the biblical pattern: a single uncaused God, a begotten but obedient Son, and a Spirit who proceeds in ordered ministry.

The political victory of metaphysics obscured this older tradition. What had once been the normative framework for understanding God's order and action was now remembered, if at all, as an aberration. The result was not only a doctrinal shift but a historical erasure—the **replacement of Christian Monolatry with Nicene Trinitarianism**, not by consensus, but by imperial consolidation.

Contrasting Theological Models: Christian Monolatry vs. Nicene Trinitarianism

To understand the depth of the theological shift initiated by Athanasius and finalized at Constantinople, we must lay side by side the two competing frameworks: the older and biblically rooted model of Christian Monolatry, and the later metaphysical system known as Nicene Trinitarianism. These are not two versions of the same theology—they represent fundamentally different assumptions about divine identity, relationship, and hierarchy.

Below is a comparative outline that highlights this divergence:

## Contrasting Theological Models: Christian Monolatry vs. Nicene Trinitarianism

| Feature | Christian Monolatry | Nicene Trinitarianism |
|---|---|---|
| Divine Source | One uncaused God—the Father alone. | One divine essence shared by three persons. |
| The Son | Begotten by the Father's will; divine by derivation. | Eternally begotten; coequal and consubstantial. |
| The Holy Spirit | Proceeds from the Father through the Son; subordinate agent. | Coequal and coeternal; same divine essence. |
| Eternity | Dynamic—relational actions occur before time. | Fixed—all relations exist timelessly and necessarily. |
| Worship | Directed to the Father alone, through the Son. | Worship equally offered to Father, Son, and Spirit. |
| Unity | Relational & Ordered—unity of purpose and will. | Ontological—unity of indivisible essence. |
| Authority Structure | Hierarchical—Father > Son > Spirit. | Flat—all persons equal in authority and being. |
| Relation to Scripture | Preserves language of sending, obedience, and begetting. | Reinterprets these as eternal, metaphysical conditions. |
| Theological Model | Ordered Monotheism—biblical, relational, volitional. | Metaphysical Trinitarianism—timeless, coequal essence. |

*This comparison makes clear that what changed was not just terminology—it was the entire conceptual system. Christian Monolatry affirms the Father's supremacy, the Son's derived divinity, and the Spirit's personal agency under both. It allows for real relation, real order, and real divine initiative.*

Nicene Trinitarianism, by contrast, removes any concept of volitional hierarchy. Begetting becomes a timeless condition; sending becomes an eternal procession; and worship, once directed singularly to the Father, is now distributed among three equal persons, each indistinguishable in essence.

This is not a minor doctrinal development—it is a systemic theological reconstruction, and one that cannot be reconciled with the earlier biblical and Jewish-Christian tradition. Christian Monolatry stands as the more faithful and coherent model, preserving both the singularity of divine worship and the relational richness of God's eternal action.

**From Theological Shift to Imperial Enforcement**

The rise of Athanasius and his metaphysical reformulation of Christian doctrine marked a decisive break from the theological inheritance of the early Church. What we now reclaim as Christian Monolatry — the belief in one uncaused God (the Father), a begotten but subordinate Son, and a Spirit who proceeds in obedient agency — was not defeated in open debate, but slowly overwritten by a new framework: Nicene Trinitarianism.

Athanasius's innovation was not merely theological. It redefined the nature of divine relationship, collapsing volitional order into static ontology. By insisting on essential sameness rather than relational hierarchy, he erased the asymmetry that had characterized biblical revelation and apostolic faith. Begetting was no longer an act of divine will — it became an eternal necessity. Worship, once directed through the Son to the Father, became distributed equally across a metaphysical triad.

Yet this doctrinal transformation did not triumph through theological consensus alone. The theological architecture of Christian Monolatry — coherent, scriptural, and deeply embedded in early Christian identity — did not disappear because it failed to persuade. It was outlawed.

In the next chapter, we will see how the Emperor Theodosius I made this theological redefinition permanent by codifying it into imperial law. The Council of Constantinople in 381 did not merely affirm a creed; it extinguished all dissent. The shift from Christian Monolatry to Nicene orthodoxy was not completed in the church councils — it was completed in the imperial court.

Thus, the story that follows is not one of theological triumph, but of political consolidation. What began with Athanasius's metaphysical remapping of the divine life would end with the criminalization of theological diversity. Christian Monolatry — the theology of the apostles and the pre-Nicene Church — was buried not by argument, but by decree.

Now we turn to the moment where theology became law — and law rewrote the story of Christian belief.

# 21

# Doctrine by Decree: How Imperial Power Forged a New Orthodoxy

In the late fourth century, the vibrant and diverse theological debates of the early Church came to an abrupt end. The question of God's nature was resolved not by further scriptural debate or ecclesial consensus, but by imperial command. In 380 A.D., with a single decree—the Edict of Thessalonica—Emperor Theodosius I transformed the Christian theological landscape forever.

The edict did not merely favor a particular viewpoint; it weaponized it. Nicene Trinitarianism, the metaphysical framework advanced by Athanasius, was declared the only legal form of Christianity in the Roman Empire.

> "It is our will that all the peoples subject to Our gracious rule should practice that religion which the divine Peter the Apostle transmitted to the Romans... We shall believe in the single deity of the Father, the Son, and the Holy Spirit under the concept of equal majesty and in the Holy Trinity. We command that those who follow this law shall embrace

*the name of Catholic Christians, while the rest, whom we judge to be* **demented and insane***, shall sustain the infamy of* **heretical dogmas***."*
— *Edict of Thessalonica, 380 A.D.*[79]

The language was unequivocal. Theodosius legally enforced ontological coequality, criminalized all dissenting views, and officially rebranded those who held to the older hierarchical frameworks—including Christian Monolatry and Semi-Arianism—as mentally unstable enemies of the state. Theology no longer emerged from the Church's discernment; it was dictated by the emperor's command.

The shift from theological dialogue to imperial enforcement reached its peak at the **Council of Constantinople in 381 A.D.** This was not a council of consensus but of consolidation, where Theodosius ensured his new orthodoxy was finalized.[80] The consequences were swift and severe:

- Bishops who did not affirm full ontological coequality were deposed.
- Clergy who upheld the traditional hierarchical theology were removed from office.

---

[79] The Edict of Thessalonica, issued in 380 A.D., is a landmark in the history of Christianity. Historians universally recognize it as the decree that effectively made Nicene Christianity the state religion of the Roman Empire. The text of the edict, preserved in the Theodosian Code, explicitly condemns non-Nicene Christians as "demented and insane" and subjects them to both divine and imperial punishment.

See: *The Theodosian Code, 16.1.2. For a modern scholarly discussion of the edict and its political implications, see: Charles Freeman, A.D. 381: Heretics, Pagans, and the Dawn of the Monotheistic State (New York: Overlook Press, 2008), 34-37.*

[80] The Council of Constantinople in 381 was convened by Emperor Theodosius with the explicit goal of ratifying his new Nicene orthodoxy. It was not a fully ecumenical council in the same vein as Nicaea; it was composed entirely of bishops from the Eastern Empire who were in theological alignment with the emperor. Historians note that the council's primary function was to depose the remaining Arian and Semi-Arian bishops and to formally extend the *homoousion* principle to the Holy Spirit, thereby completing the Athanasian theological project under imperial authority.

See: *Richard Rubenstein, When Jesus Became God: The Struggle and Conflict over the Origins of Christianity in the Fourth Century (New York: Harcourt Brace, 1999), 209-222.*

- Non-Nicene churches and alternative theological schools were shut down, and their worship was driven underground.

What had once been the mainstream theology of the Eastern Church—a subordinationist view far closer to Christian Monolatry—was now treated as heresy. This was not a theological tightening; it was a legal and political purge.

Beyond the immediate suppression, the long-term consequence was a sweeping **erasure of theological memory**.[81] With the full backing of imperial power, Nicene proponents recast the theological past in their own image. Earlier theologians who affirmed a divine hierarchy—like Origen and Eusebius—were retroactively reinterpreted as confused or problematic. Their writings, and those of others who did not align with the new formula, were destroyed, marginalized, or left untranslated.

The history of Christian theology was rewritten to make Nicene Trinitarianism appear inevitable and apostolic, while the once-dominant model of Christian Monolatry was portrayed as a fringe heresy. The result was a cultural amnesia that has shaped Christian discourse ever since. The assumption that the Trinity has always been defined as three co-equal persons is a product not of theological discovery, but of historical suppression. The early Church's most coherent and scriptural theology was not refuted; it was outlawed.

This fusion of doctrine and empire created a new model of authority that would last for a millennium, where heresy became treason and

---

[81] The victory of the Nicene party in the fourth century led to a significant rewriting of Christian history. Earlier, respected subordinationist theologians like Origen and Eusebius were retroactively branded as problematic or heretical. As historian R.P.C. Hanson notes, the "official" history written by the victors often obscured the fact that for much of the fourth century, the "Arian" or Semi-Arian (i.e., subordinationist) position was actually the dominant and majority view in the Eastern Church. The narrative of a single, unchanging apostolic faith being defended against a novel heresy was a later, politically useful construction.

See: R.P.C. Hanson, *The Search for the Christian Doctrine of God: The Arian Controversy 318-381* (Edinburgh: T&T Clark, 1988), xix-xxiii, 869-873.

orthodoxy was no longer discerned, but dictated. And yet, this story—of how Nicene orthodoxy rose to dominance not by persuasion but by political enforcement—has itself been forgotten. In the next chapter, we will uncover why this theological shift was not only enforced, but intentionally hidden from the historical record.

# 22

# Why We've Never Heard This Story

The history of Christian theology, as told in most churches, seminaries, and textbooks, presents Nicene Trinitarianism as the inevitable conclusion of apostolic faith — a pure doctrine refined through faithful councils and theological clarity. But this narrative conceals more than it reveals. It overlooks the fact that **the victory of Nicene orthodoxy was not merely theological — it was legislative, enforced, and sustained by empire**.

From the moment Theodosius I issued the Edict of Thessalonica in 380 A.D., declaring Nicene Christianity the only lawful religion of the Roman Empire, the theological landscape was no longer shaped by dialogue or Scripture. It was shaped by decree. Views that had once flourished — including Christian Monolatry — were not rebutted; they were outlawed. Their defenders were exiled, their writings burned, and their memory replaced with a version of history that served the new orthodoxy.

This chapter explores **why we've never heard this story** — how the combination of imperial control, ecclesiastical censorship, and academic pressure ensured that Christian Monolatry would not only be suppressed but **systematically forgotten**. It's not simply that this theology was lost to time; it was actively hidden, rewritten, and buried under centuries of institutional power.

What follows is not a conspiracy theory. It is a historical reality — one supported by legal decrees, conciliar acts, destroyed libraries, redacted manuscripts, and a thousand years of theological monopoly.

To understand why Christian Monolatry disappeared from Christian memory, we must examine the mechanisms that made its disappearance possible — and why its recovery is not just important, but necessary.

## *Church-State Alliance: The Systematic Suppression of Monolatry*

The theological erasure of Christian Monolatry was not accidental. It was the direct result of a strategic alliance between the Roman state and the institutional Church. From 380 A.D. onward, theology was no longer merely the domain of bishops, councils, and Scripture—it became a matter of imperial jurisdiction. Doctrine was enforced by law, and theological dissent became a criminal act.

### Imperial Enforcement After 381 A.D.

When Theodosius I issued the **Edict of Thessalonica**, he did more than declare Nicene theology as true—he declared it **the only legal form of Christianity**. This edict criminalized all other theological expressions, including the monolatrous subordinationism that had once defined the

## WHY WE'VE NEVER HEARD THIS STORY

early Church.[82]

> "We authorize the followers of this law to assume the title of Catholic Christians; the rest, we judge demented and insane. Their assemblies shall not receive the name of churches, and they shall be punished first by divine vengeance and then by our own initiative."
> — Edict of Thessalonica, 380 A.D.

This decree marked a permanent shift. From this moment forward:

- **Non-Nicene bishops were exiled** or removed from office.
- **Churches aligned with alternative theologies were confiscated** or closed.
- **Theological schools that taught subordinationist or monolatrous views were shut down.**
- **Manuscripts and writings** that contradicted the Nicene formula were destroyed or banned from copying.

For example, in 435 A.D., Theodosius II issued another edict ordering

---

[82] The systematic destruction of non-orthodox texts was a key feature of imperial policy following the consolidation of Nicene power. The edict issued by Emperor Theodosius II in 435 A.D. is a prime example, specifically ordering that the writings of Arius and others deemed heretical should be sought out and burned. This state-sanctioned destruction of literature is a major reason why the works of many subordinationist theologians survive only in fragments quoted by their opponents.
 See: Richard Rubenstein, *When Jesus Became God: The Struggle and Conflict over the Origins of Christianity in the Fourth Century* (New York: Harcourt Brace, 1999), 235-237.

that all Arian writings be located and burned—ensuring that alternative theological voices would not only be silenced but eliminated from the historical record.

## Councils as Political Instruments

After 381, ecumenical councils were no longer forums for genuine theological discourse. They became **imperial tools for enforcing uniformity**. Councils such as Ephesus (431) and Chalcedon (451) did not welcome theological diversity—they were designed to ratify imperial theology and eliminate dissent.

- **Opposing bishops were declared heretics**, regardless of their scriptural or historical arguments.
- **Dissenting traditions were not debated—they were excommunicated.**
- **Conciliar decisions were often influenced by imperial threat, bribery, and the political maneuvering of pro-Nicene parties.**

These gatherings served less as gatherings of spiritual discernment and more as mechanisms of **doctrinal consolidation** under imperial oversight.

The long-term effect was devastating. The earlier diversity of Christian theology—so clearly attested in pre-Nicene writings—was retroactively rewritten as heresy. Those who had once shaped the Church's theological vocabulary were now remembered only through the condemnations of their opponents.

What began as Christian Monolatry was reframed as Arianism, heresy, or "blasphemous innovation." In truth, it was neither new nor blasphemous—it was simply **no longer allowed**.[83]

## *Merging Doctrine and Civic Loyalty: Christendom's Theological Monopoly*

The legal enforcement of Nicene theology under Theodosius did more than suppress rival doctrines — it fundamentally redefined what it meant to be a Christian. From the late fourth century onward, **theological orthodoxy became indistinguishable from civic identity**. To reject Nicene Trinitarianism was not merely to err in doctrine; it was to stand outside the boundaries of society itself.

### The Rise of a Theocratic Church

With the fall of the Western Roman Empire, the Church did not relinquish power — it absorbed it. The bishops of Rome and Constantinople inherited the political authority once held by emperors, and theology became the

---

[83] While often presented as moments of pure theological discernment, the ecumenical councils of the fifth century were deeply enmeshed in imperial politics. Historians note that councils like Ephesus and Chalcedon were often characterized by political maneuvering, imperial pressure, and the violent condemnation of theological opponents. Their outcomes were frequently determined as much by political power as by theological argument, serving to ratify a state-approved orthodoxy and eliminate all dissent.

See: Charles Freeman, *A.D. 381: Heretics, Pagans, and the Dawn of the Monotheistic State* (New York: Overlook Press, 2008), 139-160. *Freeman details the intense political rivalries that shaped these later councils.*

foundation of civil order.

- **The Holy Roman Empire** institutionalized Nicene Christianity as the official religion of Western Christendom.
- **The papacy became both a theological and political office**, mediating between kings and peoples, and enforcing Nicene theology as law.
- **National churches** in Catholic and later Protestant regions adopted confessions of faith that mandated Nicene formulations — not just for clergy, but for all citizens.

This fusion of Church and state ensured that **to be a Christian was to be Nicene**. Dissent from this theology was not merely heretical—it was criminal.

Example: The **Fourth Lateran Council (1215 A.D.)** decreed that heretics must be suppressed not only by the Church but by **civil authorities**. This meant that **non-Nicene Christians were not only excluded from the Church — they could be arrested, imprisoned, or executed by the state.**

## Control of Education and Scriptoria

The Church's monopoly extended to **what could be known**, not just what could be believed. The institutions responsible for preserving and transmitting knowledge — monasteries, universities, and scriptoria — came under ecclesiastical control.

## WHY WE'VE NEVER HEARD THIS STORY

- **Scriptoria** were instructed to preserve and copy only those texts that supported Nicene orthodoxy.
- **Writings from earlier theologians**—even those like Eusebius of Caesarea or Theodoret of Cyrus, who held hierarchical or subordinationist views—were **selectively edited** or allowed to fade from circulation.
- **Non-Nicene texts were rarely translated, rarely taught, and rarely preserved**, meaning that much of early Christian theological diversity was lost by neglect, if not by active suppression.

In time, the **first universities** — Paris, Oxford, Cambridge — emerged under direct ecclesiastical oversight. Theology became not a field of inquiry, but a guardian of received dogma. Professors were priests. Libraries were censored. Doctrinal conformity was the price of participation in intellectual life.

The result was centuries of theological monopoly. **Alternative voices were not merely drowned out—they were never heard to begin with.**[84]

---

[84] The preservation of knowledge throughout the Middle Ages was almost entirely in the hands of the Church. Monastic scriptoria and, later, the first universities were the centers of learning, and their work was conducted under strict ecclesiastical oversight. This created a theological monopoly where only texts that affirmed the established Nicene orthodoxy were copied, translated, and taught. The works of many early, subordinationist theologians were either lost through neglect, selectively edited to conform to later doctrine (as happened with some works of Origen), or intentionally suppressed.

   See: Jaroslav Pelikan, *The Christian Tradition: A History of the Development of Doctrine, Vol. 1: The Emergence of the Catholic Tradition (100-600)* (Chicago: University of Chicago Press, 1971), 324-331. Pelikan discusses the process by which "the selection of fathers" was made, cementing a particular version of the tradition.

## Modern Seminaries and Academic Pressures: Why Alternative Views Remain Marginalized

The marginalization of Christian Monolatry did not end with the Middle Ages. In the modern era—through seminaries, universities, and academic publishing—the dominance of Nicene Trinitarianism has been maintained not through empire, but through **institutional inertia, doctrinal gatekeeping, and structural pressures**. The result is a theological environment in which questioning Nicene assumptions is often **professionally risky and academically excluded**, even today.

**University Theology Under Doctrinal Oversight**

Most Christian seminaries and theological faculties are directly affiliated with denominations that require Nicene doctrinal conformity as a condition of accreditation, funding, and employment.

- **Professors are often required to sign confessional statements** affirming belief in the Trinity and the Nicene Creed.
- **Curricula are shaped by denominational oversight**, making it nearly impossible to introduce or even discuss non-Nicene theological models.
- **Accrediting bodies** for seminaries and Bible colleges typically mandate doctrinal agreement with Trinitarian orthodoxy, further excluding alternative views from institutional legitimacy.

This system ensures that theological diversity is curtailed not at the level of argument but at the level of access. In most academic settings, **Christian Monolatry is not refuted—it is simply not taught**.

Example: A theological scholar interested in publishing a dissertation on subordinationism or alternative Christologies may find **limited or no institutional support**, and even face the loss of tenure opportunities for deviating from accepted dogma.

**Peer Review and Publishing Bias**

Even beyond seminaries, the landscape of academic publishing continues to favor Nicene perspectives:

- **Major theological journals and academic presses** are controlled by editorial boards that assume Trinitarian orthodoxy as a baseline.
- **Articles or books that challenge the Trinity** are frequently labeled as speculative, fringe, or insufficiently "Christian."
- **Research funding**, particularly for biblical or doctrinal studies, is almost always awarded to projects that affirm traditional frameworks.

This creates a self-reinforcing loop: only Trinitarian interpretations are funded, taught, and published — and because they are the only ones seen, they are assumed to be the only valid options.

While this is not a universal rule, and some academic institutions and publishers certainly foster greater theological flexibility, the majority of the landscape remains challenging. As a result, those who begin to question the traditional model can often find themselves isolated, struggling to publish, and effectively excluded from mainstream academic credibility. The gatekeeping is not always a conscious conspiracy—but it is systemically effective.[85]

---

[85] While direct imperial enforcement has ended, the legacy of this theological monopoly continues through institutional structures. Most mainstream theological seminaries and academic publishers operate under confessional standards that presuppose Nicene Trinitarianism. This creates systemic barriers for scholars exploring non-traditional Christologies, affecting everything from curriculum design and faculty hiring to peer review and the funding of research. Consequently, alternative models like Christian Monolatry are rarely given a serious hearing in mainstream academic discourse.

While this is a sociological observation, it is widely acknowledged within the field. For a discussion of the challenges of doctrinal revision, see: Maurice F. Wiles, The Making of Christian Doctrine: A Study in the Principles of Early Doctrinal Development (Cambridge: Cambridge University Press, 1967).

# 23

# The Unbroken Thread

It is no accident that you are reading these words. In a world saturated with information, a thousand other books could have found their way into your hands. But this one did. And if the journey through these pages has been as unsettling as it has been illuminating, that is only because you have been invited to witness the unearthing of a truth buried for seventeen centuries. This was not an accident. It was an appointment.

We began this book not by following a thread, but by following a Person. We sought to find the Son, the one who promised that to see him is to see the Father. And in our search, we found him everywhere, though his form shifted through the ages. We saw him as the Angel of YHWH, bearing the very Name of God. We saw him as a second YHWH, raining fire on Sodom while the Father remained in heaven. We found him in the Aramaic Targums' *Memra* and in Philo's Hellenistic *Logos*. This was the native worldview of the apostles, who presented Yeshua not as a theological rupture, but as the culmination of this long tradition—the begotten Son who derives His very life from the Father. It was the undisputed faith of the Apostolic Fathers and the great pre-Nicene theologians like Eusebius, who defended this divine hierarchy as the core of Christian orthodoxy.

This ancient, biblical model was not defeated by superior scripture or argument. It was overwritten. We traced the pivotal shift to Athanasius, who redefined God's nature from a dynamic, willed relationship to a static, metaphysical essence. This new theology, in which the Son was no longer the subordinate agent of the Father's will but a co-equal necessity of His being, was then made permanent not by consensus, but by the sword of empire. The Edict of Thessalonica did not clarify the faith; it criminalized the original version of it, branding it as insanity and ensuring that its memory would be buried under a thousand years of institutional control.

But a truth revealed by God cannot be erased, only obscured. For the reader whose theological world has now been upended, this is not an ending. It is a homecoming.

**First, we are invited into a clearer and more profound vision of the Father.** For too long, His unique supremacy has been obscured by philosophical formulas. To reclaim Christian Monolatry is to restore the Father to His rightful place as the sole uncaused, unbegotten, and ultimate source of all things. He is not one of three co-equals; He is the "only true God" (John 17:3). Our worship, like that of Yeshua and the early Church, finds its ultimate destination in Him.

Second, and perhaps most importantly, **we are invited into a more authentic and powerful relationship with the Son.** When we see Yeshua not as a metaphysical puzzle but as the Father's perfect, begotten Agent, the entire Gospel story ignites with a reality that was previously dimmed. His life is no longer a divine actor playing a scripted part; it is a story of real relationship, real struggle, and real triumph.

Suddenly, the weight of biblical truths becomes breathtakingly real.
- The Son's obedience is **real**.
- His prayers to the Father are **real**.
- His agony in the garden, where he sweat drops of blood, was not theater; it was the **real** anguish of a Son submitting to His Father's will.
- His need to be strengthened by an angel was **real**.
- His temptation was **real**.
- His death was a **real** death.

- The moment the Father turned His face away was a **real** moment of divine abandonment.

In the static model, these moments are cheapened, their edges softened by the assumption that He was simply God acting out a role. But in the monolatrous framework, they become the most profound testament to the Father's love imaginable. The sacrifice was not a divine being sacrificing a lesser part of himself; it was the **one true God sacrificing His one, true, only begotten Son.** The love that drove that act is deeper than we ever knew. The Son's victory and subsequent enthronement are not a return to a default state, but a genuine reward, **granted** to Him by a loving Father.

This changes everything. It means that we are so important to the Father that He would put His most precious Son through this unimaginable ordeal for our sake. Our value is measured by the infinite cost of that sacrifice.

This is the challenge, and the glorious invitation, this book leaves with you. This is the passing of a torch. The history has been uncovered, the framework has been restored. Now, the path forward for this generation and the next is to return to the Scriptures, not with the old lenses of tradition, but with fresh eyes and a fresh faith. The challenge is to read the Bible again, perhaps for the very first time, and see if this ancient, monolatrous truth doesn't make the entire story more vibrant, more meaningful, and more powerfully real than you ever thought possible.

The story of Christian Monolatry did not end in 381 A.D. It was buried, but it never truly died. It survived in the quiet hearts of believers in every generation who, despite the doctrines of men, held fast to a simpler faith. It lived on with those on the narrow path that few find, who knew only what the Scriptures so clearly taught: a supreme Father and His beloved Son.

It is time to reclaim this heritage—not as a novelty, but as the rightful, ancient faith of all who seek to follow the God of Abraham, Isaac, and Jacob, and His Messiah, Yeshua. This is more than a historical correction; it is a spiritual realignment. It frees us from the paradoxes of later metaphysics and invites us back into the vibrant, ordered cosmos of the Bible. It is time to return home to our **One God** and his **Son Jesus Christ**.

# A Word to the Reader

This book has traced a forgotten theological lineage—one that begins in the Scriptures, courses through the voices of prophets and apostles, flows into the early Church, and was ultimately diverted by the force of empire.

Christian Monolatry is not a fringe hypothesis. It is the suppressed foundation of biblical theology—a framework that harmonizes divine agency with worshipful order, and affirms both the transcendence of the Father and the exaltation of the Son. It allows Scripture to speak in its own terms, without being forced into metaphysical molds imposed centuries after the resurrection.

Yet to explore these truths today is to walk against centuries of tradition, assumption, and institutional inertia. You may find yourself asking:

*Can this really be true? Why have I never heard it before?*

The answer is not theological failure, but historical interruption. The enforcement of Nicene orthodoxy was not just about doctrine—it was about identity, empire, and control. And in its wake, much was lost.

But the faithfulness of God ensures that what was true never ceases to be true. The ancient path remains, waiting for those with eyes to see and ears to hear.

This work is not the final word. It is an invitation—to revisit Scripture, to reconsider theological inheritance, and to reclaim the simplicity and beauty

## A WORD TO THE READER

of Christian Monolatry. Not for novelty's sake, but for truth's.

If you've reached this point, you have already taken the first step. Whether scholar or seeker, teacher or skeptic, you now carry a new lens through which to read the Word and understand the story of the Church.

Hold it humbly. Test it honestly. And may it lead you—not into controversy—but into clarity, peace, and deeper worship of God.

**— the Author**

# Appendix: The Foundational Creeds

The following are the standard English translations of the two most significant creeds from the fourth-century controversies. Presenting them here allows for a direct comparison, clearly showing the theological developments between the two councils, particularly in the expanded section concerning the Holy Spirit.

**Appendix A: The Creed of Nicaea (325 A.D.)**

We believe in one God, the Father Almighty, Maker of all things visible and invisible.

And in one Lord Jesus Christ, the Son of God, begotten of the Father, the only-begotten; that is, of the essence of the Father, God of God, Light of Light, very God of very God, begotten, not made, being of one substance (*homoousios*) with the Father; by whom all things were made, both in heaven and on earth; who for us men, and for our salvation, came down and was incarnate and was made man; He suffered, and the third day He rose again, ascended into heaven; from thence He shall come to judge the living and the dead.

And in the Holy Spirit.

[But those who say: 'There was a time when he was not;' and 'He was not before he was made;' and 'He was made out of nothing,' or 'He is of another substance' or 'essence,' or 'The Son of God is created,' or 'changeable,' or 'alterable'—they are condemned by the holy catholic and apostolic Church.]

**Appendix B: The Niceno-Constantinopolitan Creed (381 A.D.)**

We believe in one God, the Father Almighty, Maker of heaven and earth, and of all things visible and invisible.

And in one Lord Jesus Christ, the only-begotten Son of God, begotten of the Father before all worlds (æons), God of God, Light of Light, very God of very God, begotten, not made, being of one substance (*homoousios*) with the Father; by whom all things were made; who for us men, and for our salvation, came down from heaven, and was incarnate by the Holy Ghost of the Virgin Mary, and was made man; he was crucified for us under Pontius Pilate, and suffered, and was buried, and the third day he rose again, according to the Scriptures, and ascended into heaven, and sitteth on the right hand of the Father; from thence he shall come again, with glory, to judge the living and the dead; whose kingdom shall have no end.

And in the Holy Ghost, the Lord and Giver of life, who proceedeth from the Father, who with the Father and the Son together is worshiped and glorified, who spake by the prophets. In one holy catholic and apostolic Church; we acknowledge one baptism for the remission of sins; we look for the resurrection of the dead, and the life of the world to come. Amen.

# Bibliography

Of course. It is an essential and final step. A well-formatted bibliography that includes the scholarly sources you've engaged with is a hallmark of a serious and credible work.

Based on all the citations we have worked on together from your final manuscript, I have compiled the comprehensive bibliography for your book. I have organized it alphabetically and formatted it according to the Chicago Manual of Style, which is standard for theological and historical works.

You can place this at the end of your manuscript.

*Bibliography*

**Biblical Translations**

*The ESV Bible (English Standard Version)*. Wheaton, IL: Crossway Bibles, 2001.

*Legacy Standard Bible*. Three Sixteen Publishing, 2021.

*New American Standard Bible*. 1995 Update. La Habra, CA: The Lockman Foundation, 1995.

**Ancient Sources**

Athanasius. *Against the Arians*.

*Didache*. In *The Apostolic Fathers: Greek Texts and English Translations*, edited by Michael W. Holmes. Grand Rapids, MI: Baker Academic, 2007.

Eusebius of Caesarea. *Ecclesiastical History*. Translated by Kirsopp Lake. Loeb Classical Library. Cambridge, MA: Harvard University Press, 1926.

———. *On Ecclesiastical Theology*. In *Eusebius of Caesarea: Against*

*Marcellus and on Ecclesiastical Theology*, translated by Kelley McCarthy Spoerl. The Fathers of the Church, vol. 135. Washington, DC: The Catholic University of America Press, 2017.

*Epistle of Barnabas*. In *The Apostolic Fathers: Greek Texts and English Translations*, edited by Michael W. Holmes. Grand Rapids, MI: Baker Academic, 2007.

Ignatius of Antioch. *Epistles*. In *The Apostolic Fathers: Greek Texts and English Translations*, edited by Michael W. Holmes. Grand Rapids, MI: Baker Academic, 2007.

Irenaeus. *Against Heresies*. In *The Ante-Nicene Fathers*, edited by Alexander Roberts and James Donaldson, vol. 1. Buffalo, NY: Christian Literature Publishing Co., 1885.

Josephus, Flavius. *Antiquities of the Jews*. Translated by William Whiston. Peabody, MA: Hendrickson Publishers, 1987.

Justin Martyr. *Dialogue with Trypho*. In *The Ante-Nicene Fathers*, edited by Alexander Roberts and James Donaldson, vol. 1. Buffalo, NY: Christian Literature Publishing Co., 1885.

Origen. *Commentary on the Gospel According to John, Books 1-10*. Translated by Ronald E. Heine. The Fathers of the Church, vol. 80. Washington, DC: The Catholic University of America Press, 1989.

———. *Homilies on Genesis and Exodus*. Translated by Ronald E. Heine. The Fathers of the Church, vol. 71. Washington, DC: The Catholic University of America Press, 1982.

Philo of Alexandria. *The Works of Philo*. Translated by C.D. Yonge. Peabody, MA: Hendrickson Publishers, 1993.

Polycarp of Smyrna. *Letter to the Philippians* and *The Martyrdom of Polycarp*. In *The Apostolic Fathers: Greek Texts and English Translations*, edited by Michael W. Holmes. Grand Rapids, MI: Baker Academic, 2007.

*Shepherd of Hermas*. In *The Apostolic Fathers: Greek Texts and English Translations*, edited by Michael W. Holmes. Grand Rapids, MI: Baker Academic, 2007.

**Modern Scholarship**

Attridge, Harold W. *The Epistle to the Hebrews*. Hermeneia—A Critical and

Historical Commentary on the Bible. Philadelphia: Fortress Press, 1989.

Barrett, C.K. *The Gospel According to St. John: An Introduction with Commentary and Notes on the Greek Text.* 2nd ed. Philadelphia: Westminster Press, 1978.

Bauckham, Richard. *The Theology of the Book of Revelation.* Cambridge: Cambridge University Press, 1993.

Beale, G.K. *The Book of Revelation: A Commentary on the Greek Text.* New International Greek Testament Commentary. Grand Rapids, MI: Eerdmans, 1999.

Boyarin, Daniel. "The Gospel of the Memra: Jewish Binitarianism and the Prologue to John." *Harvard Theological Review* 94, no. 3 (2001): 243–284.

Chilton, Bruce. *The Isaiah Targum: Introduction, Translation, Apparatus, and Notes.* Collegeville, MN: Liturgical Press, 1987.

Clifford, Richard J. *The Wisdom Literature.* Interpreting Biblical Texts. Nashville: Abingdon Press, 1998.

Dunn, James D.G. *The Acts of the Apostles.* Grand Rapids, MI: Eerdmans, 1996.

———. *The Partings of the Ways: Between Christianity and Judaism and their Significance for the Character of Christianity.* London: SCM Press, 1991.

Ehrman, Bart D. *How Jesus Became God: The Exaltation of a Jewish Preacher from Galilee.* New York: HarperOne, 2014.

———. *The Orthodox Corruption of Scripture: The Effect of Early Christological Controversies on the Text of the New Testament.* New York: Oxford University Press, 1993.

Fee, Gordon D. *The First Epistle to the Corinthians.* New International Commentary on the New Testament. Grand Rapids, MI: Eerdmans, 1987.

Freeman, Charles. *A.D. 381: Heretics, Pagans, and the Dawn of the Monotheistic State.* New York: Overlook Press, 2008.

García Martínez, Florentino. *The People of the Dead Sea Scrolls: Their Writings, Beliefs, and Practices.* Leiden: Brill, 1995.

———. *Qumran and Apocalyptic: Studies on the Aramaic Texts from Qumran.* Leiden: Brill, 1992.

Hanson, R.P.C. *The Search for the Christian Doctrine of God: The Arian*

*Controversy 318-381*. Edinburgh: T&T Clark, 1988.

Heiser, Michael S. *The Unseen Realm: Recovering the Supernatural Worldview of the Bible*. Bellingham, WA: Lexham Press, 2015.

Hengel, Martin. *Judaism and Hellenism: Studies in Their Encounter in Palestine During the Early Hellenistic Period*. Philadelphia: Fortress Press, 1974.

Hurtado, Larry W. *Lord Jesus Christ: Devotion to Jesus in Earliest Christianity*. Grand Rapids, MI: Eerdmans, 2003.

———. *One God, One Lord: Early Christian Devotion and Ancient Jewish Monotheism*. 3rd ed. London: T&T Clark, 2015.

Kelly, J.N.D. *Early Christian Doctrines*. 5th ed. London: A&C Black, 1977.

Orlov, Andrei A. *The Enoch-Metatron Tradition*. Tübingen: Mohr Siebeck, 2005.

Pelikan, Jaroslav. *The Christian Tradition: A History of the Development of Doctrine, Vol. 1: The Emergence of the Catholic Tradition (100-600)*. Chicago: University of Chicago Press, 1971.

Rubenstein, Richard E. *When Jesus Became God: The Struggle and Conflict over the Origins of Christianity in the Fourth Century*. New York: Harcourt Brace, 1999.

Sanders, E.P. *Paul and Palestinian Judaism*. Philadelphia: Fortress Press, 1977.

Segal, Alan F. *Two Powers in Heaven: Early Rabbinic Reports about Christianity and Gnosticism*. Leiden: Brill, 1977.

Smith, Mark S. *The Origins of Biblical Monotheism: Israel's Polytheistic Background and the Ugaritic Texts*. Oxford: Oxford University Press, 2001.

Stead, Christopher. *Divine Substance*. Oxford: Clarendon Press, 1977.

Tov, Emanuel. *Textual Criticism of the Hebrew Bible*. 3rd ed. Minneapolis: Fortress Press, 2012.

VanderKam, James C. *An Introduction to Early Judaism*. 2nd ed. Grand Rapids, MI: Eerdmans, 2022.

Vermes, Géza. *The Complete Dead Sea Scrolls in English*. Revised ed. Penguin Classics, 2004.

Wiles, Maurice F. *The Making of Christian Doctrine: A Study in the Principles of Early Doctrinal Development*. Cambridge: Cambridge University Press, 1967.

———. *Archetypal Heresy: Arianism through the Centuries*. Oxford: Oxford University Press, 1996.

Winston, David. *Logos and Mystical Theology in Philo of Alexandria*. Cincinnati: Hebrew Union College Press, 1985.

Yamauchi, Edwin. *Persia and the Bible*. Grand Rapids, MI: Baker Books, 1990.

# Further Reading: A Guide for Your Continued Journey

This book was intended not as a final word, but as an invitation to a deeper and more ancient path of faith. For those who feel called to continue this journey of rediscovery, the works of many dedicated scholars can serve as invaluable guides. While few of these authors would arrive at the same theological conclusions presented here, their groundbreaking research provides the essential, undeniable building blocks of the monolatrous framework.

The following books are not simple reads, but for the serious student, they are indispensable. They represent some of the most important scholarship on the divine council, Second Temple Jewish theology, and the origins of devotion to Jesus.

**1. For Understanding the Biblical Worldview: The Divine Council**
- **Heiser, Michael S. *The Unseen Realm: Recovering the Supernatural Worldview of the Bible*. Lexham Press, 2015.**
- If there is one book to read after this one, it is *The Unseen Realm*. Dr. Heiser was a brilliant Old Testament scholar who dedicated his life to reintroducing the Church to the supernatural worldview of the biblical writers. He masterfully explains the reality of the divine council, the "sons of God," and the cosmic geography of the Bible. While Heiser himself remained a Trinitarian, his work single-handedly recovers the lost biblical context in which Christian Monolatry makes perfect sense.

It is an absolutely essential and transformative work.

## 2. For the Origins of Devotion to Jesus in a Jewish Context

- **Hurtado, Larry W. *One God, One Lord: Early Christian Devotion and Ancient Jewish Monotheism*. 3rd ed. T&T Clark, 2015.**
- This is a landmark academic work. Hurtado, a world-renowned New Testament scholar, proves that a high, divine Christology was not a late invention but emerged almost immediately in the earliest Jewish-Christian communities. He demonstrates that Second Temple Judaism had a robust framework for a chief divine agent who could share in God's authority without violating monotheism. His work provides the historical and theological proof that the exaltation of Jesus was a natural development within a monolatrous Jewish context.

## 3. For the "Two Powers" Controversy and the Jewish-Christian Split

- **Segal, Alan F. *Two Powers in Heaven: Early Rabbinic Reports about Christianity and Gnosticism*. Brill, 1977.**
- This is a highly academic but foundational book. Segal meticulously documents how early Rabbinic Judaism condemned the belief in "Two Powers in Heaven." He argues that this condemnation was a *reaction* to the claims of Christians and others, and that before this controversy, Jewish theology was much more diverse and open to the idea of a chief divine intermediary. This book provides the crucial historical evidence for why the monolatrous framework was eventually suppressed within Judaism.
- **Boyarin, Daniel. "The Gospel of the Memra: Jewish Binitarianism and the Prologue to John." *Harvard Theological Review* 94, no. 3 (2001): 243–284.**
- This scholarly article is a brilliant exploration of how the concept of the *Memra* (the Word) in the Aramaic Targums provides the direct Jewish background for the prologue of John's Gospel. Boyarin argues that

FURTHER READING: A GUIDE FOR YOUR CONTINUED JOURNEY

what he calls "Jewish Binitarianism" (which aligns with what this book calls monolatry) was a common and accepted theology before the rabbis later branded it as heresy.

## 4. For the History of the Nicene Controversy

- **Rubenstein, Richard E. *When Jesus Became God: The Struggle and Conflict over the Origins of Christianity in the Fourth Century.* Harcourt Brace, 1999.**
- Rubenstein is a historian, not a theologian, and his book provides a vivid, accessible, and deeply human account of the Arian controversy. He masterfully shows how the triumph of the Nicene position was as much about politics, personality, and imperial power as it was about theology. This book is essential for understanding the real-world forces that led to the suppression of the earlier, subordinationist Christian worldview.

These works will not give you all the same answers, but they will confirm the historical and biblical data presented in this book. They are the tools for a new generation of believers who are willing to look past later creeds and rediscover the faith that was once for all delivered to the saints. May your journey be a blessed one.

# Glossary of Key Terms

**Anomoeanism** The theological position of the most strict and radical Arians in the fourth century. The name comes from the Greek *anomoios*, meaning "unlike" or "dissimilar." They taught that the Son was not only a creature, but that His essence was entirely unlike the essence of the Father.

**Angel of YHWH** The primary, visible agent or messenger of the unseen God (YHWH) in the Hebrew Bible. This figure is distinct from God, yet speaks and acts with His full authority, bearing the divine Name. Early Christian theology often identified this figure with the pre-incarnate Son.

**Arianism** A fourth-century theological position, named after the presbyter Arius. It taught that the Son was not eternally begotten but was created by the Father "out of nothing" before time began. In this view, the Son is the highest of all creatures but is not of the same divine essence as the Father.

**Christian Monolatry** The theological framework proposed in this book. It is the belief that the Father is the one, supreme, uncaused God who alone is worthy of ultimate worship. The Son and the Spirit are distinct, subordinate divine agents who are honored and revered but are not co-equal with the Father in origin or authority.

**Divine Council** The heavenly assembly or court of divine beings ("sons of God" or *elohim*) over which YHWH presides as the supreme king and judge. This concept is found in texts like Psalm 82, 1 Kings 22, and Job 1.

**Dynamic Eternity** A view of God's eternal nature, proposed in this book, in which God is eternally changeless in His essence but is also dynamic and relational. In this model, God can perform willed, relational acts (like begetting the Son or creating the world) from eternity, before the beginning of created time. This stands in contrast to Fixed Eternity.

*elohim* A grammatically plural Hebrew word for "gods." While it is most often used to refer to YHWH, the one supreme God of Israel, it is also used in the Bible to refer to lesser divine beings, angels, and even human rulers who represent God.

**Fixed Eternity** A view of God's eternal nature, influenced by Greek philosophy, in which God is static and unchanging in every respect. In this model, all divine relationships (like the Son's begetting) are not willed acts but are timeless, metaphysical necessities. This view leads to the concept of a single, shared divine essence among co-equal persons.

*homoousios* A Greek philosophical term meaning "of the same essence" or "consubstantial." It was the central, and most controversial, term inserted into the Nicene Creed (325 A.D.) to affirm that the Son is of the same divine substance as the Father, thereby refuting Arianism.

**Logos** A Greek term meaning "Word," "Reason," or "Principle." In the Hellenistic Jewish philosophy of Philo, the Logos was the divine, rational principle through whom the transcendent God created and ordered the universe. The Gospel of John identifies Yeshua as the personal embodiment of this divine Logos.

*Memra* An Aramaic term meaning "Word," used frequently in the Jewish Targums (Aramaic paraphrases of the Bible). The *Memra* of YHWH functions as a divine intermediary, representing God's active presence in creation, revelation, and covenant without compromising His transcendence.

**Monolatry** The belief in the existence of many divine beings (*elohim*) but the exclusive worship of only one, supreme God (YHWH). This book argues that monolatry, not strict monotheism, is the foundational theological framework of the Bible.

**Monotheism** The belief that only one divine being exists. All other so-called "gods" are considered false or imaginary.

**Patripassianism** From the Latin words *Pater* ("Father") and *passio* ("suffering"). It is the theological view, closely associated with Sabellianism/Modalism, that because the Son is merely a "mode" of the Father, it was the Father Himself who was incarnated and who suffered and died on the cross. This was condemned as a heresy by the early Church for compromising the impassibility (unchangeable nature) of God the Father.

**Post-Exilic** Referring to the period of Jewish history after the end of the Babylonian exile in 538 BCE. This era, also known as the Second Temple Period, was a time of significant theological development, seeing the rebuilding of the Temple and the composition or final editing of many biblical and extra-biblical texts.

**Sabellianism** A third-century theological view (also known as Modalism) that the Father, Son, and Holy Spirit are not distinct persons, but are simply different "modes" or manifestations of a single, undifferentiated God. It was condemned as a heresy by the early Church.

**Semi-Arianism** A term for a diverse group of fourth-century theologians who rejected the strict Arian view that the Son was a creature, but also rejected the term *homoousios* ("of the same essence"). They preferred the term *homoiousios* ("of a similar essence"), seeking to affirm the Son's true divinity while preserving His subordination to the Father.

**Shekhinah** A term from rabbinic literature that refers to the manifest, dwelling presence of God, particularly in the Temple. It is used in the Targums to speak of God's localized glory without compromising His transcendence.

**Subordinationism** A broad theological term describing the belief, dominant in the pre-Nicene Church, that the Son and the Spirit are subordinate to the Father in origin, rank, and/or authority.

**Two Powers in Heaven** A term used by rabbinic Judaism to condemn as heretical any theology that appeared to posit a second, divine figure alongside God. This charge was often directed at Jewish-Christian claims about the exalted status of Jesus, as well as some Jewish mystical traditions.